UNSQUARING
THE WHEEL

UNSQUARING THE WHEEL

COMPREHENSIVE & SCALABLE TRANSFORMATION

ACCLAIM FOR
UNSQUARING THE WHEEL

UnSquaring the Wheel is the operating manual for the printing firm of the future. It is filled with new thinking for an old industry trying figure out what it wants to be when it grows up. There will be print as we move into the future and it will be produced by firms that transform themselves. This book will tell them how to do it."

Frank Romano, Professor Emeritus
Rochester Institute of Technology

Commercial printers looking for a real world tool that will assist them to evaluate their business and provide them with a clear path forward would be well served to check out this new offering from Dr. Joe Webb and his collaborators Wayne Peterson and Prof. Chris Bondy. *UnSquaring The Wheel* takes you beyond theories and philosophical concepts. It provides an evaluation of your business and then establishes a path for improvement and success for the future. Any company that wishes to be a successful marketer of a broader range of client services should be checking this out.

John Berthelsen, Chairman
Suttle-Straus, Inc.

WOW! As Graphic Communications executives struggle with challenges associated with transforming their businesses, this brilliant collaborative project by industry experts Dr. Joe Webb, Wayne Peterson and Prof.Chris Bondy - Unsquaring the Wheel - integrates significant fundamentals that focus on the Customer, the Platform and the Resources. Engage your multi-generational teammates to explore a new business model, work with their unique UnSquaring assessment and dig into your business to build your future.

Jerry Scher,
Founder and Harrison Assessment™
Managing Partner Peak Focus, LLC

Unsquaring the Wheel weaves high level and complex concepts into the granular level of day-to-day business reality. The authors eloquently cover each topic from the ground up to 36,000 feet and then take you back down again. Let the reader beware: there are no gimmicks or 12 easy steps to get from A to L. If the reader approaches this book looking for an instruction guide you will miss the point. You won't find a program here. *Unsquaring The Wheel* is a blueprint for a methodology of thought processes, and the more you read the more the thought process becomes a natural part of the actions – and real change - required to successfully survive in this convoluted world. It is not for the faint of heart; it is for those who want to be honest of heart and face the hard realities of ourselves and our business models in this industry, and not cling to the perceptions and "best practices" we have spawned over the years so we could ignore those realities.

The case studies are painfully honest. I have been on all sides of this industry from web publication print, to graphic arts supply, technology and equipment distribution, to commercial sheetfed, to paper. There is no topic not covered, and Wayne and company outline them in cogent detail. This is a book I will read many times and wish I had to read many times over the years. The writing style is engaging and provoking and in some places so brutally honest you have to laugh or you'll cry. What is spoken here is by no means limited to the graphic arts world either. Take courage though: if you can think what you read there is great hope ahead!

Joe Fanelli, CEO
New Leaf Paper, a Public Benefit Corporation

Whether you are a big or small printer, the new book *UnSquaring The Wheel* written by three industry titans, Wayne Peterson, Dr. Joe Webb and Prof. Chris Bondy of RIT will take you on a proven journey to transform your commodity business into a meaningful and profitable enterprise. It is by far the best book ever written for the industry, and takes you step-by-step through the process of reinventing your business for the future.

Jim Schultz, Chairman, President & CEO,
Great Lakes Integrated

Business transformation is really hard work. *UnSquaring The Wheel* offers a roadmap for business leaders to begin with market-back thinking (what to do) and proceed to implementation and execution (how to do) in the transformation process.

Tom Saggiomo, President & CEO
DG3 Group

Our industry is filled with well-intentioned owners too "busy" to build value in their business so their iceberg slowly melts away and they are left with little revenue and useless equipment. Please invest the time in *UnSquaring the Wheel.* You are certain to learn: (1) you are not alone, (2) there is a way to build a vibrant business with lasting value and great enrichment, and (3) your brand is much more than a name, it is the embodiment of your purpose and your relevance to customers and prospects.

As business owners we want to move to that coveted "upper right quadrant" with coveted and "sticky" clients, deep relationships and great value added services. UnSquaring gets you there.

Kevin K. Cushing
President- Allegra Network- Alliance Franchise Brands
Former CEO and franchisee- AlphaGraphics Inc
Soderstrom WTT CEO of year 2011

UnSquaring the Wheel offers a blueprint for redesigning the traditional printing company business model — a task that confronts the entire industry.

John Snyder, President
HBP, Inc.

Nicely done! Those leaders who constantly look at the three *UnSquaring the Wheel* disciplines and determine how to improve each will gain share from those who just watch the job schedules, managing from month to month."

Terry A. Tevis, Chairman
Coloredge

Our industry is not going away. Our industry leaders are looking for direction on how to reinvent themselves and succeed in a different media industry environment. UnSquaring The Wheel is a great resource for transforming graphic communications companies. The authors share great insights beyond purchasing off-the-shelf technology and provide advice on how to transform and differentiate their product and service offering.

Paul V. Reilly, Partner
New Direction Partners

For years, many companies focusing on printing, graphic arts, graphic communication, and related areas have been floundering with many disappearing, downsizing, or consolidating. The book *UnSquaring The Wheel* and its philosophical undergirding presents methods that can really work with its "hands-on" approach. It addresses a prevailing illusion that has lead to the demise of many printing companies: "Print is great! Everyone needs print! Print is not going away!" Well, this is not true. This is "the preacher preaching to the choir" or the rabbi preaching to the minion.

What the printing industry and related industries need is the truth, and then solutions to their existing problems such as changing customer desires and needs, changing preferred ways of communicating between and among businesses and individuals, introducing new entries into the communication markets and competition therein. *UnSquaring The Wheel* is an earnest attempt to provide the printing industry with options for survival and growth today and in the future. It presents scenarios that all industry company leadership should take seriously.

Harvey R. Levenson, Ph.D., Professor Emeritus,
Graphic Communication Department
Cal Poly State University, San Luis Obispo, California

ACKNOWLEDGMENTS

Setting out on the open seas with a concept, a boatload of experience, and a commitment to deliver something unique and valuable is an ambitious journey for even the best sailors. Little did I know from the start of this project that I was partnered with two individuals that would work harder than I ever imagined and deliver collaborative work with such passion and precision. Like the spokes in a wheel, each of the *Un-Squaring The Wheel* authors provided context and experience that established a balanced equilibrium of critical thinking that was synthesized into this work. Thanks to Dr. Joe Webb and Wayne Peterson for their undying commitment to this enormous undertaking. From the onset, the churning of ideas and content and refining the work through countless hours videoconferences, emails, phone calls, and face-to-face meetings, our work in the trenches together has established a brotherly bond forever.

Thanks to RIT, Dean Dr. Lorraine Justice, Sr. Associate Dean, Dr. Twyla Cummings from the College of Imaging Arts and Sciences, the School of Media Sciences, and the Frank E. Gannett Endowment for enabling me to conduct the research on this project. Thanks to the students that worked on various aspects of the Web site. Thanks to our early reviewers for their perspective, feedback, and endorsements; especially Jon Budington, Global Thinking, Mike Panaggio and Greg Dean, DME, Randy Seberg, Direct Marketing Partners, and many others.

To all involved in this project (in addition to those recognized elsewhere): Carmel Priore-Garlock for deft editing, and RIT Press for distribution.

Thanks to my wife and soul mate Denise, for her encouragement, support, and belief in this project and all that is important to me. You are a unique and special person who is always able to find the good in everything. When I was weary with the demands and volatility of this project you provided a calming perspective that allowed me to carry on. You are the very best!

Chris Bondy
Rochester Institute of Technology
August 2015

Writing is hard work. Writing in collaboration is much harder work. And the collaborative work was done in hundreds of hours of weekly videoconferences over nearly three years. I'm grateful to Professor Bondy and Dr. Webb that "iron sharpens iron" and consistently so. The physical separation was a disguised gift at times in that we couldn't physically reach each other. Some of the dialog was pointed. That indicated the work itself wasn't yet sharp enough. For myself, I'm grateful that they stuck with it even when the going was difficult and the size of the task daunting.

The book emerged from the UnSquaring model and process, and not the other way around. Both were vetted early on by some incredibly gracious and generous industry leaders. We're especially grateful to a handful of people who invested their insight most substantially. Those are Ken Garner of Epicomm, Kip Smythe now retired from NPES, Jackie Bland who led GAMIS and then PRIMIR for two decades, Robert "BoSacks" Sachs of Precision Media Group, Jim Morgan of HBP/Balmar, David Briggs of The Lane Press, and Jerry Scherr of Peak Focus.

Personally, I'm grateful to the clients within whose companies my own work has been shaped and refined, tested and proven. Most particularly, I'm grateful to Philip Drumheller and the team at The Lane Press in Burlington Vermont, and to Bob Bennitt and his team at The Pace Group in Industry, California. Being made welcome as an "Inside / Outsider" has been a great gift.

Bob Rempfer of Amazingly Creative Inc. did much more than design and illustrate the book. He shepherded the production of the book through many iterations. All the while, he remained relentlessly upbeat and gracious. Simply saying "Thank you" is woefully insufficient. There would have been no printed book, much less a beautiful book, without you.

Finally, I'm incredibly grateful to my wife, Marilee. She's "talked me off the ledge" at times, and been relentlessly supportive both of me and of the investment UnSquaring the Wheel required. Much more than simply my spouse, she's my chief cheerleader and incredible colleague. All of my writing is materially better thanks to her thoughtful and repeated reading, her advocacy for the reader, and her adroit questions and improvements. Thank you, Angel. You're the best.

Wayne Peterson
Philomont, Virginia
August 2015

Thanks are due to my fellow authors, Messrs Bondy and Peterson. The Cross Media Innovation Center conference in 2012 found the three of us together for the first time. Cocktail tables at business meeting breaks seem to make conversations more spontaneous and interesting even for this teetotaler. It's still a fascinating conversation.

Wayne has thanked folks whose curiosity led them to our proof of concept presentation in 2013. He's also expressed gratitude to the folks essential to the production of the book, and Chris thanked those who worked with him, especially at RIT. I second all of their sentiments. I also want to thank NPES and Graphic Arts Show Company (GASC) president Ralph Nappi and former GASC vice president Chris Price who encouraged us to bring the project to Graph Expo in 2015.

I've been blessed with four careers, one in organization life, briefly in the college classroom, consulting, and industry punditry. The UnSquaring project pulled them together. The People chapter began years ago with Tim O'Sullivan, a benevolent boss while I was in college and worked part time at the Bronx Zoo's personnel department. Tim was one of the victims in the World Trade Center, and he is greatly missed daily. The Money and the Alliances chapters arose from my dissatisfaction with economics as typically taught and believed. I started to read Austrian School economics more than a decade ago and began to appreciate the grand forces that drive the way our industry gathers and allocates (and misallocates) capital. I apologize to readers who were expecting the Money chapter to be about financial ratios and receivables collections; you'll have to go elsewhere. The Alliances chapter started to form years ago in chats with my TrendWatch business partner, Jim Whittington, who was a small and family business consultant. With the Austrian School and Jim's experiences rattling in my head, I believe we deliver a different way of thinking for a capital-constrained industry.

Life as a pundit began with my first column in WhatTheyThink in 2003. The publishers deflected complaints from printing's old guard, and that's appreciated to this day. The criticisms gave me great ideas for columns and books and encouraged me to keep challenging the common wisdom.

Finally, Mrs. Webb. Annie is my partner in life's journey. I knew it from the start forty years ago. Projects and books are disruptive to everything, and that's when you're working alone! This project was not just three consultants trying to coordinate schedules and work. It all ripples through their families and other obligations, with all of life's highs and lows. They share our struggles and triumphs as we do theirs. After more than 35 years together, Annie's thoughtful navigation remains flawless and a providential blessing.

Joseph W. Webb, Ph.D.
Wake Forest, NC
August 2015

FOREWORD

L ast year, I had an opportunity to read "Marketing Myopia"—a classic Harvard Business Review article written by Theodore Levitt. In
it, he explains how myopic businesses lose sight of their client's needs
and eventually fail. My favorite analogy focused on the rail industry. At
the beginning of the 20th century, rail was the nation's dominant mode
of transportation. But as the years progressed, highways were built, cars
improved, and air travel became mainstream. By 1950, automobiles had
overtaken trains as the primary method for transporting people—rail
has been focused on freight ever since. Sound familiar?

Just like you, I've been asked, "So, what do you do?" hundreds of times.
At cocktail parties, reunions, the countless social gatherings my wife
throws. "I'm in the printing business" is my kneejerk response, but it's
a poor description of what I do. It's one of the last vestiges of my early
understanding of the business I've been in my entire adult life.

In 2001, I became the CEO of Global Printing—the commercial firm
where I've worked since graduating RIT. My entry into a C-level position began with the company slogging through a difficult recession, a
failed business model, and little cash. Through many experiments (code
for failure), lots of education (more failure), and a paradigm shift in our
collective thinking, Global has transformed itself. I no longer see myself

in the printing business, and now I know I never was.

If not printing, what business were we in? From our founding in 1978 and up until the technology boom, bust, and subsequent recession of 2001, Global focused on producing publications and business stationery. We built the perfect operation to fulfill these needs to our clients. But in 2002, as the marketplace began to recover, we realized our customers were experimenting with new online technologies, and our printing business lagged behind the growing economy. The online world was beating us at our own game—providing a lower-cost method for disseminating content.

Our initial reaction confused everyone. We weren't printers anymore; we became marketing service providers. We spoke of variable data and digital print, and later we moved on to QR codes and augmented reality. We changed our sales pitch, but our only marketing service was printing, and our clients weren't buying. Our myopic view focused on what we could make. We weren't asking ourselves why our clients would need it.

We began to meet with our clients as a strategic resource, and it became clear they needed help transitioning from print to online. We started to understand the change we needed to make, and knew it would require radical investment.

We created a new division named Global Thinking. We hired creatives, strategists, and technologists from outside the printing industry. We essentially bought the education we didn't have to understand the technological change we were facing.

Unlike us, our clients were never in the printing business. They had used print to promote their ideas, sell their products and tell their stories, and these needs continued to exist. Moving into the online space was the logical next step. The reality that they would need both an online and offline strategy created opportunities. How could we bring efficiencies to the process of using print?

As we helped move content online, we saw new opportunities for print-in-message delivery. Combining offline print experiences with online marketing required new thinking about process. This gray area between the old technology of print and the new world of online media was in need of innovation.

What is innovation? Printers get conflicting advice on this. Most focus inwardly on their equipment. Do your customers buy make-readies? Do they ever ask how fast you can make ready your press? Hopefully not, but I still hear print CEOs talk about how they differentiate themselves through their equipment lists. Talking about ourselves, our certifications, our commitments to the environment, our new "service provider" name and logos – none of this is innovation. In fact, it's counterproductive.

So what does innovation look like?

Ask your customers, because innovation begins when you focus on them. Attend your clients' meetings, read their publications, and critique their websites. Ask yourself what they are trying to accomplish. You might have some good ideas.

Know that innovation always wins, and fighting it will waste time and resources. Explaining how print grows trees will not bring back a cancelled print publication.

Innovation never stops. Don't feel confident that your current product offerings will ever be good enough. At Global, confidence lies in our belief that we've created a new thought culture, possess a willingness to learn, and maintain a nimble organization—we can keep up.

And finally, innovation is growth. If your business isn't growing, it's shrinking. Surviving, cost cutting, and downsizing are not long-term business plans. Growth through innovation is the only way forward.

So back to the rail industry, why didn't they build automobiles, push for more highways, or invent the airplane? They owned the transportation market, had access to the customer base, and had the resources to innovate. Instead, they focused inward, making faster locomotives and offering services like mail delivery. They believed they were in the train business. They failed to understand their clients' need was transportation, not trains.

I've learned to love a good recession. 2001 gave me the opportunity to lead this company, and the "great recession" of 2008 gave us the opportunity to grow through our ideas. Difficult economic times create climates of change—where the old methods no longer work, and clients seek outside ideas on how to improve. As Global clients' needs change, so will our business. When I think back on Global's transformation, I'm struck by how difficult it was to see what now appears obvious. Moving off the "tracks" of our printing presses required us to understand our much larger, client-focused universe.

Evaluating a business without bringing in bias and ego is nearly impossible—like representing yourself in court. And self-evaluation without process almost always fails. Our industry has lacked the resources and tools to educate business leaders on methodologies for cultural improvement and true innovation.

On first reading, Unsquaring the Wheel looks like Global's playbook for change. It's not a how-to guide, but a framework on how to think logically about your business.

So get out of your office, turn off your phone, be humble, and start reading. You're about to be thrown off your rails.

Jon Budington, President
Global Thinking
Global Printing

UnSquaring the Wheel: Comprehensive & Scalable Transformation
by Chris Bondy, Wayne Peterson and Joe Webb

UnSquaring the Wheel

unsquaringthewheel.com

ISBN-10: 0692519645

ISBN-13: 978-0-692-51964-6

First Edition 9 8 7 6 5 4 3 2 1

Printed and bound in Canada

TABLE OF CONTENTS

1

STRATEGY AND BUSINESS MODELS:THE CASE FOR TRANSFORMATION

by Wayne Peterson

"Graphic communications is an industry in wholesale transition."
— Tom Saggiomo, CEO, DG3

As communications changed globally, graphic communications as an industry was largely asleep at the switch — and we woke too late for many companies to change course and secure viable futures for themselves. Much of the blame has been thrown at changing technologies, but there's much more to the story. We believed some things that simply blinded us to the emerging future.

- We believed that a growing population, ever-widening use of our products, and fifty years of gains in incomes and affluence guaranteed our health and our growth as an industry.

- We believed that there was no real substitute for our products and services. We believed that an ongoing "war on waste" and gains in productivity would be sufficient to offset any decline in perceived value and unit pricing.

- We believed that we could apply process controls and industry standards so effectively to print production that consistently high mechanical reproduction quality would continuously drive variability out and costs down.

- And we believed that those things, taken together, would ensure a future that looked much like the decades-long industry expansion to which we were accustomed.

Unfortunately, what we believed wasn't trustworthy or proven true. In essence, we lost – against ourselves by TKO.

We've long prided ourselves on being an industry of small- and medium-sized businesses (S&MEs). And we believed that the small size and relative youth of most of our businesses equated with entrepreneurship and innovation. Unfortunately, we were wrong about that, too. Few of our businesses were genuinely innovative. Rather, most of them were founded by owners who had worked within other graphic communications companies, and who had assumed that they could do the same thing only a little better. This worked for decades, until it didn't.

As global communication changed, few graphic communication companies were innovative and entrepreneurial enough to see change approaching and capitalize on it. Only a handful ever developed new technology or a market approach of their own. Most implemented applied technology, sold or licensed to them by others. Few of those integrated various technologies effectively, rather than employing them in isolated islands. And that left graphic communications firms vulnerable to changes they were ill-equipped to understand, much less to leverage effectively.

Technology, Communication, and the Paces of Change

A tremendous amount of attention from all sides is being paid to new and emerging technologies. And that noisy pace of changing technology is providing a giant distraction, one that is very difficult to tune out or to see past. Unfortunately, the seduction of emerging technology is masking a fundamental change in the business strategies and the business models needed to successfully lead graphic communications companies of all kinds and all sizes today. Even more basic elements of the whole graphic communications industry are changing, too. And while technology has played a role as a change driver, looking solely at technology ignores issues that are even bigger.

Why we communicate has not changed. We communicate to inform, to persuade, to entertain, and to transact. So the purposes remain consistent. The media change, and so do the methods by which we communicate. The content and the format in which we communicate certainly changes— but not the purpose. The most substantial change in communication is that immediacy now has greater value than does perceived quality. "Now-ness", convenience, and the ability to alter communication on the basis of behavior.

The need to communicate grows ever-stronger, creating new opportunities for graphic communications companies. However we choose to communicate, and for whatever purpose, our customers will continue to have a driving need to communicate with their customers, members, constituents, investors, and audiences.

A further complication to defining and executing a successful business strategy is the relative pace of change among five significant business elements: emerging technology, applied technology, platform, product and services, and customer segments.

1. Emerging or Breakthrough Technology

Emerging technologies represent intervals of advancement, capability, and innovation in a particular field of technology. Emerging technologies can be incremental or disruptive.

An emerging technology is considered incremental when it delivers the next level of expected capability in a natural progression of advancement and capability. An example of an incremental-emerging technology might be the next release of the iPhone.

However, emerging technologies are considered disruptive when they deliver innovative capabilities that provide a new or "breakthrough" advancement and capability that change the way we interact. An example of a disruptive-emerging technology might be the initial launch of the apple digital wrist watch. This is a disruptive technology because it provides technology innovation that changes the way we use a wristwatch.

2. Enabling or Applied Technology

We need to distinguish between enhancing technology and displacing technology. The speed with which displacing technologies can take hold makes all technology decisions difficult and short-term. Calculating the Net Present Value (NPV), or breakeven point, for a technology investment tells us that the likelihood that a technology can be purchased and be useful long enough to be depreciated over five or more years is falling fast.

3. Platform

Platforms change as applied technology is integrated. And so platforms change at a slower pace than do either breakthrough or applied technology. Pre-media processes, for example, look very little like they did as little as 10 years ago. The entire method by which plates are created for conventional offset reproduction looks nothing like it did. The supporting (incremental or enabling technologies) technologies changed much faster than the core technologies (burning a plate) did the overall process itself. But the process did change.

4. Products and Services

Products and services change much slower than technologies or platforms. While the technologies and the processes used to deliver those products and services may change, the output changes much slower. The methods used to create and deliver some printed products have changed radically. For example, the workflow to produce a printed magazine is substantially different than it was only a decade or two ago. However, the product received by the end-user is nearly identical to what it was 20 or even 50 years ago. But the products themselves do change over time. New products appear, and some vanish.

5. Customer Segments

Customer segments change, too, but far more slowly than do technologies, platforms, or products. For graphic communications companies, this is the great good news. Publishing companies as a category have existed for much more than a century. Advertising and marketing communications firms have existed for nearly as long. Associations date back to the Revolutionary War in the United States, and the list goes on. The need to communicate continues unabated, and long-term customer segments can still be identified and developed effectively.

Technology Migration

A business strategy based on the application of a specific technology or group of related technologies is a high-risk undertaking. Those strategies typically overlook one of the core behaviors of nearly all technologies: They migrate into the hands of the end user. A handful of examples should make this behavior clear.

The advent of word processing didn't merely simplify the lives of secretaries, typists, and transcriptionists. Rather, it eliminated the need for a third party to create typewritten documents. It made it easy for the originators to do it themselves. It also made it incredibly simple to quickly draft a document and then take it through multiple editing cycles without the need to re-keyboard the text. And so while early word processors were installed in typing pools, and in the offices of secretaries and legal transcriptionists, that didn't last. The technology migrated into the hands of the individual creating the text in the first place. The benefits were immediacy, convenience, and reduced expense.

The advent of desktop publishing, which put text formatting and page creation tools onto a personal computer platform, quickly allowed anyone to build a document incorporating multiple typefaces, illustrations (including illustrations in color), and whatever page layout they desired. Desktop publishing did not merely improve the lot of art directors, editors, and production artists. Instead, it enabled the end-user who needed the document to create it herself. Typographers, color separators, layout artists, and other specialists vanished in the wake. Investments in enabling technologies to perform third-party services proved ill-advised, particularly for color separation firms who often had millions invested in drum scanning, proofing, image setting, and CEPS equipment. Not even service bureaus were insulated as imaging to film was supplanted by imaging directly to plates.

All of these technologies capture sophisticated knowledge, build it into rules and routines, automate its application, and eliminate the learning curve and investment necessary to share that knowledge. Crafts whose skills could be translated into logic, arithmetic, ...and mathematics presented the most obvious opportunities. Therefore, the likelihood that any service provider can build a sustainable advantage based on a non-proprietary technology is very low. Those technologies will continue to migrate into the hands of the end-user. That means service providers, including legacy print service providers, need a different foundation on which to build. Significant investment in enabling technologies isn't sufficient, nor is it trustworthy.

Why MUST your business exist?

That question is vital because it is so rarely asked or effectively answered.

A hard look at the purpose of a business is rarely done for several reasons. Most often, that's because the answer we expect is unsavory: profit for the business owners. Rarely does anyone get excited about enrichment of the business owner, not even the owners themselves. Fortunately, that's always the wrong answer. Theodore Levitt (1986) made clear that profit is not and cannot be the central purpose of a business. He wrote:

> "... to say that profit is a purpose of business is, simply, morally shallow. Who with a palpable heartbeat and minimal sensitivities will go to the mat for the right of somebody to earn a profit for its own sake? If no greater purpose can be discerned or justified, business cannot morally justify its existence. It's a repugnant idea, an idea whose time has gone." (6)

Profit is a result of actions, a signal to stop or to continue doing something. It is never a purpose in itself.

Peter Drucker (1974) answered the question aptly and accurately when he said, "There is only one valid definition of business purpose: to create a customer. " (61) Levitt (1986) amplified Drucker's assertion: "To say that they should attract and hold customers forces facing the necessity of figuring out what people really want and value, and then catering to those wants and values. It provides specific guidance and has moral merit." (7)

If Drucker was right — and I believe he was precisely correct — the question of purpose cannot be answered without describing who the enterprise intends its customers to be, and how the enterprise intends to create value for those customers. Now we're on to something. So let's frame the question a little differently, and as the first of a critical series of questions.

When you begin the tough work of developing a strategy, there are a handful of essential questions:

- Why **must** your business exist? That's a different question than, "Why does your business exist?" How would your customers suffer, and what would they be missing if you ceased to exist? How do you intend to make your customer's lives better?

- What about your business is utterly unique and valuable to your customers?

- What about your company in action best demonstrates the value you intend to create and deliver?

- Who are your intended customers, and why should they want to become and be your customers?

Those very tough questions go to the heart of your customer relationships and whether there is anything about you on which a durable competitive advantage can be created. It takes a tough-minded look at those tough questions to know that you're building something lasting and of real value. It's a tough-minded response to the tough circumstances of an industry in wholesale change.

Labels aren't enough

Many graphic communications companies have dropped references to print, mail, bind, or other services from their names. And they've relabeled themselves something related to marketing. Often the word "marketing" is part of the new name. The default description for these relabeled entities is marketing services provider. The MSP label isn't sufficient in the eyes of customers for several reasons.

First, customers generally don't buy it. When a name is changed and the service offering is nearly identical to what it was before, customers describe the change as irrelevant or disingenuous. Using the term "marketing" is to make a claim of marketing expertise and capability.

Second, bolting new services onto an existing business model isn't enough either. When the existing business model remains focused on execution, offering to execute more things adds relatively little additional value.

Third, what customers expect from the relationship with a supplier has changed. Re-labeling without changing how the company behaves, or changing the style and structure of the relationships it creates, makes clear to the customers that little has changed other than the name.

In the face of large-scale changes about the relationships customers will value with a supplier, both strategies and business models need to change in response.

The Legacy Business Model

A business model is the blueprint for an economic engine. A business model describes how value is created and captured. It is a practical process by which a company creates and offers products and / or services valuable enough to attract and retain customers. It describes why those customers are willing to pay enough that the company can capture and retain a portion of the value for itself, in order to fund its future and to provide the business owners with a return on investment.

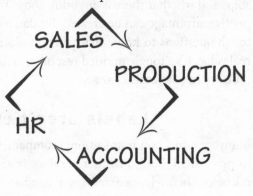

Graphic communications as an industry is built around a nearly universal business model: sell it, make it, ship it, bill for it. While companies within the industry make and do a variety of things for a variety of customers, nearly all of them adopted the same organizational structure: sales, production, distribution, and accounting. Many roll production and distribution together, and add human resources as the fourth leg for the table. Companies with nearly identical structures, and with roles that are nearly interchangeable are the result. This was the historic job shop business model. And its structure was intended to make a company highly effective at executing what someone else had already determined to do.

Produce and Distribute

This is the original business model for commercial printing. It has as a number of advantages. It is easily scalable. It can be customized for the type of printed product. It focuses on efficiency, and therefore, on cost reduction. It enables the application of available and specialized technology. And it encompassed the small piece of the communication process for which customers expected the printer to be accountable. The printer had little or no involvement in the creation of content, nor in choosing where it should be distributed.

Design, Produce, and Distribute

Many commercial printing companies found it effective to add creative services to their original duplication and distribution services. Most of these were focused on design and art direction, while some added copywriting. However, the focus continued to stay on the "how?", rather than on the "why?" and "what?"

Design, Produce Distribute, Track / Measure

The next common stage in the development of a larger service offering was adding tracking and measurement of what has been done. While it still stays focused on execution, this does add an element of "What happened?" to the services provided to the client. It remains focused on activity, but begins to acknowledge the importance of results.

Diagnostics, Design, Produce, Distribute, Track / Measure

This next development stage is a sea-change. Here, for the first time, the graphic communications company is involved with the customer to determine what the customer needs and what outcomes the customer should seek and expect. The interaction with the customer is entirely different. Much of the value being created comes when the graphic communications company equips and enables the customer to make the best possible decision about what they should do. Often this takes the form of multiplying options, or creating choices the customer did not know they had. Here, the advice and counsel are often perceived as more valuable than the simple ability to execute what is decided. Customers have become very savvy. They tend to recognize that they do not know all of the options available, nor do they see all of the risks inherent in each of those options. And while customers for decades have relied on their suppliers to keep them out of trouble, graphic communications companies have been wary of providing too much pushback in fear of being branded difficult to work with.

Diagnostics, Design, Duplicate, Distribute, Track / Measure, Results.

In this development stage, the supplier assumes responsibility for the results created. Literally, this means that the graphic communications company is accountable for the business results created and measured for that customer. This closes the loop and completes the process. The supplier is now actively involved to help the customer decide what it is in the customer's best interest. Once they have enabled the customer to do exactly that, they measure and report the results, and then accept responsibility that the results delivered what they lead the client to expect.

Neither the strategy nor the structure of the typical graphic communications company is well-suited for delivering this kind of customer value. Even if the supplier was willing to accept responsibility for the results, few firms are equipped to do the Needs Analysis or to measure the business results. And therein lies the gap: The old business model cannot and will not support it.

Research to Strategy

One more development stage deserves note, and this one wraps itself around all of the sequential steps described in the others. Some companies are able to look at an entire market segment, rather than at a more narrowly defined group of current customers. And they may not be serving those large segments at all at present. The objective is to find an unserved or under-served market that has real needs the company can meet. Once a highly textured understanding of that segment has been created, a strategy can be crafted to meet those unmet needs, largely eclipsing the efforts and offerings of conventional competitors. The best example of this is Vistaprint. Vistaprint's growth had much less to do with applying a web-to-print process effectively, and much more to do with identifying an under-served market segment and crafting a strategy to serve it exceptionally well.

Why start with strategy?

Mention business strategy in a conversation, and I can guarantee that some eyes will roll toward the ceiling, while others glaze over. Few things sound as obscure, excessively academic, or impractical as "business strategy." Frankly, that's tragically unfortunate. Because unless you get the strategy right, nothing else is likely to be effective unless by accident.

A strategy is only good if it eliminates your uncertainty about why you're acting, what you're going to do, and how you're going to do it. In essence, strategy is a designed response to a challenge, a response that creates a durable, competitive advantage. It needs to clearly describe where to play, how to compete, and how to win. All three elements are essential because a strategy is incomplete until it describes specific actions that will be taken.

A business model will always be subordinate to a strategy. Tinkering happily with the generation of a business model before there's clarity and strength to the business strategy can certainly be entertaining. However, it is unlikely to be especially fruitful, no matter how stylish or pretty the diagram. If a business model is elevated to a primary focus, the enterprise runs the risk of copying what others are doing and diluting the differentiation on which every competitive advantage is based.

Unfortunately, that leaves us facing another of Peter Drucker's (1974) assertions: "Because its purpose is to create a customer, the business enterprise has two — and only these two — basic functions: marketing and innovation. Marketing and innovation produce results; all the rest are 'costs.'" (61) Essential are the creation of new and better value for the customer, and engaging potential customers around that value. So a strategy must focus on creating demand for a company's products and services by meeting customer needs in a way that no one else can.

Strategy, Tactics, and Logistics

Three terms need clear definitions: strategy, tactics, and logistics. A good definition of strategy is a plan of action or policy designed to achieve a major or overall aim. If there's a three level pyramid, strategy is at the top. It takes the highest, broadest, and longest view. It deals with those things that define an entire company.

Tactics are actions carefully planned to achieve a specific end. Where strategy is overarching, tactics will typically focus on a single step or single objective. Tactics are vital, but subordinate to, strategy.

Logistics is the detailed coordination of a complex operation. For most graphic communications companies, this is "operations." It is the most foundational "how-to."

The Structure of a Real Strategy

My best metaphor for an effective business strategy describes three simple elements: Diagnostics, prescription, course of treatment. It is a sequential, three-step process that we've used for over two decades. And it parallels the process described by Richard Rumelt (2011).

Diagnostics defines the problem or challenge by assessing the situation internally and externally. Few things are less useful than finding a marketplace opportunity for a company that lacks the capability or resources to pursue that opportunity. The external diagnostics are critical because they are the only thing which prevent us from acting on assumption. There are no facts or truths about the marketplace or about your customers inside your four walls. The only thing that exists inside are perceptions and opinions.

Next comes the work of crafting the **prescription.** Once the diagnostics are done, both internally and externally, the hard work of marrying capability with opportunity begins. And it must be customer-facing. In essence, the prescription describes the marketplace opportunity by describing the needs and problems of real customers. It then describes the capabilities and resources of the business enterprise that will be used to meet those needs and problems directly.

A **course of treatment** must be designed once the diagnostics and the prescription are completed. That's where the development of a business model really begins. No matter how accurate the diagnosis nor how pow-

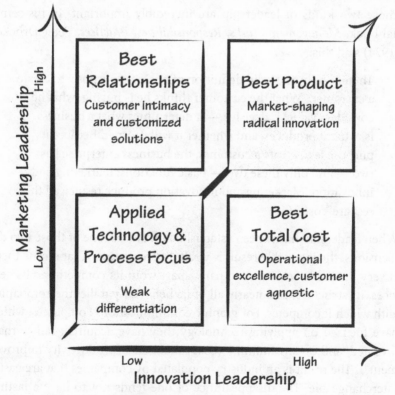

Adapted from *The Discipline of Market Leaders*, Treacy and Wiersema, 1997

erful the prescription, unless that prescription is actively used in a course of treatment, no value is created. The patient doesn't get better. So where can a strategy take you? And what kinds of strategies lead to a competitive advantage that is durable? For graphic communications companies who find themselves with little competitive advantage and who look to their customers much like their competitors, there are three options.

Marketing Leadership and Innovation Leadership

The quadrant diagram is useful because it shows where most graphic communications firms must begin (where they find themselves now) and where it is possible to go.   Most industry firms find themselves in the bottom left quadrant. Applying the technology drives the business. The primary focus is on process improvement and application. In that quadrant, companies demonstrate little marketing leadership and little innovation leadership.

Those two kinds of leadership are incredibly important. In his seminal book, *Management: Tasks, Responsibilities, Practices,* Peter Drucker (1974) said this:

> There is only one valid definition of business purpose: to create
> a customer. What the customer thinks he is buying, what he
> considers value, is decisive — it determines what a business
> is, what it produces, and whether it will prosper. Because its
> purpose is to create a customer, the business enterprise has
> two — and only these two — basic functions: marketing and
> innovation. Marketing and innovation produce results; all the
> rest are 'costs'. (61)

When leadership hasn't been established on at least one of those two dimensions, the inevitable result is weak differentiation. That means there is very little that sets one company apart from its competitors. Its services, its structure, and nearly all of its behavior parallel the companies with which it competes. For graphic communications companies, which have focused on applying technology they have acquired, rather than invented, and on streamlining (cost reduction / "productivity improvement"). The result is an industry populated by companies that are easily interchangeable. The disappearance of one tends not to have a lasting negative effect on the customers of that company. They can quickly and easily begin doing business with another one that looks and behaves very much like the first.

Three Paths Out of the Trap

There are three opportunities to create a strategy to get out of that trap. Each requires developing leadership on at least one of those two dimensions.

Innovation Leadership: Some companies can escape the trap by focusing on genuine innovation, while still remaining customer-agnostic. By that I mean these companies are indifferent to their customer's businesses. They focus on operational excellence, and they innovate to achieve it. Not satisfied simply to buy and apply technology or capabilities from outside, they focus on their own processes and systems. They move away from methods of work and structures that are usual and customary. While they may not create much of their own technology, they tend to be highly effective technology integrators. Where their competitors may have islands of technology, these firms tend to avoid that trap. They build highly integrated systems and workflows with a strong focus on the services that those systems are intended to deliver, and the customer value that those systems are intended to create.

Marketing Leadership: Other companies can best escape the trap through marketing leadership. These companies work hard to become experts in their customer's businesses. They leverage their expertise and intimacy to create highly customized products or services that are very valuable to a narrow range of customer organizations. These firms pride themselves on building deep and strong customer relationships. That means that no single individual within the graphic communications company owns a customer relationship. Instead they built multiple and parallel relationships with key people inside the customer organization, and at multiple levels. In the best cases, the lines between the two organizations begin to blur. Often, these companies will take on processes or responsibilities originally managed by the customer organization itself internally. This path out of the trap doesn't depend on deep technical expertise or upon proprietary technology. Instead, it depends on the ability to help customers accurately diagnose their own challenges and opportunities, and then to collaborate with those customers. The result is co-created services which are tailored tightly to an individual customer and which create very substantial perceived value.

Both: The third path out of the trap leverages leadership on both dimensions. These are companies that have developed a deep understanding of their customer segments, and it equally deep ability to innovate. This is the best product or a best service model. And this is where market-shaping, radical innovation appears. Often, the needs being met have been unmet for some time. The possibility that those needs could be met is often unrecognized until the company brings its service offering to market. Underserved customer groups, many of which have been overlooked, are often the targets of these firms.

Specific and Actionable

Whichever strategic direction is chosen, a strong strategy will make it very specific. It will describe the ideal customer to whom the company's offering should be most valuable. It will intentionally exclude those potential customers for whom the company can create little or no unique value. That means a strong strategy is not only inclusive, but it is intentionally exclusive, as well. And that's what enables companies with strong strategies to remain focused and to avoid distraction. Customers who value a best total cost offering will typically have little interest in deep intimacy with a supplier, nor in highly customized service offerings. What is valuable to that customer is the intrinsic product alone. Companies whose strategy is based on best relationships understand this. Then they neither compete for, nor do they compromise to win relationships with, customers who most value a best total cost offering. Companies whose strategy is based on best total cost will avoid pursuing customers who value customer intimacy and who are looking for highly customized, highly effective services from a handful of suppliers.

Four Bases for Competitive Advantage

There are two sides to the coin of an effective strategy. The two work perfectly in tandem. One is an end, and the other is a means. The end is creating a competitive advantage that is durable. The means is creating superior value as the optimal customers would describe it.

An artificial conflict is sometimes proposed between those two. And companies can get off track if their focus turns toward their competitive position relative to a specific group of competitors, causing them to take their eyes off their customers. But to suggest that there is a fundamental conflict between creating the outcome of a durable competitive advantage and the means of customer value misses the point. Competitive positioning must play a role in any effective strategy. Behaving as though competitors and competing offerings are irrelevant, or saying so outright, is hubris.

It's much more effective to see the means and the end as inseparable. But that also requires us to see the basis on which we can create customer value sufficient to create a durable competitive advantage. Marty Neumeier (2007) has aptly described four bases from which we can do this: Means of Production, Capital, Intellectual Property, and Brand.

1. Controlling the Means of Production

The first basis from which we can create customer value and a competitive advantage is the control of the means of production. In the graphic communications industry, this has been very difficult to achieve. That's because the means of production is available to anybody who wants to buy or lease it from an equipment or technology vendor. And there has been nothing to discourage them from selling, leasing, or licensing their means of production to anyone who could afford to buy it. In fact, failing to do so would have been anti-competitive. But without a proprietary means of production, there is nearly no hope of creating exceptional customer value and a durable competitive advantage.

2. Employing Raw Capital

The second basis from which companies have created customer value and a competitive advantage is raw capital. Companies that have control of or access to significant capital can leverage it in a variety of ways to create customer value, not all of which apply that capital to acquiring the means of production.

3. Intellectual Property

The third basis from which we can create customer value and competitive advantage is the leveraging of unique intellectual property or intellectual capital. In essence, that means we're leveraging the knowledge or know-how that's unique to us. It requires patent or copyright protection in many cases. But it also requires that the intellectual capital or intellectual property goes deep enough to create real value. That can often take the form of expertise in the customer's business, and services that have been tightly tailored to customers of a particular kind. When those services are based on a unique process, they become defendable as intellectual property.

4. Brand

The fourth basis from which we can create customer value and competitive advantage is building a strong brand. Customer value is always perceived value. Much of it is intangible. And yet it is real because customers demonstrate a willingness to pay for the perceived value that is delivered by a strong brand. As you will see, a brand is really a gut feeling (largely emotional) that one holds about a product, service, or company. That gut feeling can deliver a wide variety of different kinds of value.

For most graphic communications companies, the last two of these four bases offer the best opportunity to create enough customer value to build a durable competitive advantage. Proprietary technology or production capability is a pipe dream for most. So is lots of readily available, inexpensive, and undeployed capital. But that's not fundamentally bad news. Most companies can develop deep customer expertise, a strong brand, or both.

A Different Business Model

If the job shop business model is no longer sufficient as a foundation on which exceptional customer value can be created, what is the alternative? One very viable alternative is the model of a professional services firm. Most often, that looks like a blend between a consulting practice and an advertising agency. It's a business model based on leveraging the knowledge and capabilities of the firm to diagnose the needs and opportunities of a customer, and to propose the best options for meeting those needs and leveraging those opportunities. The business then delivers the services that have been proposed, while tracking and accepting responsibility for the results.

This business model requires a structure and capabilities that go well beyond sell-make-ship-bill. The most radical difference is on the sales side. This business model requires an entirely different kind of customer relationship. That demands a different sort of salesperson with a radically different skill set. This business model also requires the capability to do the diagnostics and to craft solutions. It no longer rests on the simple ability to find tasks that others have already determined need to be done.

Many variations and adaptations of this model are possible, of course. At minimum, it needs to be tailored to specific customers and customer challenges. Ideally, it's focused on an under-served customer group whose needs are not being met very well by others, including the other job shop graphic communications firms against which the company has been competing.

Because this strategy and the business model necessary to support it don't rely primarily on process expertise or high productivity, one of its benefits is the contrast it creates with larger firms who are offering a "best total cost" promise to their customers and to the marketplace.

What is necessary?

To execute an entirely different kind of strategy, and to build a business model to support it, graphic communications companies of all sizes will need to do a number of things that they've never had to do well until now. On the customer-facing side of the business, there are three:

First, they need to develop an understanding of brands, and they need to build one.

Second, they need to manage business development as a systematic process, bridging the artificial gap between marketing and selling.

Third, they need to create an intentional customer experience that delivers everything the brand has promised.

References

Drucker, Peter F. 1974. *Management: Tasks, Responsibilities, Practices*. New York, Harper & Row.

Levitt, Theodore.1986. *The Marketing Imagination*. New York: Collier Macmillan.

Neumeier, Marty and American Institute of Graphic Arts. 2007. *Zag : The Number-One Strategy of High-Performance Brands : A Whiteboard Overview*. Berkeley, Calif., AIGA: New Riders.

Rumelt, Richard P. 2011. *Good Strategy, Bad Strategy : The Difference and Why It Matters*. New York, Crown Business.

Treacy, Michael and Frederik D. Wiersema.1997. *The Discipline of Market Leaders : Choose Your Customers, Narrow Your Focus, Dominate Your Market*. Reading, Mass., Addison-Wesley Pub. Co.

2

CASE EXAMPLES: TALES OF TRANSFORMATION

We learn fastest through metaphors and stories. (McDrury & Alterio 2003) And since *UnSquaring the Wheel* sets out a radically different path for the transformation of a graphic communications firm into something very different, it's reasonable to ask for examples of companies that demonstrate why it is vital and viable. We offer three of those stories here. The first is a cautionary tale of a company that failed even to begin the process. The second describes a company in the midst of that process, and is gaining traction steadily. The last describes a company that has reinvented itself and created a durable competitive advantage in the process.

References

McDrury, Janice, and Maxine Alterio. 2003. *Learning Through Storytelling in Higher Education : Using Reflection and Experience to Improve Learning.* London: Kogan Page.

CAUTIONARY: PADGETT PRINTING

by Joe Webb

Padgett Printing was founded in 1903 in Dallas, Texas. In 1989, the company had revenues of $8 million, by 2007, and the company had grown to $32 million. In a 2006 article in *American Printer* (Padgett Printing), Padgett was described as having "an impressive array of equipment." Padgett's CEO stated, "We have the right technology, suppliers, people and customers."

The company went through two periods of transformation. As one of the owners of the company, Winfield Padgett, remarked, "A lot of companies are enamored with metal, machinery and technology. We have never lost sight of the market, customers or financial structure." In *WhatTheyThink* (Sherburne), Padgett Printing is " ...often cited as an example of a conventional printer making the leap to marketing and other value added services."

There was a significant restructuring in the company in 1990, when they hired their first non-family CEO. The new CEO directed significant investments into computing and management information systems.

In 1999, Padgett became the first North Texas printer to install a digital press. In 2001, they added mailing services, in 2005, website development services, and in 2007, they added kitting and fulfillment operations.

This approach was a "build it and they will come" strategy—an incremental way of adding new technologies and new services.

Padgett faced many issues and challenges in the years to come:

- A customer with ten $40,000 print and mail campaigns per year stopped the program.

- Another customer found a full web printer that beat the prices of Padgett's half-web.

- A customer with financial problems reduced their kitting and fulfillment orders.

- A multimillion dollar insurance company decided to try to do everything online. This was compounded by postal rate changes and a general decline in direct mail.

To combat these losses, the company started to offer incentives to their sales representatives. This turned out to pose serious problems for the company financially. Many of their programs did not work, so they changed sales managers in 2008 and 2011.

Sales volumes went up, but they only added unprofitable jobs to an eroding sales rate. This meant that they were being very efficient at producing unprofitable things.

Then a deadly event occurred. An audit showed that their controller had embezzled $3.5 million over a six-year period. (Sherburne)

What Lessons Can Be Learned from Padgett Printing?

The first lesson of Padgett is to understand the nature of technology and the printing business. Its technology acquisitions were made at a time when the overall industry was growing. Growth can mask sins; tough market conditions shine the light of day on them.

Unfortunately, the Padgett story is not pretty. Many printing companies have used the same strategies for decades, treating each new equipment purchase as the means to increase sales or enter new markets. They may have considered each of them as "profit centers" with separate profit and loss statements, believing that accounting sophistication would allow them to manage their business better. There are times when "build it and they will come" works. It is actually a tenent of some classic economic theory that supply creates demand. But that is the essence of entrepreneurial risk: The market cannot understand many products until they use them. But it is not a strategy that can stand alone. Padgett, like many companies, had an idea that their equipment purchases would work out, not because of entrepreneurial savvy, but because they were mimicking the actions of risk takers who had gone on before them. While they were profitable for a time, they got not the rewards of entrepreneurial risk, but the moderate returns of floating along with the marketplace.

Keeping older technology in a business can seem like a good idea if the loans and leases are completely paid and sales related to that equipment cover the remaining costs. One does not see, however, how those resources might be deployed elsewhere in different opportunities. Management expert Peter Drucker (Peter Drucker) had a phrase he used often in his writings: "Feed tomorrow, starve yesterday." (2006) This is a very important business strategy. Padgett Printing made investments for the future in technology, but they did not allow or force their older investments to wind down. While the company was adding new services that made the company appear on the cutting edge of technology, they had older product lines that seemed profitable, but were not. New products and services were not integrated into the rest of the company.

There is a good metaphor for this integration. Learning to play classical guitar can be very difficult, and the difference between a virtuoso and a competent player is noticeable. There is a difference between playing notes adequately, compared to playing music that flows with a dramatic quality. This seems to be what happened with Padgett Printing. They could play the notes (that is, have the equipment they could operate well in separate departments), but not play music (that is, have an integrated company with a well-crafted strategy and implementation).

The problem with Padgett was not that alone. It was not understanding the future of their marketplace. How could losing major customers to digital media be a shock to them? Trying to solve their sales problems with contests and higher commissions only created new problems. Bad tactics can kill great strategy. Bad tactics often come about because of bad strategy or obsession with financials, rather than about customers.

The focus on individual investments ("We can make money if we own this equipment"), rather than anticipating market needs ("These are problems we can solve for our clients") meant that they did not understand what was driving the decisions that their customers were making.

Padgett added many new products, but did not really understand what was happening to the overall demand for the products they were offering. There was demand "out there", but they did not know its size, nature, or scope.

This means that they had what economists call "malinvestment." This is a misallocation of resources. When that happens, it means that scarce financial resources are used for the wrong things.

Padgett seemed to have problems understanding that planning and budgeting are not the same. As for many printing companies, their planning processes involve heavy reliance on budgeting and tracking of revenues and costs. But planning is different. Planning involves understanding the future. Planning requires developing alternative scenarios for them to adequately prepare management and have a complete understanding of the marketplace. Their cumulative incremental actions through budgeting were not planning.

Finally, having proper financial controls in a company is essential. How a controller could "get away" with embezzlement is not just a crime by the controller, but the sign of a serious deficiency in management. Audits, especially of a company of the size Padgett was, should be welcomed. And there is good reason to use different auditing firms, or at least different auditor personnel, over time. Audits should be welcomed as verification of honesty in accounting practices and the identification of areas where fraud or misuse of resources can occur.

There is also another benefit of audits with a good accounting team that goes beyond the verification that bookkeeping and tax compliance are correctly done. Having a good accounting review is also about managerial accounting. It is about making sure that job costing and investment evaluation methods are relevant to the market and will allow management to have the right and relevant information they need.

The multi-year deceit of embezzlement went on behind the backs of management. While they were trying to fix the "shiny objects" of sales, attention was diverted by the very function that should have provided warning signals for their situation was corrupt.

There were so many issues going on inside Padgett, but there was not a single one that caused the downfall. Companies have survived embezzlement, but Padgett's was the final nail in its coffin. Businesses need to have a robust health that allows them to survive disasters, but that only comes from strategy.

Strategy is the cure for incremental decision-making. Incremental decisions are those that are made when new situations occur; decisions are made as they are needed. These kinds of decisions are always necessary in business, because there are always unexpected situations about which management must make decisions. The best companies seem to anticipate the challenges of sudden adversity.

Even when not facing adversity, the best run businesses make incremental decisions in a strategic context where the criteria for their decisions have already been clearly stated and are well-defined. Their plans, culture, and history give them a broad and well-reasoned perspective. It's hard to blindside companies such as those.

References

Drucker, Peter. *The Effective Executive.* HarperCollins US. January 3, 2006. http://www.harpercollins.com/9780060833459/the-effective-executive

"Padgett Printing." Padgett Printing. May 1, 2006. http://americanprinter.com/industry-content/hvto-industry-news/padgett-printing.

"Peter Drucker." Wikipedia. Accessed August 6, 2015.

Sherburne, Cary. "Padgett Printing Closes, President David Torok Gives Insight." July 25, 2011. http://whattheythink.com/articles/51854-padgett-printing-closes-president-david-torok-gives-insight/

DEVELOPING:
PACE LITHOGRAPHERS

---

by Wayne Peterson

Pace Lithographers was established in 1975 by Carl and Bob Bennitt as a commercial printing company in Southern California. In 1989, Bob Bennitt succeeded his father as President and has led the company ever since. For decades, Pace was known as a provider of commercial printing to businesses in the Los Angeles area. Pace customers included organizations in the financial, non-profit, higher education, healthcare, retail, and manufacturing sectors. Pace built a reputation for personalized customer service and exceptionally reliable performance.

By 2007, Pace faced diminishing demand for traditional print services. Bob Bennitt (2015) turned his attention to figuring out how to reinvent Pace. Here's how he describes that challenge:

> The market, and Pace along with it, was about to dramatically contort, evolve on the fly without a net, and transform forever. The survival of companies has been determined by their ability to evolve and adapt, their tolerance for risk, and their determination to be relevant and necessary to their clientele. Tens of thousands of printing companies that employed a "strategy of hope" are no longer with us. (telephone conversation with author)

In 2008, Bennitt led Pace to begin a transformation. The company name was changed from Pace Lithographers to Pace Marketing Communications in 2012, and then to The Pace Group in 2015. Bennitt (2015) describes the process this way:

> The journey hasn't been obvious or easy. It has required intuition and a willingness to invest in and develop systems, sophisticated technologies, and staffing on the go. In 2006, 100% of our revenue was from commercial printing. Now, in 2015, that's no longer the case. Over 25% of our revenue, and climbing, now comes from other offerings. (telephone conversation with author)

Service Offering

Pace now offers marketing strategy and execution. That means the firm actively advises its clients about what they should consider doing in addition to enabling them to execute what they choose to do. The two offerings are welded together seamlessly. And the range of services Pace offers to its clients includes secured and variable data management, digital and conventional printing, digital marketing, warehousing and fulfillment, mailing, marketing resource centers, and Asian marketing consultation. Bob Bennitt (2015) described the developing service offering this way:

> And, most recently, we've added creative strategy and design to our offering. We've nearly completed our transition from a commercial printer into a reputable provider of marketing strategies and execution. Our retainer income for engagements that require MRC's, warehousing and fulfillment, creative services, and strategic marketing consultation is climbing steadily. This is evidence that our clients have accepted, even welcomed, Pace's position as a preferred resource for marketing strategy and execution. (telephone conversation with author)

Investment and Clients

Bob Bennitt (2015) describes the investment that the transformation of Pace required this way:

Our transformation has required continued financial investment in the skillset creation and development as well as the recruitment of talent, especially a new sort of business development talent. This has been expensive, and has required patience, forward-thinking, and risk-taking. Additionally, it has been demanding on the company culture as it blends new and different personalities.

...

Pace's evolution from a printer into a provider of marketing strategy and execution began where all business should begin – with the identification of, and a commitment to solving, our clients' needs. We believe one of our roles is to be the "eyes and ears" for our clients when it comes to discovering and vetting emerging technologies and techniques. Over the previous eight years, we have collaborated with our clients to introduce them to what have become the new offerings of Pace. We have been in a constant state of learning new technologies and offerings while we simultaneously make those offerings available to clients. It has been somewhat like learning to crawl, then walk, then run, while at the same time teaching others to do the same. (telephone conversation with author)

That's how Bob Bennitt (2015) describes the relationships with clients on which his transformation of Pace has been founded. He continued:

Our success has been the result of having extremely loyal clients who were willing, even eager, to invest in us as we developed our skills in the new areas of digital offerings, relevant one-to-one campaigning, data management, variable data printing, secured data, warehousing and fulfillment. Over the years, these engagements have actually grown deeper, into enterprise-level relationships. In effect, they have funded the evolution of the company into the unique, turn-key provider it is today. (telephone conversation with author)

Business Development

An essential step for Pace was a business development organization different than the printing sales force that had been effective for Pace for decades. Bob Bennitt (2015) describes that change this way:

> Not all account executives have the experience to provide expert consultation as marketers. These are legacy printing reps, and their expertise is not necessarily in adept business development. But they take great pride, and are successful, in caring for clients whose needs are mainly print-related. To build a team of business developers who can engage clients with our comprehensive portfolio of marketing offerings, Pace has successfully recruited and developed talent that comes from outside the printing environment. These have included digital marketers and creative marketing professionals. Given Pace's portfolio of offerings, we can engage with clients at several different points of entry, including print, data, creative, marketing strategy, mailing, marketing resource centers, digital, even secured data. Each member of our sales team tends to specialize in specific offerings and verticals. (telephone conversation with author)

Raving Fans

The continuing transformation of Pace has turned customers into raving fans. One Pace client recently described the company this way:

> To me, they are everything a business partner should be. They not only deliver on their commitments, they offer ideas and options that enhance the success of my projects. They "get it" that I need their expert advice and critical thinking as much as I need their technical operational capabilities. And now they have brought this same commitment and craftsmanship to an array of new offerings. They have strategically and elegantly evolved into a marketing communications company, which is just so impressive to me.

Results

Bob Bennitt (2015) describes the financial results of the transformation this way:

> Our financial performance shows sustained revenue growth and sustained profit growth as well. We are growing. And the growth is coming from a variety of sources, both new and legacy. In addition to our transactional revenue in print and other core offerings, we are growing monthly retainers and revenues for engagements that require MRC's, warehousing and fulfillment, creative services and strategic marketing consultation. This is evidence that our clients have accepted, even welcomed, Pace's position as a preferred provider both of marketing strategy and execution.
>
> The key to our success has been to honor our commitment that we exist to serve our clients. This is our quintessential value. Everything we think and do is imbued with that value. We trust in it. What we do may change, but never how we do it or why. (telephone conversation with author)

References

Bennitt, Bob, telephone conversation with author, July 20, 2015.

TRANSFORMED:
DME

by Chris Bondy

DME is a full-service direct-marketing agency with more than $100 million in revenue. It has found its success with a full complement of cross-media services. DME has roots in digital printing and direct mail. However, this is only one of many channels they are deploying in a grander strategy of pursuing vertical markets through highly targeted campaigns. DME serves fast-paced, vertically integrated marketing environments with a focus on data-driven and results-oriented targeted communications.

Benefitting from its unique ability to incorporate leading technology with meaningful application for marketers who need to measure results, DME has spun off several businesses. In the years since its founding, the company has pursued non-print media, as well, building a comprehensive cross-media and multi-channel capability for its clients.

It wasn't always this way. Mike Panaggio founded DME in 1982 and had seven employees at that time. Today it has 500, with most working in its 11-acre Daytona Beach production facility. As the company grew, it had to deal with resource issues, changing customer needs, and unique integration of technology and processes.

In the early to mid-1980s, DME filled a void in central Florida in direct mail. It quickly expanded its mailing capabilities regionally and nationally with a hybrid litho and monochrome digital workflow. In the 1990s, DME identified the need for innovation upstream, so it developed software applications to automate direct mail creative processes (Design Assistant) and multi-channel prospecting for financial planners (Response Mail Express, or RME). DME also opened a 92-seat Customer Interaction Center (CIC) with 150 professionally trained operators to process inbound/outbound telecommunications. The integration of call center services with direct mail was innovative. It became a powerful differentiator for DME, allowing them to produce and track campaigns – a strategic plank that DME leverages to this day.

In the early 2000s, DME pioneered the use of full-color digital press technology and personalized color printing, paving the way for full-color personalized direct mail and personalized photo books. In 2003, DME launched a proprietary cloud-based platform (Red Rocket) that fueled acquisition and retention programs in the automotive market. This added front-end capability enabled further growth at DME and the acquisition of an expanding fleet of Xerox iGen, HP, and Xeikon digital presses. DME's success in the automotive vertical market expanded to include a spin-off partnership called DMEautomotive.

In 2010, DME expanded its consumer offering with personalized greeting cards, gift wrap, and keepsakes through its Personalized Gift Sources portal. DME further expanded its B2B reach in 2012 through a strategic partnership with Office Depot, offering their customers customized and branded web-to-print platforms. In 2013, DME released a web-to-print portal (DME Connect) for both B2B and B2C clients.

DME now operates as DME Holdings with a staff of over 500 focusing on personalized cross-media communication strategies. Its client roster reads like a *Who's Who* of Fortune 500 leaders in healthcare, finance, sports, hospitality and automotive fields.

Issues and Challenges

DME faced a number of challenges over the years as they transformed into a leading marketing services provider.

One challenge DME faced, as a direct result of trying to incorporate leading edge technologies into its operation, was integration. Mike Panaggio found it to be a difficult area in the early years, but because they had a larger strategy to guide them, they worked through those challenges in a systematic way. In turn, they built a team of integration experts that he now considers to be a major competitive differentiator for DME.

DME needed a platform approach because they had many different technologies in the company, and not all of them were designed (nor imagined) to work together. This meant that their own DME technical staff had to integrate solutions from a variety of vendors in a meaningful way to serve their customers and for their own efficient production.

This kind of approach requires a "can do" business culture where creativity is regarded as important. Integrating technologies from different vendors is hard. There is much trial-and-error involved, and the knowledge of solving those problems needs to be stored and shared with others. The fact that it involves trial-and-error means that management tolerates a learning process of failure and the expenses associated with it. Those expenses are covered by the value created in reducing production costs and increasing product value.

Cultures tolerate paradox. The same culture that tolerates the failures inherent in creating cutting-edge product integration also has tight controls on its costs and an insistence on measurable results. This means that recruiting the right personnel and maintaining an environment that includes constant training and creativity is essential.

DME is also decentralized, and division managers have a great deal of autonomy in determining their needs for investments. The decisions of these managers are considered to be their own responsibilities. This means that implementation (and integration) is handled at the lowest level possible. Investments that don't work out are also their responsibility to divest and to regroup from, in sharp contrast to them hanging on to poorly performing investments, which are constant drains on financial results. Greg Dean, Executive VP, Marketing and Technology states that at DME, "… we are on constant watch for business, technology, and cultural change. Our competency is determining the difference between a trend and fad and reacting with meaningful solutions to intercept the needs of new trends".

The Customer

DME's value proposition is focused around its consultative approach, which involves uncovering the needs, disconnects, and gaps in a client's existing marketing and sales programs. This consultative selling approach targets specific vertical markets and aims to deliver measurable communications solutions. That means that DME has a detailed understanding of marketing and communications, and has an expectation that they will be judged on the ROI of the programs they work on. It also puts DME in the role of an expert whom clients come to rely on for their experience in results, not just for production costs.

As DME has understood the objectives of their clients, rather than just their needs, they have increased their range of product offerings. For example, the company is not just involved in direct mail, but also in telemarketing approaches to direct marketing programs. They have also added video and digital media production, and web development. The company also has a studio that creates personalized videos to supplement direct marketing programs.

The sales process does not wait for requests for bids before engaging with clients and prospects. DME approaches clients with a team that assesses the client's sales and marketing approach, looking for gaps of opportunity to improve performance with programs that drive customer acquisition, retention, or improved response to conversion costs.

The company focuses on results measurement and using the right communications tools at the right time. Most of the client programs include telemarketing, print, Web, and video components. This includes reporting of those results to the client and measuring their effectiveness.

The Platform

The company started with offset and early versions of digital printing, customizing offset "shells" with digital personalization. As production digital color equipment came to market and was improved, the company reduced its need for offset. Personalization software became a major investment.

A key aspect of the company's transformation from having a production focus to having a business focus has been its perspective on technology. The company's attitude toward technology is that it has to serve a purpose. While you can admire and be fascinated with technology, Mike Panaggio has always concentrated on what the technologies can deliver from a business perspective, and he relies on his integration team for their investment assessments.

This does not mean that the company resists technology. They have a department, DME Labs, that develops new product offerings with the company's current capabilities and also investigates new capabilities they may want to acquire. Greg Dean says that, "our equipment doesn't define us—our service does. DME provides unique solutions for our customers that are enabled by technology, not led by technology."

Some of the products DME Labs has developed include personalized wrapping paper (Personalized Gift Sources), photo products for the college market (Replay Photos), and another photo composition product (RocketLife). These products are enabled though interactive applications on the DME cloud portal that allow users to make design and layout decisions, including personalization. The job content and job instructions (or intent) are sent to the DME production facility for final print production, finishing, and delivery.

DME is on the constant probe for B2B and B2C market gaps and areas where they can add value. DME has the proven ability to uncover distinct unmet market needs. It then determines a creative way to meet those needs in the form of new services that are enabled through its technology platform and applications development expertise.

DME considers data management skills as a critical service for clients and as a key business differentiator. They emphaze measurement of effectiveness and analytics, but the company also has an in-depth understanding of data resources that they might acquire on behalf of their clients. DME understands market segmentation and targeting. They know how to manage, clean, and merge lists to make certain that recipients are presented with the right message —whether by direct mail or online.

The Resources

The DME workforce represents a significant point of leverage and differentiation built off of a foundational commitment to attract and retain a diverse and creative team. Since the time of DME's inception in the early 1980s, the graphic communications industry has had to reconcile an extremely large range of skill sets. A complete range of information technology, software development, data management, and systems integration skills are now required— in addition to the traditional skills associated with print and the graphic arts. For DME, the recruiting of employees with unique skills that can be integrated into the mix is a strength that not only extends their reach, but also innovates though a culture that promotes ideas and experimentation. Mike Panaggio has created an environment that supports the ideation process with a "fail fast" mentality. Mike says that this culture enables his team to take risks on new ideas and drop those ideas quickly if they do not show promise – or expand on them if the ideas have traction.

"We are constantly looking for top talent and learning how to creatively harness and retain that talent, as well as eliminate staff members that do not contribute," states Panaggio. DME is always on the lookout for creative, high-tech employees who understand a particular vertical market or application, and can complement the current team and the solutions DME offers.

Significant and creative relationships with suppliers and customers provide unique ways of engaging the market to maintain DME's margins and differentiation. In addition to having a strong workforce, the DME team has developed strategic relationships with several key suppliers who provide DME with "early adopter" access to new technology and, in some cases, co-development partnerships. The DME leadership team has also established strategic relationships with their customers through new and innovative business models, such as the Office Depot and Toyota auto dealership groups.

DME continues to innovate with its customers, services platform, and the internal and external resources it has formed to engage the market.

DME is committed to continuous development of a technology platform that drives relationship building. The DME platform provides automation through web-to-print portals and virtual storefronts, all designed to help their clients deliver and measure targeted programs that are "emotionally engaging".

THE FIRST DISCIPLINE

ENVELOPING
THE CUSTOMER

by Wayne Peterson

For decades, most graphic communications enterprises treated their customers as ancillary to their organizations and interchangeable with each other. In essence, they were seen simply as sources of demand for the physical products those enterprises were built to manufacture. The business need behind the customer's demand was immaterial and meaningless.

In a job shop organization, everything is optimized around workflow. The focus is on reducing the ways in which customer orders are different, and on standardizing and refining. Differences between customers are seen as chaotic and as a threat to a smoothly running operation. So walls are erected. And the responsibility to filter out the chaos of customer behavior, preferences, and differences is shared by salespeople and customer service people. That chaos characterizes many graphic communications firms even now.

In essence, the customer never was the primary focus. And graphic communications firms were never organized around their customer's preferences and core needs. So it's little wonder that customer attachment to many of those firms is low. It's little wonder that few of them have developed a durable competitive advantage. And it's little wonder that so few create value sufficient to defend them against commodity-level pricing pressure.

Changing that situation -- actually making it substantially better -- depends on embracing customers, rather than stiff-arming them. In practice, that means building a business strategy and a business model to support it that envelopes the customer.

We've already described the relationship between business strategies and business models. This book describes several different self-sustaining, virtual cycles. This discipline describes the first and the most central of those cycles. It begins with a strategy for creating a particular value for a particular set of customers, and then describes how to implement that

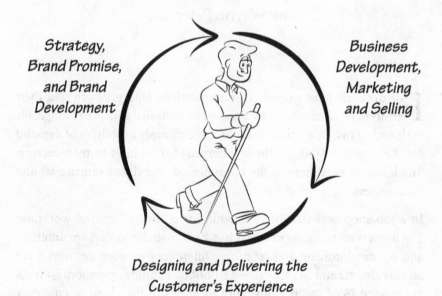

Strategy,
Brand Promise,
and Brand
Development

Business
Development,
Marketing
and Selling

Designing and Delivering the
Customer's Experience

strategy effectively. It's a multi-step, relentless process that expresses a customer-facing strategy as a brand promise, builds a meaningful and strong brand on that promise, crafts a business development process that integrates marketing and selling, and then designs and delivers a customer experience that fulfills the promises made and the value that's expected. Fulfilling those promises and expectations confirms the strategy, reinforces the brand, and begins the cycle again. It looks like this:

The customer stands in the center of that self-sustaining cycle or process in a way that customers of graphic communications firms have rarely done before. The entire discipline is built around the needs of a group of customers the firm can surround with resources, products, services, and experiences that are worth having in the eyes of the customer and are more valuable than those attainable elsewhere. It's an intentional and designed process to create a customer group that can be defended effectively from firms that are currently direct competitors, and from substitutes, as well.

For nearly all graphic communications enterprises, a durable competitive advantage must now be built around a set of customer relationships. Understanding and choosing how those will be created and maintained, as well as how value will be created and delivered to those customers, is the foundation of UnSquaring your own wheel and for your getting traction.

3

BRAND

by Wayne Peterson

"Walk the damned talk!" That's how one executive expressed her frustration with graphic communication vendors who want to pitch doing business with her, but who don't practice for themselves what she preaches and lives. What puzzles me? Graphic communications companies who have taken on a "marketing" label and who are frustrated when marketers don't take them seriously because they fail to practice effective marketing to build their own brands.

Effective branding is much more than simply coordinating the appearance of your logo on everything from your building and trucks to your shirts and coffee mugs. And while advertising specialties can be useful, simply labeling things with your logo and updating style of your website (and making it mobile-friendly) misses the point. Marketing is not simply social media, direct mail, sales promotion, and some advertising. All of those activities are in support of one fundamental process: building a brand.

Why should a graphic communications company be concerned about building a brand? We've described already an industry wholesale transition, and we've made clear that customer expectations have changed substantially. That has made your company's brand much more important than it has ever been before. Here's why:

The brand is the most basic, most vital foundation of a sustainable business model. A brand is what a person both believes and feels about a product, service, or organization. It is that gut understanding which determines how that person will behave toward that product, service, or organization. So a brand isn't entirely about the rational. It's also very much about the emotional. It's not merely what someone knows or thinks about your company. It's how they feel that determines how they will respond and act (Roberts 2005). The most loyal, enthusiastic, and strongest customers have been aptly characterized as "raving fans" (Blanchard & Bowles 1993). And there's no such thing as a being raving fan without having a powerful emotional attachment to that brand.

Brand Stages

Strong brands are built intentionally (Aaker 1996, Bedbury & Fenichell 2002). A customer's perceptions move through distinct stages as their understanding of and attachment to a brand grows.

1. Unknown

When a brand is unknown, there is very limited awareness of the company outside of its current customers. Those customer relationships have been created almost solely through direct selling activity. The company depends on the word-of-mouth of its current customers and on the work of salespeople to make potential customers aware of the company and what it offers.

2. Known

The very first positive step is moving from no awareness at all to knowledge that the brand exists. Basic name recognition has been created, along with a understanding of the company's basic service offering. Minimal investment has likely been made in a brand strategy, and little development has been done beyond naming and development of a logo. Promotion tends to be sporadic. Even if there is awareness of the company in the minds of its prospective customers, the brand is not easily distinguished from its competitors.

Novice marketers sometimes celebrate being able to measure that first level of brand awareness, but awareness doesn't equal preference. If buying decisions were largely rational, rather than emotional, that might be enough. But it isn't.

3. Known for Something

At this step, there now is market-wide awareness of the company, its service offering, and its basic positioning. As awareness of a brand grows, customers can describe what the product, service, or company does. Their understanding may be very specific, even if not comprehensive. By now, some investment has been made to promote the company, and that has been focused on its core service offering and capabilities, and on features and benefits. Sometimes there are references to customer outcomes or customer results in the brand's messaging. The company is tightly identified with a particular service offering and is easily compared with competitors.

Again, novice marketers will sometimes celebrate being able to measure the specificity of customer awareness. That temptation is especially seductive if the company believes that product features and general benefits will drive buying decisions. But even specific knowledge about the company, and its products and services, tends not to have much effect on buyer behavior.

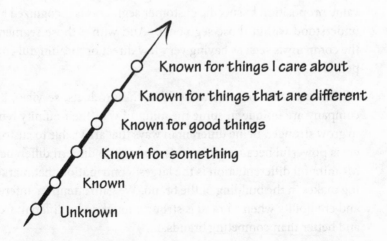

4. Known for Good Things

Customer affinity for a brand begins to develop when that brand is known for things considered to be generally good. When product or service performance is understood to be generally good, and when the company itself is understood to be a good corporate citizen, customers will describe feeling mildly positive about the brand. It is at this stage that customers will consider doing business with the brand, especially in the absence of stronger brands.

At this stage, there is widespread awareness of the company, and its personality or style. A brand strategy has been created. Initial investment has been made to make the company known for admirable traits, including being of service to its customers. The company has begun to talk about its customers, rather than about itself. And direct comparisons with competitors are beginning to become difficult.

5. Known for Different Things

The next stage is reached when a company is identified with specific customer segments. And within those segments, the company is known for creating at least one kind of unusual value. Ongoing investment is being made in customer communication and brand development. Customer segments have been consciously chosen and are widely understood within the company. Messaging is clear and very consistent. Adaptation of the company's core value proposition to specific customer segments is recognized and understood within those segments. And within those segments, the company is seen as having very few direct or meaningful competitors.

When customers become aware that the products, services, and company are unique in some meaningful way, their affinity tends to grow stronger. Being different in ways that are visible to customers is powerful because our minds are built to discern differences. Meaningful differentiation is the largest contribution that marketing makes in the building of the brand. We gain attention, interest, and credibility when a brand is strong enough to be different from and better than competing brands.

6. Known for Important Things

The brands that are strongest are those that are different in ways that are important to the customer. At this stage, the company is very well known in its chosen customer segments, and it is known for creating value that's important to many customers in those segments. Ongoing investment is being made to reinforce the brand presence within those segments. Customer affinity has been created, and current customers would actively regret the loss of the brand. The company is an "anchor brand" in its space, thus customers have great difficulty comparing it with any competitor.

These are the brands that stand for something that the target customer considers very important. To those customers, these are the brands that matter. These are the brands with which customers identify themselves. It gets expressed like this: "Those are the kind of people I want to do business with. It's my kind of company"

If your potential customers cannot effectively research your company and gain a coherent picture of you (the value you create, who you exist to serve, and your competitive position), then you won't get the opportunity to pitch anything at all. Frankly, they won't return your salesperson's call, much less give that salesperson an appointment. Period. End of story. Elvis has left the building!

Why Now?

When the "job shop" business model still worked well, few graphic communications companies needed to have much concern about their brands. For such companies to grow and thrive, a minimal level of awareness on the part of the marketplace, effective direct selling, simple and straightforward service offerings, and the consistent delivery of those service offerings were required. It may not have been easy, but it was simple. Then everything changed.

Whether we like it or not, this is the era of the branding of everything. It's a blessing and a curse. Seven-year-olds sporting logowear from head to toe might fall into the "curse" category. But ignorance of the power of well-developed and well-managed brands is its own curse. The era when firms selling B2B could ignore their brands and rely on product/service features and benefits is behind us. A strong brand is no longer tertiary or optional. It's the main thing. Philip Kotler (Kotler, Pfoertsch et al. 2006) sums it up this way:

> Industry consolidation, a tepid global economy and ex-changeable market offerings are driving competitive forces. In such an increasingly competitive environment, it is not enough anymore to just offer great products and services. By establishing a brand and gaining a favorable competitive position in the marketplace, businesses can successfully set themselves apart from the pack. (34)

Graphic Communications, as an industry, is in trouble largely because we've been product-oriented (that is, print-oriented), rather than cus-tomer-oriented. We defined ourselves as being in the printing business, rather than in the communications business. We've been focused on pro-ducing and distributing, rather than on enabling our customers to com-municate effectively and to achieve what they want to achieve (which is much more than printing and distributing some piece of communica-tion.) And because we focused so tightly on print as a technology or pro-

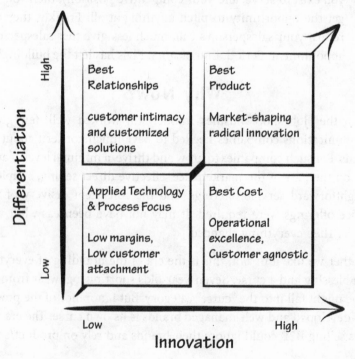

cess, rather than on the end results desired by our customers, we allowed others to take customers away from us. In essence, because we didn't effectively fill the needs our customers have, that need was filled by others, instead of by us.

For decades, most customers have viewed graphic communications companies of all kinds as service providers. They view us as being able to execute elements of larger programs and projects. Catch that—it's important. They believe we are equipped and skilled at executing what someone else has already determined needs to be done. Even worse, they view us largely as sellers, rather than marketers, because we are focused on our need for volume (in order to cover our overheads and drive down unit cost), rather than on their needs. One point of supporting evidence for that belief is a damning piece of our own behavior: We spend a great deal to communicate technical capabilities and product features, while we have spent nearly nothing building strong brands. Since so many of our customers are marketers of one stripe or another, they understand that technical capabilities are about us, while brands are about them.

Many, if not most, printing, mailing and related graphic communications companies were created when the founders made this assumption: "We can do the same thing only better." Rather than look at customers with fresh eyes, the founders tended to look at the businesses in which they had worked before and identified things they could do better. So, their strategies were reflective rather than new. They were based on incremental improvement, rather than on innovation. Few graphic communications companies demonstrated much capability to lead through innovation. Pair that with the low demonstrated ability to lead through differentiation, then finding most graphic communications companies in the bottom left quadrant of the adjacent diagram makes perfect sense.

Building a Brand

The strongest brands weld together an organization's purpose and strategy, and then face the customer to express it effectively. That means there are four elements we need to bring into focus: Organizational Purpose, Strategy, Brand Promise, and the Brand itself.

Purpose: A powerful brand distills and captures a compelling purpose. And the core purpose expresses the good that the brand exists to do in

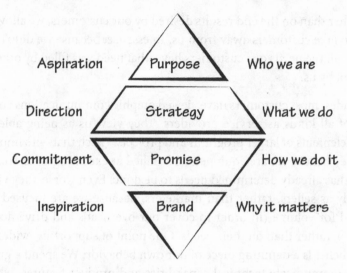

Aspiration	Purpose	Who we are
Direction	Strategy	What we do
Commitment	Promise	How we do it
Inspiration	Brand	Why it matters

the lives of its customers. Which of your customer's aspirations do you exist to fulfill? What do you inspire your customers to do or to be?

In different ways, all of the strongest brands express that core ideal. A single unifying idea is the source of any brand's power. That idea captures the essence of a brand. But it also captures its ethos. Ethos is the characteristic spirit of an organization that's apparent in its beliefs, aspirations, and behavior. This is central because people gravitate together around common sets of ideas and beliefs. Sharing values and beliefs fosters the development of trust. Simon Sinek (2009) said it well:

> Great companies don't hire skilled people and motivate them; they hire already motivated people and inspire them. People are either motivated or they are not. Unless you give motivated people something to believe in, something bigger than their job to work toward, they will motivate themselves to find a new job and you'll be stuck with whoever's left.(94)

There's danger here, too, and the danger here is hyperbole. Newsflash! Your business enterprise isn't going to change the world. Therefore, your purpose should not be so grandiose that it slides into the absurd. Empty statements of aspiration aren't the point. The history of paths paved with good intentions isn't especially encouraging. Therefore, this needs to be practical and grounded in marketplace reality. For employees, a clear purpose is vital if they are going to be fully engaged. A purpose needs to be larger and more important than enriching the business owner or trading time for income. If it is to matter, the enterprise must be about more, about something larger. It must be purposeful. You don't have a purpose when you decide what it is and declare it. You have a purpose when you create consequences for acting contrary to that purpose.

The two keys here are scale and balance. Your purpose should reflect a scale appropriate to your enterprise, a purpose that's within your reach and grasp. Your purpose should be meaningful to each of your stakeholder groups: customers, employees, and owners/shareholders. So any statement of purpose should survive these two questions: "Is our purpose one we can fulfill ourselves, with our resources?" and "Is our purpose meaningful to all of our stakeholders?"

The best news is that since your core purpose is to make and keep a customer, you can clearly describe who your customers are intended to be, the value you intend to create for them, and how they will benefit. While you're not running the Peace Corps, and altruism isn't the single, superordinate driver for your enterprise, all of your stakeholders should have an affinity and appreciation for being of service to your customers in ways your customers find meaningful and valuable.

Strategy: Strategy describes how purpose is going to be fulfilled. Suffice it to say that where purpose is aspirational, strategy is directional. When purpose is welded to a clear strategy, something powerful begins to happens—aspiration becomes specific and actionable.

Ted Levitt (1991) describes the importance of strategy this way:

> A strategy that doesn't speak explicitly about customers and the competitive environment will surely fail to generate and sustain a proper level of customer and competitive consciousness in your company, especially in the important nooks and crannies where the real work gets done. People will speak with technocratic simplicity about doing certain specific things, but without regard to why and for whom. (114)

An effective strategy has three elements: a diagnosis of the situation, rules of engagement describing how the situation will be addressed, and integrated actions taken to execute the strategy.

The diagnosis needs to be simple so that it cuts through the cloud of complexity to those elements of the situation that are essential. It can often be described as a simple story. This is not about listing objectives or aspirations. It is about describing the structure of the challenge — in essence identifying the gap between what is and the purpose that's been described, and explaining why that gap exists. The diagnosis answers the question: "What's really going on?" How we understand and describe the situation is what leads to the creation of real value for the benefit of your customers.

The rules of engagement (or the course of treatment, or course of action) are not a list of objectives or goals. The rules of engagement take the challenges identified in the diagnosis and identify where sources of advantage can be leveraged to tackle the challenge. This is about a method to meet the challenge. The rules of engagement describe what you will and what you won't do. In essence, they set boundaries, describing how you'll create value, how you'll compete, and how you won't compete. This is an exercise in focus that builds on the diagnosis and which pays attention to

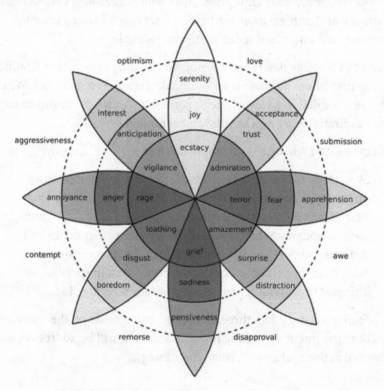

what the diagnosis has identified as being important. Done well, the rules of engagement resolve the uncertainty about what to do.

Finally, a strategy is about what specific actions will we take to execute the rules of engagement. It is the hard work of strategy to decide which priority takes precedence. Taking action is often painful. As long as strategy remains at the level of intention and concept, any conflict between strategy and the organization, or among initiatives, remains unresolved (which often leads to a rat's nest of organization defensive routines.) The pain of taking action cannot be avoided, though. Prioritizing and taking action will always be painful to those whose initiatives and priorities are different.

The specific actions taken must hang together. They must be in concert with each other and subordinate to the rules of engagement. The coordination of those actions is intentional, and it is imposed. In fact, strategy only becomes visible when it becomes a set of actions in concert that is imposed on the enterprise.

Brand Promise: Aspiration and direction, and purpose and strategy, need to be made clear, concise, and resolutely customer-facing. The very best way to do that is to capture both in a compelling brand promise. A statement of brand promise is the necessary final building block upon which a brand is built. It's the framework or superstructure to which the visible elements of the brand are fastened.

A strategy describes who a company's customers are intended to be, the value the company intends to create for those customers, and how it intends to do so. The best way to express all of that, while ensuring that it is completely customer-facing, is to express it as a brand promise. Because, just as business purpose drives strategy, strategy needs to drive brand.

Coherent brands are those where the understanding of the company held by its customers is in concert with the understanding held internally. They are also those brands where the promises made by the brand are in concert with each other and are consistently delivered in its customer experience.

A brand promise is a stake in the ground. It describes what your customers are entitled to expect when they become and remain your customers. A compelling brand promise effectively answers a handful of questions:

How will their organizations benefit?

How will their business results be better?

How will their working lives be better?

What commitment are you making that is stronger and more valuable than the commitments your competitors are making?

What will you always do, every time, without fail?

What will you never do — no matter the urgency or cost?

What commitments will you refuse to make because they contradict your purpose?

What do you want your customers to experience, and how do you want them to feel about that experience?

A brand promise is a very concise statement describing the value a customer is entitled to expect when they become your customer and for the duration of time that they remain your customer. It describes the outcomes the customer gains and the experience they have with you along the way. Another way to say it is this: A brand promise describes what your customers get and how they get it.

A brand promise is the foundation on which all branding, marketing, and selling activity needs to stand. But that's not all it is. It's also the standard of measure against which each and every result can be compared. It's where good performance metrics begin. That makes it the ideal basis from which to craft a business model because a business model answers the question: How do we fulfill our brand promise?

Therefore, a robust brand promise will speak to what we desire the customer to think, but also to what we aspire for them to feel. Yet, talking about what we want the customers to feel starts to sound squishy and suspicious to tough-minded, results-driven business people.

We could easily and happily avoid dealing with the whole messy realm of feelings if customers made their buying decisions rationally. If buying decisions could be reduced to and be based upon a comparative analysis distilled to a spreadsheet, we would have no need to pay attention to what customers feel. However, far too much research conducted over far too long has demonstrated conclusively that even business-to-business buying decisions are not solely rational (O'Shaughnessy 1992, Howard & Howard 1994, Solomon 2015). In fact, we tend to make decisions very quickly and almost entirely emotionally. We then gather facts to rationalize and defend the decision we've already made emotionally. This is called post hoc rationalization. Ted Levitt (1991) described it this way: "The buying behavior of businesses is heavily emotional, more so even than a consumer buying cosmetics in a retail store" (116). So when crafting a brand promise, we have no choice but to clearly describe what we aspire for the customer both to feel and to think if our intention is that they take action in response.

To push this just a little farther, I would suggest that a strong brand promise has both aspirational and inspirational elements. In other words, it should answer this pair of questions: Which of your customers' aspirations do you exist to fulfill? What do you inspire your customers to do or to be?

Examples of Brand Promises: So what does a compelling and effective brand promise look like, upon which a brand can be intentionally built?

Pace Marketing Communications, City of Industry, California:

Pace Marketing Communications exists to create exceptional results for our clients, as our clients measure and define them. We earn our long-term client relationships and their trust in us by doing just that. In practice, this means that:

We define our success entirely by the results our clients are achieving from the campaigns and projects we execute for our clients.

We will not limit what we do. Instead, we will seek out and use any resource, technology, or medium that will deliver the results our clients need and expect.

We will align ourselves with our clients in highly interactive, high-trust relationships where much of the value we create is the delivery of the best advice and counsel they can find anywhere.

LANE PRESS
On *Your* Page™

The Lane Press, Burlington Vermont

Lane Press will be your trusted surrogate: Helping you succeed is the very fiber of who we are, how we do business, and how we measure our success. In practice, this means:

We will act on your behalf, as we believe you would when you are not present to act for yourself.

We will do those things for you that distract you from maintaining a laser-like focus on your core business.

Our actions will always be guided by the commitments that you have made to your customers, reflect the passion you have for your business, and evidence nimble, innovative, and creative thinking.

We will collaborate with you in ways that make things easier and not harder, that treat our relationship as a long-term commitment, and above all, that value trust, honesty and integrity.

We will do this by continuously developing our knowledge of how content is created, distributed, and funded; and with a deep and nuanced understanding of your business, your customers, and your culture.

We will be "On Your Page".

The Brand Itself

If the brand promise is the superstructure, the brand itself distills the brand promise into a powerful and memorable idea that has three elements: identity, narrative, and experience.

Your brand is not merely your logo, name, and tagline. Identity matters, as we'll see, and certainly those are important branding elements. But your brand is the central idea with which you're identified, the core narrative that your customers and the market tell about you. Your brand is how you are defined and described—factually and emotionally—by those to whom the brand matters most. The narrative, identity, and experience that make up your brand need to reinforce each other and to work in concert with each other.

Shortly after his return to Apple in 1997, Steve Jobs addressed these remarks to a group of Apple employees: "To me, marketing is about values. This is a very complicated world. It's a very noisy world. And we're not going to get the chance to get people to remember much about us. No company is. So we have to be really clear on what we want them to know about us" (https://www.youtube.com/watch?v=vmG9jzCHtSQ).

The intentional development of a brand is how you get and stay clear about what you want people to know and feel about you. And there are two groups for whom your brand is vitally important. The first group is your customers and potential customers. The second group is your employees.

The experience that your employees have with your brand is the mirror image of what your customers will have. Your employees are service performers and service providers to your customers. Their interaction with your customers will make or break your brand because your customers' actual experiences with your brand will always define the brand for them. Therefore, your brand is and should be vitally important to your employees. They need to be immersed in and saturated by your brand. Berry and Parasuraman (1991) describe this immersion and saturation:

> Internalizing the brand involves explaining and selling the brand to employees. It involves sharing with employees the research and strategy behind the presented brand. It involves creative communication of the brand to employees. It involves training employees in brand-strengthening behaviors. It involves rewarding and celebrating employees whose actions support the brand. Most of all, internalizing the brand involves involving employees in the care and nurturing of the brand. Employees will not feel part of nor act out the brand unless they understand it and believe in it. (129)

Howard Schultz, the founder of Starbucks, (Schultz & Yang 1997) described this effect perfectly:

> Our competitive advantage over the big coffee brands turned out to be our people. Supermarket sales are nonverbal and impersonal, with no personal interaction. But in a Starbucks store, you encounter real people who are informed and excited about the coffee, and enthusiastic about the brand .... Starbucks' success proves that a multimillion-dollar advertising program isn't a prerequisite for building a ... brand -- nor are the deep pockets of a big corporation. You can do it one customer at a time, one store at a time, one market at a time. (247)

Therefore, all three elements of your brand need to speak to your customers and to your employees simultaneously. The graphic on the next page shows those relationships:

Brand Identity: Your logo isn't your brand, and neither is the combination of your logo, name, tagline, and color scheme. In some combination, they are simply your trademark or service mark. But the imagery or symbols (including your name) that identify you are important. They make an essential contribution by serving as a simple anchor or a form of shorthand that encapsulates your brand. Therefore, those elements that identify your brand should work in concert with each other and be used consistently.

Name: There are limitless ways to name a brand or company. And since for the majority of readers, the two are identical, we'll treat the two as one: The company is the brand. The three most typical options are naming the company for the founders (Smith, Smith, Smith, Smith & Smith), naming it for a process or product (Graphic Graphics), or giving it a purely conceptual name (TriXenoTech). There are, of course, combinations of those three in wide use, as well (Smith Graphics).

Regardless, strong names exhibit a handful of characteristics, including these five most important ones:

Memorable: Is the name distinct enough to set it apart from others in the space and become memorably tied solely to you? Does it sound and function like a noun?

Short: "The Ping-Pong Paddle with the Flashlight in the Handle Company" isn't a good choice for many reasons. Most important, it is simply too long. Long names inevitably get shortened in use. Dodge that bullet if you can.

Simple: Is your name easy to spell and easy to say? If not, go back to the drawing board. A jumble of random consonants or unrelated syllables may sound "high tech," but it isn't likely to work well in use. A good method to avoid the jumble is to pair a noun with a verb or a noun with an adjective. Dropbox is a good example.

Engaging: Will people like saying it? Does it roll off the tongue easily? This can slide into the "too cute" or "too clever by half" realm easily if you're determined to take yourselves too seriously or if you assume that everyone seeing it will get the joke. But a name should be winsome in a fashion that makes sense in your context. PerfectBlast could work well if you're in the precision demolition business, but less well if you're an email marketer.

Relevant: Is there an appropriate connection between your purpose and the name? Randomness in naming is a drawback rather than an advantage. Again, Dropbox is a good, positive example. Gravee and Fairtilizer aren't.

Icon: A logotype isn't the same thing as a brand icon. In use, a logotype is a simple graphic element typically paired with a name to provide a visual anchor or point-of-reference to speed identification. They are the descendants of trademarks. And logos are easy to create badly. In the worst cases, the art bears no relationship to the name or your brand promise. In far too many cases, the art is indistinguishable from other, too-similar logos.

The additional effort required to move beyond a logotype to create a brand icon is well worth it. A logotype is static and flat. An icon can move beyond those limitations, and include movement (animation) and sound. It can move even farther and become an avatar— the brand embodied in a character (simple or complex) capable of movement and action. So a rush to execute a flat and static logo is usually ill-advised.

A brand icon should reflect the emotional attachment you intend your customers to have with your brand. That means the icon should have a clear sense of personality. And if the icon isn't in concert with the style of those customer relationships, discard it and try again.

Tagline: The best taglines are distillations of your brand promise. Catching the essence and the spirit of your brand promise in a handful of words can reinforce both your name and icon. So while they are not absolutely essential, they are often at least very helpful.

Taglines get executed badly when they don't either differentiate the brand from competing brands, nor communicate the value of its innovation clearly. Most often, taglines fail when they fall into one of the following traps:

> They are hackneyed— overused to the point of being mean-ingless. Saying you are the service or quality leader is saying nothing. Claiming that you can be trusted, counted on, or that you care are equally trite.

> They do nothing more than tell us what we already know. If you're a printer, mailer, fulfillment specialist, or marketing services provider, a tagline that spells that out will do little more than insult your customer's intelligence. They already know.

> They yell "Me too!" If your tagline could be applied just as easily to any competing company or brand, start over. So do that. Put your tagline against the name or brand of your primary competitor and test for fit. If it fits them as well as it does you, then begin again.

> They point to the obvious. If your tagline points to the mini-mum offering that all competitors must provide in order to play in your space, then you haven't said anything meaningful because you haven't pointed to anything that sets you apart.

> They are stiff, static, and lifeless. When there's no discernible personality in a tagline, it loses power.

Can your tagline effectively answer the question: What do you stand for? BMW has had one of the most recognizable and longest-standing tag-lines of any well-known brand. And it is instructive. The ethos or spirit of the brand is unrivaled performance. The functional benefits are reliabil-ity, agility, and acceleration. The emotional benefits that BMW offers are feeling cool, feeling admired, and feeling empowered. The tagline cap-tures the essence of all those elements inherent in BMW's brand promise. That's why "The Ultimate Driving Machine" is so apropos as BMW's tagline. It captures in one short statement what BMW stands for.

Brand Narrative

Seth Godin (2005) described how behavior gets changed. "Facts don't change people's behavior. Emotion changes people's behavior. Stories and irrational impulses are what change behavior. Not facts or bullet points." He was writing about useless conferences and meetings, and how to change them. However, the core truth applies directly to brands.

Narratives are about action and emotion— doing and feeling. And narrative explains why the testimonials of actual customers and case examples or case histories are so effective to influence the behavior of your current and prospective customers, either to remain your customers or to become your customers.

Two stories are being told about strong brands. The first is the story brands are telling about themselves. The second is the story that their customers are telling (to themselves and others) about the brand. And with the advent of social media, the two are converging quickly into a single narrative being co-created and told both by the company (including its employees) and by its customers.

A core narrative is more important and more powerful than all of the investment and effort in the development of a tangible and visual brand identity. When your employees, customers, and prospective customers can frame a cohesive narrative about your brand, almost nothing can dislodge your brand from that position in their minds and hearts.

A core narrative about your brand will follow a pattern. It's the same pattern that effective screenplays use, often described as The Hero's Journey. And in this, your customer is always the hero.

Act One: We meet the buyer (the Hero) and understand her current, ordinary life. We learn what she does every day, the goals she seeks to achieve, and the mission she works to fulfill. We learn how the Hero's responsibilities relate to our products and services.

Act Two: The Hero encounters the challenge. There is always a challenge: an opportunity that's difficult to grasp, a problem that evades solution, or a threat that appears on the horizon. It is a core challenge, not merely an inconvenience. Likely, the failure to address the challenge poses a threat to the success of his or her entire organization. We learn about the ways the Hero has attempted to meet the challenge with insufficient success or at too high a cost. We learn why the attempted solutions were flawed and ineffective, and why partial solutions are unsatisfactory and insufficient.

Act Three: We see how the Hero learns about the resource of your brand, reacts initially, finds herself intrigued, and discovers what sets your brand substantially apart from your competitors. And we learn how the Hero discovers that your brand will fulfill her needs and aspirations, delivering both tangible and emotional fulfillment.

Those narratives are incredibly powerful when told in the first person. They explain why your brand matters and why it matters to that specific customer. When those narratives can be aggregated and common themes described that are illustrated by individual customer experiences, the central brand narrative becomes nearly impossible for one unhappy customer or one envious competitor to discount or displace. That's because what's embedded in that narrative is how your customers feel when doing business with your brand, including

how they feel about what they can now do,

how they feel about what they now understand,

how they feel about the opportunities they are capturing, and

what are the challenges they are now meeting effectively.

Brand Experience

The experience of having contact with your brand and doing business with your company is explored in a chapter of its own because the delivery of your customer experience is how your brand ethos comes to life. Within the customer discipline, it's an entire vector.

Your brand experience is what builds your customer's attachment to your brand. Their earliest experiences build their awareness and some measure of trust as they experience your consistency and performance on their behalf. Next, their experiences build their understanding of your relevance and their active preference for your brand as your competitive differentiation becomes clear. Finally, their experience builds their affinity and emotional attachment as they discover and value the "everything else" they gain from a relationship with your company and your brand.

Summary

Brands are so powerful that it is little wonder that the brand is often the most important business asset, often accounting for 10% to 50% of the market value of a company as a going concern.

Effective brands align your employees with your customers, your culture with your reputation, your behavior with your differentiation, and your promises with reality.

Your enterprise is built on a purpose with the customer at its center, a strategy for delivering benefits to the customer that are relevant and distinctive, a brand promise that articulates your purpose and strategy, and a brand that captures and embodies narratives that begin with the customer's issues and describe solutions in language that is direct, practical, compelling, winsome, and memorable.

Your brand describes functionally what you will do for your customers, competitively how you will be different in a positive way, and emotionally how they are entitled to feel when doing business with you.

Because brands are living experiences, they have both aspirational and inspirational dimensions. Which of your customer's aspirations do you exist to fulfill? What do you inspire your customers to do or to be? And what are you doing with your brand?

References

Aaker, David A. 1996. *Building Strong Brands*. New York: Free Press.

Bedbury, Scott and Stephen Fenichell. 2002. *A New Brand World: 8 Principles for Achieving Brand Leadership in the 21st Century*. New York: Viking.

Berry, Leonard L. and A. Parasuraman. 1991. *Marketing Services: Competing through Quality*. New York: Free Press.

Godin, Seth. November 13, 2005. *How to Run a Useless Conference.* http://www.encyklopedia.in/viewtopic.php?f=74&t=4660.

Howard, John A. 1994. B*uyer Behavior in Marketing Strategy.* Englewood Cliffs, N.J.: Prentice Hall.

Kotler, Philip, Waldemar Pfoertsch, and I. Michi. 2006 *B2B Brand Management.* Berlin: Springer.

Levitt, Theodore. 1991. *Thinking about Management.* New York: Collier Macmillan.

O'Shaughnessy, John. 1992. *Explaining Buyer Behavior : Central Concepts and Philosophy of Science Issues.* New York: Oxford University Press.

Roberts, Kevin. 2005. *Lovemarks : The Future Beyond Brands.* New York: PowerHouse Books.

Schultz, Howard. and Dori Jones Yang. 1997. *Pour Your Heart into It: How Starbucks Built a Company One Cup at a Time.* New York: Hyperion.

Sinek, Simon. 2009. *Start with Why: How Great Leaders Inspire Everyone to Take Action.* New York, Portfolio.

Solomon, Michael R. 2015. *Consumer Behavior: Buying, Having, and Being.* Boston: Pearson.

4

BUSINESS DEVELOPMENT

by Wayne Peterson

For graphic communications companies, any war between marketing and sales was over before it started. Marketing as a business discipline never made it onto the field. In fact, for most Graphic communications firms, there is no marketing function and there has never been one. Sales has reigned supreme on the customer-facing side of the business.

Enabled by the job shop business model, the marketing activity of most small- to medium-sized enterprises (SMEs) has been ad hoc, sporadic, and treated as an event, rather than an ongoing process. Those companies who added marketing resources used them in support of direct selling activity, often to reduce the time that expensive salespeople spent on distracting activities or activities which the salespeople could not execute especially well — advertising, sales promotion, and lead identification.

Then, as we've noted already, everything changed. Suddenly direct salespeople became less effective as they became less valuable and less necessary in the customer's eyes. Customer buying and vendor management patterns shifted and changed, leaving the salesperson much less able to define reality in the eyes of the customer. (Holland & Young 2010) Companies unsupported by strong brands and not anchored as "thought leaders" in the customer's mind's found themselves unable to get to the table even to offer their services. The advent of digital, social, and mobile media has enabled customers to vet potential vendors quickly and easily, long before a first conversation with a salesperson. Potential customers can easily interact with peers and colleagues in similar firms, getting a clear sense of the potential vendor before deciding to accept any overture from a salesperson.

The situation grows more and more difficult for unbranded and poorly marketed companies where nothing plows the road in front of the legacy salespeople. And yet, many Graphic Communication companies defend the status quo while bemoaning their inability to identify, recruit, retain, and channel effective salespeople.

We're beyond the point where efficient selling activity (enough contacts, enough calls, enough bids, enough meetings) can meet the revenue needs of most companies. If it was ever a "numbers game", it is no longer. Despite that reality, some companies still resort to punitive and tightly controlling metrics when disappointed in the top-line revenue results. But even highly effective direct selling activity is proving insufficient when that's the only effort being made. Something needs to change.

Marketing and Selling, or Business Development?

"Marketing" and "Selling" are good terms. But "Business Development" has the benefit of a single term encompassing all the work of creating new customers. Where Graphic communications companies have seen marketing as subordinate to and supportive of direct selling activity, Business Development takes a wider view of the whole. And hiding in that key term is a vitally important reality: marketing and selling are no longer separate processes. Business Development is the integration of marketing and selling into a single process. For Graphic communications, brand development, marketing (including marketing communications) and selling aren't even links in a chain. They are simply signposts showing us where we are in a cyclical process flow.

In his perennial bestseller, *The Seven Habits of Highly Effective People*, Stephen Covey's (1989) second habit is "Begin with the End in Mind." For business development to be effective and sustainable in a Graphic communications firm, that's the essential starting place: at the end. Because Business Development is a process, rather than an event, it can be designed in the same way that any other business process is designed. And as is true with the very best processes, it should begin with the outcome and work upstream. You have to answer the questions: "What are we trying to do? What kinds of customer relationships are we working to create?"

The perfect place to begin is by looking at the very best customer relationships you have now. In most cases, there are only a handful of them. And regardless of the industry segments occupied by those customers, or the specific products and services they are buying from you, those very best relationships will look very much like each other.

Business Development as a Process

The obsolete "funnel" model has been replaced with a continuous cycle of customer interaction. Picture a circle of customer touch points that includes both outbound and inbound interaction, and both virtual / digital

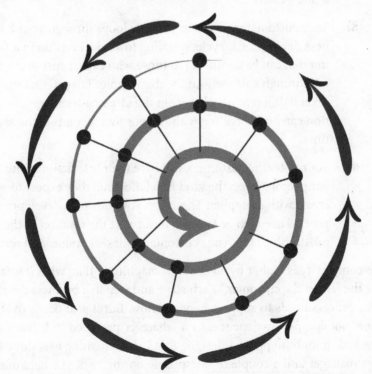

interaction and interaction with a salesperson. From any point on that circle, a customer can move directly to a buying decision. More to the point, their path will be their own, rather than one that you design or prescribe.

This has four significant implications for building a business development process:

1. Customers will not simply follow any linear path you design, step-by-step. Instead, they will reach for whatever resource and whatever point of contact makes the most sense to them at the moment. This applies to potential customers, of course. But it also applies to current customers preparing to make renewal or additional purchase decisions.

2. Your opportunity to create value does not begin when the salesperson makes contact. In fact, your first opportunity to create value -- and the point where customers expect you to offer value -- is much earlier than when most would reach for a salesperson.

3. Your customers will make multiple loops through your business development cycle, spiraling toward a decision in a fashion that can be confusing to those who expect customers to fall through a funnel. And with multiple "buyers" that means several different people within the same customer organization can be interacting with various touch points at the same time.

4. Your potential customers will base their interactions with your company on the kind of relationship they expect to create with a supplier. Therefore, your business development process needs to be tailored to support the creation of the relationships that your customers will seek, value, and retain.

The complexity is higher by an order of magnitude than what it was before the "era of the customer." Each stage and step in a business development process needs to support a logical flow. But it also needs to stand alone, not completely dependent on whatever preceded it. It takes diligent and thoughtful process design. This isn't something best done by a sales manager and a couple of salespeople on the back of a napkin over drinks. Unfortunately, that's just how many business development processes have been created.

The balance of power between a B2B sales person and potential customer has shifted radically. The information advantage once belonged to the salesperson. He or she had control of information that buyers considered necessary or even vital. Now, your potential customers can access information remotely — from you, from your competitors, and from your current and former customers. Daniel Pink (2012) describes the change this way:

> When buyers can know more than sellers, sellers are no longer protectors and purveyors of information. They're the curators and clarifiers of it – helping to make sense of the blizzard of facts, data and options. (56)

Therefore, your customers no longer believe that direct interaction with the salesperson is essential early in their decision processes. When they do reach for a salesperson, they will often present that salesperson with a well-informed series of questions. And that tends to turn the tables on most legacy selling methods that depend on the salesperson controlling both the conversation and the questions being asked. Salespeople describe this change as "being put on the defensive" by customers who have, or seem to have, more and better information than does the salesperson. Some potential customers will come to believe that they have sufficient information to take your company out of the running without ever reaching for a salesperson, and without ever responding to a salesperson's overtures.

Post-The Great Recession, the number of people involved in buying decisions has continued to increase, but primary decision-makers have largely retaken authority that was steadily being delegated into the hands of committees, teams, and other groups. As organizations have gotten leaner, the layers to which authority had been pushed out have been jettisoned. However, the primary decision-maker (who has the authority to give the final "Yes", rather than those who can make a "No" stick somewhere in the process) is now typically at a higher level in the organization. Therefore, business development processes need to target decision-makers at higher levels, regardless of the relationship style that the customer would prefer to develop with a chosen supplier.

That's an apparent contradiction many salespeople find confusing: More people are involved in the selling and decision process, but final authority is concentrated in one individual at a higher level. It's made identification of the ultimate decision-maker harder.

The Best Relationship

Organizations of all kinds are actively segmenting their suppliers. Regardless of the motivation driving that segmentation, effective and sustainable business development depends on your ability to anticipate and prepare for it. Aligning a business development process with both the buying process encountered most often, and with the kind of relationship that the customer desires, is essential. Both the objective and the path to reach it are critical.

It is likely that your very best customers have segmented their suppliers, as well as grouped them. In fact, those engaged in actively supplier management are consistently trying to understand your behavior, and what's important to you. This runs contrary to what most salespeople believe: that relationship management is one-directional, from the supplier to the customer. Jonathan O'Brien (2013) described some of that thinking this way:

> Imagine you could sit invisibly in a supplier sales meeting.
> What would they say about your company, you and the stake-
> holders in your business they interface with? Suppliers' sales
> planning meetings are often like planning battlefield tactics,
> except the meeting takes place in a swanky office, not a tent
> in the middle of a field. Suppliers have just one objective and
> that is to grow and maintain the accounts that are important to
> them. If this includes your company, then you will be the sub-
> ject of discussion at sales meetings. Suppliers will debate what
> they need to do to develop the relationship so that they are in
> prime position. This will include tactics for engaging with you
> and key stakeholders.
>
> Not every account is of interest to the supplier, and the sup-
> plier has only so much resource to put into growing and
> maintaining their accounts, so this will be directed at the ac-
> counts that are seen as priorities. There are accounts where the

supplier will not be hugely interested, perhaps because they are difficult to service, unprofitable or have poor terms within the contract. In this case suppliers may adopt a deliberate strategy to either do the minimum to maintain the account or even manage the account out of the business. It is vital you understand how the supplier sees your business, because there is great risk if you see the account as strategic (portfolio analysis) but the supplier sees the account as one to manage out. The analytical tool we use here is called supplier preferencing, and it should be used in conjunction with portfolio analysis.

Nearly all supplier segmentation methods can be distilled down to two factors: how important is the supplier to the organization, and how difficult would that supplier be to replace? That leads to a simple segmentation scheme, like the one illustrated below.

The diagram identifies four quadrants within which a supplier relationship can fall. It is a mistake to assume that only the strategic quadrant

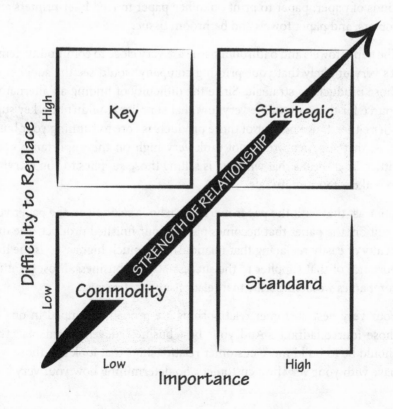

at the top right is it desirable space within which to build a lasting and profitable customer relationship. Different customers are seeking different kinds of value and, therefore, different relationships with suppliers. In the same way, not all readers of this book are leaders of companies equipped and are prepared to build strategic relationships with their customers. You may be structured to do something very different.

This is an important starting point for two reasons. First, it should clarify the sorts of relationships you're best prepared to create and keep. Second, it should clarify the relationships that your very best customers find most appropriate and most valuable. In other words, it starts the process of aligning your business development process with a valuable and attainable objective — more relationships like those with your very best current customers.

Let me give you an example. Let's take paper. Your business buys more than one kind of paper. So let's imagine for a moment that you're a printing company. As a printing company, you will buy at least three different kinds of paper: paper to print on, office paper to feed laser printers and copiers, and paper towels and bathroom tissue.

The paper towels and bathroom tissue are very close to commodity items. It's very unlikely that your printing company would see the supplier of those products as strategic. Since the difficulty of finding an alternative source for those would be very low, that supplier wouldn't be a key supplier either. Since neither of those products is core to running your business, that supplier would not rank very high on the importance scale either. That means that whoever is selling those supplies to you is trying to make a commodity sale.

Contrast that with the paper merchant who is selling you the paper you print on, the paper that becomes part of your finished product. The difficulty of easily replacing that relationship is much higher. So is the importance of that supplier to the success of your business. Most printing companies would describe that relationship as strategic.

Your very best customer relationships are probably grouped in one of those four quadrants. And your best business development objective should be to build more customer relationships that look like those you have with your very best customers. So determining how your very best customers see their relationship with you as a supplier is where to begin designing a business development process.

Where would your best customers put you? Is your objective to create more relationships like those? Most likely it is. And that will tell you the kind of sales process you'll build. Not only does your process need to fit your company or practice and your customers, it needs to fit the quadrant you're targeting.

News flash: There is no "one best, one-size-fits-all" sales process that's appropriate for all four quadrants. At least there's not one that works equally well in all four quadrants. The easy, thoughtless response could be to jump to the strategic quadrant, concluding that nothing else makes sense. However, that's rarely the case. There are strong and profitable relationships that customers will quickly flag as key or standard. If your product or service really is customer-agnostic, even commodity relationships can be appropriate and profitable. There's the rub and the opportunity.

Too often, sales methods are applied where there is no real fit. Let me explain through a pair of examples. Let's go back to our hypothetical printing company for a moment. Imagine that you are the owner or president of that hypothetical printing company. And imagine you are approached by a salesperson from a company that supplies paper towels, bathroom tissue, and other janitorial supplies. Imagine that the seller's voicemail to you indicates that he or she wants to create a strategic relationship with you. Can you already picture yourself staring at the telephone in disbelief? The disconnect is huge between the importance of that supplier to your business and the objective the salesperson has described.

Let me give you another example. Imagine that you are still the owner or president of my hypothetical printing company. But imagine that a seller approaches you from a paper merchant who wants to supply the kinds of paper that become part of your finished product. Imagine hearing a voice mail message that talks solely about unit cost. No mention is made of availability, range of products, extension of credit, training and other resources, or the quality of the business relationship. If, for you, the relationship with the paper merchant makes them a strategic supplier, how much traction will the one-dimensional approach focusing on unit cost likely have with you?

The sad reality is that both of those examples are drawn from actual events. Neither was effective. Neither led to any kind of serious interaction between the person selling and the person buying. And an owner or company principal made both overtures. So identifying the quadrant that best describes your relationship with your very best customers isn't just an academic exercise. It is the first piece of information you need to choose the sales process you are going to build. So, which quadrant is yours?

Most Supplier Relationship Management efforts within customers' organizations will focus on reducing the importance of a given supplier relationship since it is much harder to create additional options and to reduce the difficulty of replacing the supplier. In the same fashion, most business development efforts will focus on increasing supplier importance, since you have little control over the external environment and the number of competitors, substitutes, and replacements for your product and service offering. Therefore, a strong business development process will follow one of two wide paths. It will aim to increase your importance, moving you from a commodity supplier to a standard supplier, or it will increase your importance and move you from a key supplier to a strategic supplier.

Designing a Business Development Process

The obsolete funnel model is no longer useful to describe marketing, sales, or the two combined into a single business development process. Therefore, a number of factors will have a significant effect on the business development design process.

No complete and clean hand-off can be expected between marketing and sales. That means there is no point where your process will move completely from inbound to outbound, or from virtual to human.

Very few sales are now made between a single buyer and a single salesperson. Certainly, most high-value purchases involve a buying committee or team. While only one individual typically has the authority to give final approval for purchase, nearly all the team members will have veto authority and the power to say "No." Therefore, your business development process will need to weave a fabric of relationships between people in your organization and people in the customer organization.

Your business development process will almost certainly include digital, social, and mobile access to information, resources, and tools for which your prospective customers will reach first. Those are essential if you're going to be included as the customer buying process begins.

Your business development process will likely include far more customer touch points than at any point in the past. Your company won't be compared simply with your direct competitors. Instead, your prospective customers will compare their interactions with you to their interactions with Amazon, Southwest Airlines, Zappos, Apple, and others. They will expect you to enable a great deal of self-service for them beyond simply making basic information available.

Therefore, it's now necessary to build an understanding of how customers manage the supplier selection process in your particular market space, however you've defined it. That moves beyond understanding the supplier quadrant in which your very best customer relationships fit. To that we need to add the process by which your customers are willing to put you there. And we need to understand who within those very best relationships are the decision-makers empowered to say the ultimate "Yes". Where, how, and who are the three vital pieces of information we need to understand in order to tailor a business development process specifically to your organization.

Customers move through predictable, very broad stages in the development of any relationship with a supplier. While the detailed and specific stages and steps in your business development process need to be tailored to your customers and the value you deliver, it's helpful to understand customer development from 30,000 feet above.

Customer Journey Stages

The earliest stages of the "customer journey" are all during customer formation – the process the customer goes through becoming your customer. Customers move from knowing to feeling to doing, from information to emotion to action. When business development, sales, or customer-

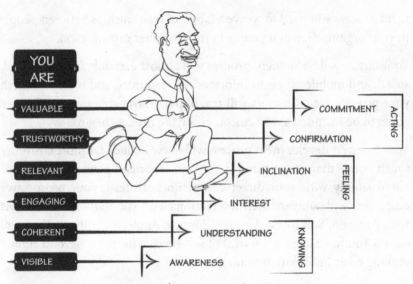

YOU ARE			
VALUABLE	COMMITMENT		ACTING
TRUSTWORTHY	CONFIRMATION		
RELEVANT	INCLINATION	FEELING	
ENGAGING	INTEREST		
COHERENT	UNDERSTANDING	KNOWING	
VISIBLE	AWARENESS		

First Steps in a Customer's Journey

formation processes don't work, it's usually because the emotional / feeling piece is missing or ignored.

When multiple people within a customer organization are involved in the process of choosing to begin doing business with you, each one moves at their own pace through the same early stages. How they take those steps can vary widely. But the steps described in the graphic above show why each one is connected to an element of your business development process. Your visibility enables a customer to become aware of you. The coherence of your messages and content enables a customer for form an understanding of you. Behavior and content that are engaging enable a customer to develop active interest in you. Behavior and content that are relevant enable the customer to develop an inclination or affinity for you. Behavior that's trustworthy enables a customer to develop confidence in you. And, finally, the creation, communication, and offer of real value, enables a customer to make the commitment to do business with you.

Most funnel or pipeline diagrams that chart separate marketing or sales processes will miss one or more of these steps. Marketing will often focus on the first three or four. Sales will often focus on the final three or four steps. And if there's a turf battle between marketing and sales, it is often for the middle two steps. In the worst-case scenarios I've seen, marketing has focused only on the first two steps with sales focused on the last two. Meanwhile no one was engaging the customer around the middle two, leaving the customer cold and the process broken, while marketing and sales pointed fingers at each other.

Awareness

Customers become conscious of a company and its offering when the company is visible. Most often, companies are invisible because they are either silent or speaking only rarely. The two most effective B2B tools to create real and sustainable visibility at present are intentional brand building and content marketing. We've described brand development already. Content marketing is essential to understand in B2B business development now. And in B2B business development, content marketing must be both interactive and media-agnostic.

It isn't news that the era when one-way, outbound marketing communication was effective in the B2B space is behind us. Interactive content marketing doesn't simply mean a rudimentary presence on social media, enabling customers to find content of interest, and post reactions or responses to it. Rather, it means that the company is working to become a primary, authoritative, and valuable voice within its competitive space. While "thought leadership" is already an over-used and inelegant term, it does carry the message that content needs to be meaningful and useful for potential and current customers.

Content marketing also needs to be media-agnostic. The knee-jerk assumption now is that content marketing should be primarily or exclusively digital if it is going to be interactive and effective. And that's simply a shallow and false assumption. Direct mail content marketing can be highly effective because it is tangible. The fact that direct mail delivers meaningful and useful content in physical form has a couple of powerful advantages — visibility and persistence. The entire piece of direct mail is visible at once if designed with that intention. That's not the case for most digital marketing messages, and especially not for email. The fact that so many marketing messages are delivered via email and so few are now delivered via direct mail works in the favor of direct mail, too. It's the exception rather than the rule, making it more visible. Beyond that, it is persistent in a way that email is not. Email messages (as well as other digital marketing messages) can easily be skipped over, even if the recipient intends to return to them later. That's true even for content marketing where the content may be genuinely interesting and actionable. Direct mail tends to persist because it is easy for the busy recipient to set it aside, drop it into a backpack, or put it somewhere that it will be handled multiple times.

Cross-media and interactive communication is the foundation of gaining real visibility with the decision-makers of prospective customers.

Understanding

Effective interaction with potential customers doesn't need to be exhaustive or even comprehensive. Leaving decision-makers intrigued is a good thing. But content marketing created to benefit the potential customer and build real interest does need to be coherent. Far too much content marketing fails to be planned and well-integrated. Instead, individual pieces of content and individual messages seem to have no clear context. Randomness rules too often. Be wary of listicles, cute memes, and other randomness.

Coherence tends to follow effective planning, and that should include an editorial calendar. Rather than starting each month (or even week) with an empty slate, an effective content plan should describe posts or articles organized around themes and sequenced appropriately. A series of articles or posts tends to be much more powerful than any stand-alone piece of content.

However it is offered (inbound or outbound, digital or tangible), the content that's intended to help your potential customers know you needs to be coherent so that a clear picture of you emerges. That means you'll speak with a consistent voice, and you'll share a substantial understanding of your organization in the process.

Interest

The expectation sales has long had of marketing is that marketing will deliver "warm leads" to sales. And that points clearly to the importance of the middle two steps and an intentional emotional engagement of the customer. What the customer feels energizes what the customer knows, leading to what the customer does. Knowledge alone doesn't lead to action. It never has.

Genuinely "warm" potential customers are warming because there's a developing emotional engagement. Both sales and marketing tend to point fingers at each other, debating who has responsibility to warm the potential customer, and to enable and encourage that emotional engagement.

Personality matters in this. The personality of the company / brand, and the personality of the salesperson (when a B2B salesperson is necessary and valuable) both energize the customer's emotional engagement. There's a magnetic, emotional pull that leads to the some degree of preference for you over other options and competitors. Without that emotional pull, there's little reason for a customer to develop confidence in you, and to make a commitment to you.

The first step in that emotional engagement is active interest on the part of the potential customer. And that happens most quickly when the company and salesperson both behave in ways that are winsome. When learning about a potential supplier, the same three factors that define a positive customer experience (Manning, Bodine, & Forrester (2012) are the primary questions asked:

> Can this company meet my needs?

> Would this be easy?

> Would I enjoy this?

> Manning et. al put it this way:

> ... customers perceive their experiences at three different levels: meets needs, easy, and enjoyable. Every time they interact with a product, a service, a person, or an automated system, they judge how well the interaction helped them achieve their goals, how much effort they had to invest in the interaction, and how much they enjoyed the interaction. (11)

And it is those last two questions that are most important to answer. It is also those two that go unanswered by most B2B business development processes. We work hard to create compelling answers to the first of those three questions. We focus on features and benefits, sometimes even on advantages, that demonstrate the degree to which we can and will meet the customer's need. But we miss the other two, to our disadvantage.

Substantial indications that the company will be easy and pleasurable to work with are essential if the necessary emotional engagement is going to begin for the individual customer decision-maker. And this is where intentional and intelligent brand-building makes a substantial contribution to your business-development process. According to Ben Parr (2015), here's why:

> We rely on reputable sources to direct our scarce attention, and thus we pay more attention to those sources in the process. These reputable sources are individuals, groups of people, or organizations that have developed well-known reputations for their work, their knowledge, or their expertise. The Reputation Trigger is the leveraging of reputable sources and figures to direct attention. By either reestablishing yourself as a reputable figure, such as an expert, or receiving the endorsement of a reputable source, you can shift attention toward you and your message remarkably quickly. In fact, the reputation effect accelerates as a reputation becomes stronger, which is why reputation matters when it comes to attention. (136)

Parr sums up the case he is making this way:

> A reputation is the embodiment of a person, company, or idea's credibility and worthiness. It is the credibility and worth that determine whether something is worth our time and long-term interest. That's why reputations are important shortcuts for quickly determining who is worthy of our attention. When simply hearing your name makes people pay attention, you have become a master of attention. (160)

We attract and hold interest when we're engaging, when we're worth listening to because we're offering value in advance of expecting anyone to do business with us.

Inclination

The second positive emotional stage is when the potential customer feels an inclination toward doing business with you (rather than with someone else) when they have a need for the value you ultimately offer. This begins when the potential customer senses that you might be directly relevant to them.

Relevance that triggers a feeling, an inclination toward you, isn't fact-based. It's not the result of a careful marshaling and evaluation of an exhaustive series of features, benefits, or even advantages. Rather, inclination emerges when the potential customer begins to frame a story about you and how you might relate to what's important to that person.

> Storytelling is all the rage is business today. But storytelling is far more than an engaging form of information transfer or an addictive form of entertainment. It's how we make sense of the world. The job of the conscious mind is to automatically produce a story to make sense out of our perceptions and reflections. Those stories – or schemas, metaphors, and mental models – are how we connect the abstract content of our minds into recognizable patterns. *And the easier it is for our minds to conjure a pattern, to make a particular association, the more confidence we have in our invented story* [emphasis added]. (Asacker, 2013, 73)

When the pieces fit, when a personality clearly emerges, and when the potential customer begins to see how she could relate to you, an inclination emerges. It's that process of forming a story about you that inclines the customer toward you if there are enough pieces of narrative about you for the customer to formulate a cohesive story in her own mind.

We choose to do business with companies that are "our kind of people" or "our kind of company". Relevant content and relevant revelations about you, become the building blocks necessary for a customer to create a story about your company that leads to the inclination to do business with you should the need arise. In essence, you're equipping the potential customer to describe how you'll behave.

Confirmation

Two different actions follow the earlier steps as a potential customer becomes an active customer. The first is confirmation. At this point the potential customer has an inclination toward doing business with you, has become aware of you, formed a coherent understanding of you, has experienced some active interest in you, and created the framework of a story about you. Confirmation is making sure that all of those pieces of knowledge and emotion are warranted before a commitment is made. And that's why being trustworthy is so important.

This is when and where the potential customer takes the actions necessary to confirm that all of the pieces fit and hang together. Frequently, this is the action of checking references and vetting your firm through social media and similar sources. For some potential customers (especially when the relationship is mission-critical) background checks of various kinds are involved, including a look to see if others substantiate all of your claims.

Evidence supporting that you are who you claim to be, that your assertions are factual and truthful is what's sought and vetted. Woe to you if your claims don't hold up under scrutiny.

Commitment

The last of these early stages of the customer's journey is the action of making a commitment. And that's a process in and of itself. What enables the customer to complete that process is your offer of genuine value.

"Value Proposition" is a term that's been ill-used as a catch-all descriptor for a collection of features, benefits, and (sometimes) advantages offered generally to a market. A real value proposition is specific in the value it describes, which is meaningful only to a specific customer, and only in the context of that customer's challenges and opportunities. It's that sort of highly specific value that enables a customer to take the action of making the commitment to do business. Strong business development processes include the information gathering necessary to understand the customer's real context, and the challenges and opportunities large (important and urgent) enough to warrant taking action. From that information gathering, a series of individual value propositions can be crafted that speak to that specific customer in language that's meaningful to them. So this demonstration of value that enables a customer to take action is uniquely tailored for that individual customer rather than some generalized proposition offered to all potential customers indiscriminately.

Each customer's journey will include these six large stages. And any effective business development process will enable the customer to move easily and steadily through them. Effective business development processes will always be targeted to create relationships that customers can easily confirm are appropriate and valuable, and with companies who meet their needs, with whom it is easy to do business, and who make the whole process enjoyable from beginning to end. It's a tall order, and that's why it calls for a well and intentionally designed process rather than random sales activity and disconnected marketing communication.

References

Asacker, Thomas. 2013. *The Business of Belief: How the World's Best Marketers, Designers, Salespeople, Coaches, Fundraisers, Educators, Entrepreneurs and Other Leaders Get Us to Believe.*

Covey, Stephen R. 1989. *The seven habits of highly effective people : restoring the character ethic.* New York: Simon and Schuster.

Holland, John R., and Tim Young. 2010. *Rethinking the sales cycle : how superior sellers embrace the buying cycle to achieve a sustainable and competitive advantage.* New York: McGraw-Hill.

Manning, Harley, Kerry Bodine, and Forrester (Firm). 2012. *Outside in : the power of putting customers at the center of your business.* Boston: Houghton Mifflin Harcourt.

O'Brien, Jonathan. 2013. *Negotiation for purchasing professionals.* London ; Philadelphia: Kogan Page Limited.

Parr, Ben. 2015. *Captivology : the science of capturing people's attention.* First edition. ed. New York: HarperOne, an imprint of HarperCollins Publishers.

Pink, Daniel H. 2012. *To sell is human : the surprising truth about moving others.* New York: Riverhead Books.

5

CUSTOMER EXPERIENCE

by Wayne Peterson

What they get, and how they get it. graphic communications firms of all kinds tend to get the specifications right. It's rare that companies deliver something the wrong size, in the wrong colors, or on the wrong substrate. We get the quantities right, the content right, and the distribution right. But while we tend to manage the specifications well, we don't tend to be as effective at meeting the expectations customers have of how business will be conducted, and how the relationship will be created and managed.

The management of customer relationships has moved from simple delivery of what was ordered to include a significant service component. That's not news, and most companies are focused to some degree on delivering service that's good or better. However, only a handful of companies I can identify have begun to focus on creating experiences that customers desire and value. That's why everything in this book and the model we've built is aspirational: There is a climb that begins with making products, then moves through delivering service, and finishes with creating intentional experiences.

Customers expectations are changing in significant ways, based on their experiences with other supplier relationships and buying processes, whether B2B or not. Customers who can track Amazon orders step-by-step wonder why they cannot track the fulfillment of an order with you in the same way. Customers who can customize the build of a Mini Cooper (at the dealer or online), and then get updated automatically on every step of its path from factory to dealer, wonder why you can't provide the same insight. Customers who can order Scotch Whisky from Master of Malt after reading both staff and user reviews, and then have it shipped from London to most locations in the US in a matter of days, wonder why you cannot customize a user interface to show them only what they want to see. These same customers will also look to you to offer them the opportunity to see feedback from your other customers on their experiences with your company.

We're in an era where customers want interactions that are both frictionless and self-service. And that extends even to how they learn from your firm. Over the last 24 months, ethnographic research I've conducted with the customers of my clients made clear that those customers want a number of new experiences. A common one is the ability to interact effectively with their preferred supplier through a mobile-friendly customer interface. And they want this interaction to occur without the need to craft a request in prose and then email it to a CSR who will transcribe the request into some MIS or ERP system before it can be acted upon. Customers literally want to check schedules, place orders and reorders, pull from inventory, manufacture on demand, and ship anywhere without ever leaving their chairs in meetings. And that's not all they want. It's just one example. The days are behind us when we could create raving fans simply by having an effective customer service department that's adequately staffed.

Customer Satisfaction is Meaningless

Ordinary metrics that track customer satisfaction are meaningless. A simple story will make that clear: I fly almost weekly, and I have only two remaining criteria for being satisfied with an airline flight. First, the airline needs to take me where I paid to go — not somewhere else for any reason. Second, the airline needs to keep the number of takeoffs and routine landings exactly equal. (And, no, "any landing you can walk away from" doesn't qualify.) I have only those two remaining expectations. The airlines, United in particular, have pounded any other expectation out of me. Anything more would be unrealistic, unreasonable, and setting myself up for disappointment.

In the span of five weeks, my experience with United Airlines included the following:

- United was more than three hours late four times. It was on time barely half the time.

- United cancelled my flight three times.

- United rescheduled me to fly from a different airport more than 30 miles away from the one I was standing in, and left it up to me to get there quickly.

- United put me in the upgraded seat I paid for only about a third of the time.

- United's MileagePlus system is unable to retain my full name (in a format that the TSA will recognize for their Trusted Traveler / PreCheck program) despite two calls to try and get the problem solved. On the second attempt, United disconnected the call (hung up on me) after an hour and 18 minutes.

- One United flight was the replacement for one cancelled the day before. The replacement flight left three hours later than it was scheduled. It arrived only six minutes before the crew would have "timed out" after working the maximum allowable hours.

But, and this is a big "but", if United had asked whether I was a "satisfied customer" I'd have said "yes." And I'd have been telling the truth. My two remaining criteria were met. I got where I paid them to take me, and the flight took off and landed safely.

I don't expect to be well-treated, catered-to, listened-to, or accommodated. I know better. Since I have little choice but to use United, I've adjusted my expectations to match the system. But meeting my lowered expectations doesn't mean that United should expect my loyalty or expect me to encourage others to choose United. When asked, I'd offer the opposite advice. And yet, if United had asked me if I were satisfied, I'd have said "yes" and meant it. They met my minimal expectations. And that's why "satisfaction" is meaningless.

What matters much more than satisfaction is creating customers who will honestly tell you that you meet their needs, make it easy, and make it fun.(Manning, Bodine, & Forrester 2012) Do it right, and you turn them into raving fans and active promoters of your company and brand. There's such a strong correlation between financial performance and customer promotion that raving fans are worth creating. (Manning, Bodine & Forrester 2012)

Brand Promise and Customer Experience

Exceptional and effective customer experiences aren't about how well you mimic the best you can find – whether Disney, Nordstrom, The Ritz-Carlton or anyone else. The best customer experiences are uniquely tied to your company and are anchored directly to your brand promise. These experiences reinforce your brand and set you apart because they fulfill everything you expressed in your brand promise. These experiences deliver the best value to your best customers. In the minds of customers, a genuinely premium brand is expected to deliver a premium experience, not merely a premium product coupled to an ordinary or mediocre experience.

Not all customers are created equal. And not all deserve equal treatment in some egalitarian fantasy of fairness. Not all customers are paying or should pay the same price for a service. In fact, the absence of tiered pricing in use is a great indicator that you're telling the marketplace you believe your product or service is a commodity, and is directly comparable to anyone else's. Not all customers should receive the same customer experience, nor should they be encouraged to expect it. (Peppers & Rogers 2004) Your very best experience needs to focus on your very best customers.

What your customer experience must always deliver, however, is what you promised. Your customer experience brings the customer's journey full circle, demonstrating that you are a great choice of supplier because you are fulfilling the expectations you created. And those expectations should be tailored to the specific customer's desires and needs. Therefore, building a great customer experience isn't done in a vacuum. It begins with your brand promise, along with those things you've decided your customer has a right to expect from you as you do business together. In essence, your brand promise puts you in the customer's debt, and your customer experience pays that debt in full, and then some, when done effectively.

The Elements of a Strong Customer Experience

Branding your customer experience ties together your specific services, products, processes, and organizational culture. This experience will be unique to your organization and your customers. And your customers will experience it both rationally and emotionally. A strong customer experience includes these common elements discussed below.

Learns, Understands, Adapts

The context of the strongest and best customer experiences is the customer's circumstances and needs. Period. And that context is entirely scalable, depending on the scope of customer needs you're equipped to meet. Customers describe exceptional customer experiences using statements such as: "They know me." "They've learned my particular needs, and understand me." "They've adapted to my special needs and circumstances, which makes them a really valuable partner."

Developing a customer experience that's strong and growing stronger requires creation of processes to learn your customer's circumstances and needs, to make what you've discovered available throughout your organization, and to make that learning transferrable. Therefore, building a strong customer experience is as much about excellent discovery as it is about excellent delivery.

Meets Needs Worth Meeting

Great customer experiences are consequential -- they have weight. Both scale and scope matter. The "when" and "how" may matter as much to the customer as does the "what." A customer's needs for a product or service in a matter of hours can signal that it is important, as well as urgent. A routine product delivered exactly at the appointed time and precisely in the appointed place may be especially valuable to your customer. Therefore, those become key and critical elements of that customer's experience. To meet needs that are worth meeting, you and the customer must have agreed on circumstances that are worth changing, and are within your capability to change.

Needs worth meeting typically have an outcome that lasts beyond the moment of service delivery. Too often, firms focus on the "moments of truth" delivery of a service experience while ignoring the lasting effect. In the age of universal connections, social media, and social publishing, that's a high-risk oversight. A lasting perception or effect can be created when you meet a need that's worth meeting. The very best customer experiences are genuinely memorable because they are valuable.

Enables and Equips

Great customer experiences are usually growth experiences, too. They deliver what it takes for the customer to do more and do better than they could before. This flows from a focus on customer outcomes. Customers who walk away from contact with your company better able to meet their challenges, to grasp their opportunities, and to defend against their threats will rate the experience as useful and valuable. In fact, those are often their specific objectives from interaction with your firm, whether you can see it or not.

Most adults, especially most business managers, are lifelong learners, whether they have parallel learning styles or not. Meeting the immediate and visible need or situation may be less than half of the expectation the customer brings to the contact. Not only do many want to resolve the immediate challenge, but they also want to know how to face the same thing better next time – how to see it coming from farther away, how to more effectively multiply their options for meeting it, how to create a larger scale win. The best customer experiences deliver that growth opportunity. That's why genuine customer education is nearly always part of an exceptional customer experience, especially in a B2B setting.

Centers on the Customer, Not on the Company

Among the very worst ways to build out a customer experience, or CX, is to stay welded to a production or service workflow. That's the ideal place to begin, but a terrible place to put down roots. Products and services have no essential value in and of themselves. They become valuable when they fulfill a specific customer desire or need. Therefore, the best customer experiences center on the delivery of value in the customer's eyes as a primary focus, and they make the methodology of doing so secondary.

For graphic communications companies, this is among the toughest pivots to make. For generations, the production and distribution process has been brightly lit and on center stage. That's why operations and manufacturing managers could get away with berating salespeople with the invective: "Go sell what we do." The change I'm describing moves the spotlight to the needs, opportunities, and threats that are faced by the customer and then are met in your customer experience. That means delivering what customers need, solving and resolving the challenges they face, enabling them to do more than they can without you.

Delivers Value

All of the value delivered to your customers cannot and should not be anchored solely to your product and service. Your customers should also see the experience itself as having real value. To determine whether a customer experience is genuinely valuable (rather than simply "nice" or "pleasant"), there are three questions worth asking of each element in that experience.

1. **Is it helpful?** Is the outcome of that interaction useful to the customer? Does it create some practical value? Is that usefulness measurable?

2. **Is it surprising?** Is the experience and the outcome surprising? Exceptionally strong customer experiences create superior value that's usually unexpected. Surprise is a key element of delight. And if the objective is customers so delighted that they become active promoters of your company and brand, are you creating value in ways they find positively surprising?

3. **Is it innovative?** This is a really loaded question for most graphic communications firms. Innovation is tough. Are you creating value in your customer experience that's genuinely new? Are you creating more value now than you were in the same kind of interactions a year ago? If not, why not? The creation of new value, and its delivery in the customer experience, is how a customer experience strengthens both a brand and a firm's competitive advantage.

Organizational Culture and Customer Experience

It takes a customer-focused culture to deliver on a brand promise. We've already made the case that your brand needs to be as meaningful to your employees as it is to your customers. That relationship between your brand and your employees is essential to a strong customer experience because those parts of the experience that are delivered to your customers by a live human will be as strong or weak as the affinity and engagement that employee has for your company and your brand. But the impact of a culture built around a customer-facing brand promise isn't limited solely to employees who are delivering front-line experiences in direct contact with your customers. The impact of that culture is just as essential for those who support front-line employees, who equip them, and who lead them. It provides the context within which you have a fighting chance of genuinely fulfilling your brand promise.

Your employees won't deliver a better experience than they themselves receive (whether the floggings continue or not). Your employees won't convey more value than they themselves perceive. (Heskett, Sasser & Schlesinger 1997) When an employee finds the delivery of service to a customer either tedious or meaningless (a distraction rather than their core mission), a customer experience initiative will rarely get off the ground. It will never prove sustainable. Therefore, the culture needs to value and celebrate the delivery of your customer experience, and it needs to welcome only those capable, willing, and engaged enough to deliver that experience.

Selection of employees involved directly in the delivery of your customer experience must be unconventional. It needs to begin with traits first and move only secondarily to competencies. And that's precisely the reverse of the typical pattern. In essence, it is essential to recruit and promote for those things you cannot change, and to train for those things you can. Let me repeat that. It is essential to recruit and promote for those things you cannot change, and to train for those things you can. Far too often it is technical competence (or "experience" as a surrogate for technical competence and capability) that's the first order selection criterion. Yet, that forces the organization to tolerate and adapt to members who don't share the same values, same sense of mission, and same drive to be of service. (Peppers & Rogers 2004)

The selection of the employees who will be delivering your customer experience directly, who will be responsible for its design, or who will be responsible to manage the people and processes that deliver your customer experience should be understood as choosing those who will embody your brand promise as ambassadors or avatars for your brand. (Kinni & Disney Institute 2011)

Let me give you an example: My wife and I live near a Cheesecake Factory restaurant. It's also between our home and the airport. My wife will often drop me off for a flight and pick me up on my return, giving us more time together. When I have an evening flight, we'll often arrange a "date night" before she delivers me to the airport. And the hostesses at our local Cheesecake Factory baffle me.

To a one, they are attractive, young women. And to a one, they rarely smile at a customer. Now, they do smile and laugh among themselves and with the wait staff. But when a group of customers walk in their demeanor becomes cool, aloof, almost haughty. It's amazing to watch.

Their interactions with customers are perfunctory, scripted, and minimal. Worse, nothing about those interactions is genuine – not the greeting, not the "enjoy your meal." Not a one of the hostesses we've encountered understands that her role is Director of First Impressions, and the person most likely to set the tone for the customer's entire experience. Even worse, when there's a wait, nothing about their behavior is intended to reset the customer's clock at intervals, improving the customer's perception of being appreciated, welcome, and important. None of them check back with customers, nor offer an apology for an extended wait. Rather, their demeanor signals that their roles at the Cheesecake Factory are really beneath them, as are their customers. It's distasteful at best.

I suspect that you have people in direct contact with your customers who behave no better. Do you?

Design

The building of a customer experience often triggers a conversation about the cost of doing it, and whether it implies a commitment to higher costs in order to deliver that experience once it is designed. The assumption behind that "either / or" construct was legitimized by Michael Porter (1980) beginning in 198 when he asserted that two of three generic competitive strategies were cost leadership and differentiation. While Porter himself made clear that a firm can use them singly or in combination, they have been widely misunderstood as mutually exclusive. They are not. In fact, when well designed, a strong customer experience can reduce the long-term expense of serving and retaining customers.(Stickdorn & Schneider 2011) And that's only one reason that intentional design is critical to the creation of a strong customer experience.

Structure of a Designed CX

The design elements of a specific customer experience are well beyond the scope of this introduction. However, the design should have the following attributes:

Stressless: The emotional labor involved on the part of the customer should be as low as possible. Therefore, especially for a repeating customer, there should be nothing about the experience that triggers stress or make the customer reluctant to go though the experience regularly.

Seamless: Connections matter. When a customer needs to move from one part of your organization to another to get something done, the quality of the experience drops quickly in the eyes of the customer. Worst is when the customer needs to act as a go-between with different parts of your organization or service. From beginning to end, the customer should be able to move smoothly step-to-step in a seamless flow.

Frictionless: The number of actions required by the customer to complete the cycle should be as few as possible, and none of them should be repetitive. If your customer experience requires that the customer provide the same information multiple times and in multiple ways, you're creating friction. If the customer is required to do things purely in service to your process, system, or policy that don't add value in that customer's eyes, you're creating friction. If any part of your experience slows or stalls the customer's progress while your system catches up (or, worse, if it intentionally restricts the customer's progress), you're creating friction.

Flawless: The reliability of the customer experience can have only a single standard of measure: flawless performance. Every instance where the experience is less than flawless gives the customer reason to believe that she isn't receiving the value she was promised and for which she paid. Every instance where the experience is less than flawless calls into question the wisdom of choosing that supplier. Every instance where the experience is less than flawless costs you an opportunity to surprise and delight that customer, and it costs you a raving fan as well.

In its best form, a strong customer experience can be truthfully described as clean, simple, fast, and easy–with each of those terms being described with what customers believe them to be. A strong customer experience is intentionally consistent, very reliable, and highly repeatable. It is the best sort of strong business process because it was deliberately designed to be.

Addicted to Screens

Contrary to the knee-jerk assumption, the solution to every need in a customer experience is not the creation of an application or an interface. A customer experience is not synonymous with a user interface, or UX. In fact, recent research is showing correlations between time viewing screens and sleep disorders, breast cancer, depression, and obesity. (Artificial Light 2015) That means that experience designers need to take a step back from beginning to build wireframes as a customer need is identified or a customer interaction is analyzed.

The most elegant customer experience may intentionally eliminate interactions that were previously required, reducing the need for a customer to do anything because the experience delivers an outcome effortlessly. The results simply appear. Automating processes and leveraging technology shouldn't be seen as welded to building an interface. That's getting far too little payback from the application of technology.

Processes and Systems

Steve Jobs said it best: "You've got to start with the customer experience and work back toward the technology – not the other way around." Beginning with the end in mind means starting with the experience you intend to deliver, designing processes to deliver it, and then determining the systems, resources and even the technology necessary to do so. Unless the outcome is primary, there's no way to plan change that's anything except incremental and based on your existing structure, too.

Processes and systems trump structure when it comes to CX design. It's especially important that processes precede and supersede structure when a CX is being designed because it is so tempting to bolt the CX onto existing structure. When the existing structure includes silos and departments created to support a legacy production workflow, the risk is that the design of a customer experience will be seen simply as a "nice to do" effort, worth little more than applying lipstick to the proverbial pig.

But when the designed CX process is made primary, and the production workflow made subordinate to it, a great deal of change becomes possible. Legacy structure can be realigned because a real context has been designed for it, all created to deliver a specific and strong customer experience. And that's why we've spent so much time looking deeply at Service Delivery.

Beyond Touchpoints

Identifying, improving, measuring, and refining existing customer touchpoints is the starting point for CX design. An organization that's never focused on a customer experience needs an opportunity to build muscle and gain experience working on processes that are specifically customer-facing, and are developing interactions intended to benefit the customer directly. But that's merely the launching pad. Identifying routine and repeating customer touchpoints (that is, those parts of your service creation and service delivery process that are visible to your customers) simply prepares the organization to begin building a strong customer experience. To swing a company's people to focus externally rather than internally, there's nowhere else to start. It's the first step to moving from "what they get" to "how they get it." But the risk in staying there is that the customer experience will forever be anchored to a service or product delivery process. It will fail to stretch beyond it to find and meet other, unrelated customer needs that are going unmet now.

Metrics

Peter Drucker repeatedly said: "What gets measured gets improved." He was right, and his admonition applies to CX just was well as it does to any business discipline. A strong customer experience is designed for measurement. It's measured in terms meaningful to the most important party in the equation: the customer.

A customer experience is not a "soft" business discipline as it is often labeled. Instead, it's bedrock on which corporate performance rises or falls. Moreover, the measurements that can be applied to a customer experience are stronger predictors of future performance than are most financial and operations metrics. Customer metrics track changes in customer behavior and customer sentiment long before those changes having effect on financial or operational performance. Customer metrics can signal changes even better than sales activity metrics when applied well.

For the sake of simplicity, I recommend three initial metrics that should be used to track the effectiveness of a customer experience over time.

The Net Promoter Score

In 2003, Frederick Reichheld (Reichheld et. al 2011) introduced the results of two years of research to leverage a discovery made by Enterprise Rent-A-Car. Enterprise had discovered two things: They could ask their customers only a pair of questions that would enable them to forecast profitable growth by location, and they could focus only on the percentage of their customers who gave them the highest rankings to get there. Reichheld described the Enterprise approach as "riveting." And it set him on the trail to vet and refine that approach, distilling it down to one powerful question. The result, described in the December 2003 issue of the *Harvard Business Review*, is the Net Promoter Score (NPS).

The NPS demonstrates a strong correlation between two apparently unrelated factors: the willingness of a customer to recommend a brand, product, service, or company to a friend or colleague, and the relative growth rate of that firm as compared with its competitors.(Reichheld et. al 2011) The correlation between customer enthusiasm (rather than merely satisfaction or expressed intention to repurchase) and revenue growth is direct and high. We consider the NPS one of the essential metrics to track the real world effectiveness of any customer experience.

Customer Retention

Tracking and measuring customer retention is the best predictive, customer-facing measure of profit growth or decline. For two decades, I've been analyzing and correlating customer retention and profitability for graphic communications companies. And the correlation remains exceptionally strong. Those companies who retain the highest percentage of their customers year-over-year also deliver industry-leading profit performance. Those companies that exhibit high customer turnover (or churn) do not demonstrate industry-leading profit performance. Ever.

The drivers are easy to understand and intuitive. Lower churn means lower overall customer acquisition expense. And there's a direct correlation between the length of customer relationship and the profitability of that relationship. It comes both from reduced price pressure and from the reduced expense of serving customers whose needs and expectations are known well.

Customers At Risk

When something goes sideways and a customer is disappointed or distressed, too often the response ends when the customer stops voicing their feelings. We do worse than assume everything is fine. We pretend that it is. That gets expressed as "No news is good news." The statement is bunk. Here's why:

What's called the "Iceberg Effect" is at work here. Unhappy (frustrated, disappointed, or distressed) customers will typically reach for a manager or executive to voice what they feel only 10% of the time. They will communicate what they feel to their closest connection in your company (a salesperson or CSR, typically) about 25% of the time. That means 65% of the time, they don't say a thing to anyone in your company. But they aren't silent or inactive. They will tell peers and colleagues about their experience. And they will vote with their feet, moving their business elsewhere without ever telling you why. That's terrifying. And that's why it is so important to prompt customers to complain. That's right, you need to prompt them to complain by asking them to do so. And once they complain, you need to craft two parallel responses: Insure that the situation is resolved completely as I'll describe below, and insure that the customer is tracked going forward until you know that the relationship has been restored for a predetermined period of time.

Few clients of mine are tracking an At-Risk list of customers when I first contact them. They don't recognize the value in alerting the entire company when the next project is coming in from a customer they've disappointed or frustrated. And so it gets treated as ordinary, usual, customary, and "no big deal". That's despite a salesperson who likely has fought for the opportunity to re-earn the trust and confidence that was squandered, and is hoping that the next project will go flawlessly. What gets measured is what gets improved. So tracking jeopardized relationships for several months at least after they were put in jeopardy is essential.

Service Recovery

In any customer experience, things will go sideways once in a while. That means that a well-designed service experience includes more than simply a map showing everything going swimmingly. That's the first iteration, of course. But recovery when something goes sideways deserves to be just as well designed.

Strong customer experiences do more than merely fixing whatever went wrong. The best ones move past the fix and neutralize the customer consequence. That means making the customer whole and then going beyond to neutralize the consequences. (Yes, that runs directly contrary to common terms and conditions of sale that try to eliminate responsibility for consequences of service failures.) The key focus here is not simply fixing the problem or repairing the failure. The key focus is restoring the relationship, rebuilding the confidence of the disappointed customer. That requires follow-up after the effort is made to restore the relationship to ensure that the consequence was neutralized, and then some.

Summary

The value of a strong customer experience is impossible to overstate. It differentiates you in the eyes of your customers, reducing the risk that your offering will be seen as a commodity. It defends and supports the ratio between your price and the value your customer perceives. It enables your customers to make good decisions, and to justify continuing to do business with you in the face of competitive and substitutionary options. It is the place where new value is not only created, but also delivered to your customers to turn them into raving fans. It is precisely where the rubber of your newly round wheel meets the road.

References

"Artificial Light May Be Unhealthy". 2015. http://www.wired.com/2015/03/artificial-light-may-be-unhealthy.

Heskett, James L., W. Earl Sasser, and Leonard A. Schlesinger. 1997. The Service Profit Chain : How Leading Companies Link Profit and Growth to Loyalty, Satisfaction, and Value. New York: Free Press.

Kinni, Theodore B., and Disney Institute. 2011. Be Our Guest : Perfecting the Art of Customer Service. New York: Disney Editions.

Manning, Harley, Kerry Bodine, and Forrester (Firm). 2012. Outside In : The Power of Putting Customers at the Center of Your Business. Boston: Houghton Mifflin Harcourt.

Peppers, Don, and Martha Rogers. 2004. Managing Customer Relationships : A Strategic Framework. Hoboken, NJ: John Wiley & Sons.

Porter, Michael E. 1980. Competitive Strategy : Techniques for Analyzing Industries and Competitors. New York: Free Press.

Reichheld, Frederick F., Rob Markey, and Frederick F. Reichheld. 2011. *The Ultimate Question 2.0 : How Net Promoter Companies Thrive in a Customer-Driven World.* Rev. and expanded ed. Boston: Harvard Business Press.

Stickdorn, Marc, and Jakob Schneider. 2011. *This Is Service Design Thinking : Basics, Tools, Cases.* Hoboken, NJ: Wiley.

THE SECOND DISCIPLINE

CREATING
A PLATFORM

by Chris Bondy

The word "platform" has a variety of different meanings — all of which come down to the actionable word, "enabling". Whether you are referring to a platform as a strategic position, a communication or cultural vantage point, or a physical or technological infrastructure, the "platform" discipline for *UnSquaring the Wheel* focuses on new business models that are aligned with current and future market requirements.

The Platform Discipline is a three-legged stool that consists of Technology, Process, and Services. These three legs, or pillars, are essential to enabling the ideal-state business model for graphic communication service providers. Each pillar is highly dependent on the other two. In fact, each pillar can be dysfunctional if it lacks careful integration with the other pillars.

Without appropriate processes, your advanced technology can be wasted. Without defined processes, or the stable technologies behind them, your services can be unsupportable. When processes are not driven from true market needs and value-added services that customers are willing to pay for, those processes can be restrictive and burdensome. In all, having a strategic and market-driven integration of technology, process, and services is the key to enabling the breakthrough delivery of your cross-media communication services, as well as the new revenue and profit streams associated with being in sync with your market.

When creating a platform for your operation, you need a consistent way to approach and respond to each of the three platform elements listed above. The first critical step in building your platform is to establish an architectural framework for the analysis, selection, and integration of **technology.** To ensure that your operation is both efficient and predictable, the platform approach also requires that all your critical **processes** are defined, documented, and followed. Finally, your platform needs an approach to **services** that presents your firm in a manner that high-value work can be discovered, proposed, and delivered in a manner that delights your customer and preserves your profit margins.

Each of the primary pillars (technology, process, and services) that make up the platform discipline are covered in detail throughout the subsequent chapters. This chapter provides a high-level description of the concepts in hopes that it gives you an overview of what is needed to create your platform.

The three key elements of the Platform Discipline (Technology, Process, and Services) all work together in a unified way provide a framework or structure to address these significant questions you will face in your transformational efforts:

1. How do you configure of your operation with respect to the various technologies available?

2. What processes do you develop to help streamline your operation in order to deliver consistent and predictable results?

3.   What approach to your services offering should you take in order to be in sync with customer needs and aligned with your company's profit goals?

Answers to these questions are covered in detail in each one of the chapters that make up the Platform Discipline. In this section, we introduce you to the Platform Discipline and the concept of building a platform.

Technology

With technology, it is important to ask "What" and "Why" questions up front before you acquire the technology. What are the drivers for this technology and why should we care? Two important questions need to be asked:

1.   Is there market demand for a product or services that is enabled through this technology?

2.   Will the operation be more effective by use of this technology?

The answer to both these questions needs to be "Yes" when making a substantial technology acquisition.

UnSquaring the Wheel provides insights into the layers and components that make up the architecture of a graphic communications technology platform. The discussion begins by building from the core print production workflow, then expanding from that familiar place to incorporate additional layers that enable new services and a more streamlined production process.

As a service provider, when you understand the structure of the technology platform, it is easier to evaluate your current capability with new technology to consider whether it fits and whether it will bring value to your customers and your company.

In additional to defining a technology platform, graphic communication firms need to establish a market engagement approach for custom projects that is based on an iterative development approach. A "build-it-and-they-will-come" approach is not practical. Breakthrough companies in the graphic communications arena have found that designing a technology platform, and then engaging with lead-customers that have flexibility, can provide a solid approach to technology acquisition that can both be paid-for and tested as services are rolled out. Combining the technology platform approach with iterative market engagement is discussed in detail in the Technology chapter.

If we agree that the two-fold benefit of operational effectiveness and customer value is essential for the acquisition of technology, we can proceed with a filter that helps us not to get too enamored with the next "new" thing. Ultimately, in the graphic communication services business, we are driven to deliver a complete range of cross-media communications in a quality, timely, and cost-effective manner.

Decomposing technology requirements in the cross-media value chain into a technology reference model is helpful in two ways. First, it can identify where you are with respect to the model. And, second, it can evaluate how various complementary and disruptive technologies will fit within your framework.

Disruptive Technologies

Graphic communication firms need to embrace and integrate the deployment of content to all media in much the same way that they have done with print for decades. This requires that firms understand the management of all types of content and "collections", as well as the processing of data, so that specific content can be directed to individuals at any time in any media.

Breakthrough firms that have integrated content and data into their offering with a cross-media channel deployment are well positioned for the future. Advances in cyberinfrastructure, or "cloud computing", provide a much easier and cost-effective on-ramp and should be considered for any software across the workflow. Incorporating these disruptive technologies into the traditional and digital print offering is discussed in the Technology chapter.

Building a Technology Platform

Building a technology platform is a complex, costly, and time-consuming activity. It stands to reason that establishing an approach to building the platform is not only important, but it may be the difference in your long-term viability. With the cost and complexity surrounding technology decisions, taking the time to properly investigate your options is essential.

The Technology chapter provides insight into the following platform creation steps:

- Assessing your existing operation
- Determining your gaps and priorities
- Prioritizing your customer needs
- Establishing an integration plan/priority
- Learning how to integrate through iteration
- Becoming an Agile Project Management expert

Each of these steps is sequential. They should be done over and over again for each technology acquisition until the process is an inherent cultural and procedural aspect of your operation. Companies who have established a successful technology platform follow a process similar to the one listed above. (Those companies are discussed in detail in the Technology chapter.)

However, there is more. The technology platform is only one of three critical components of the platform. Process and services pay an equal role.

Process

The Process chapter provides insights into three key areas that will drive cost out of your operation and new revenue streams into your operation through new products and services. Companies with mature process management competency deliver work with precision, repeatability, scalability, and in a cost-effective manner. Process maturity is simply having a good repeatable recipe for all critical activities and the cultural discipline to follow that winning recipe.

In this chapter, we explore processes as they relate to:

- Operational Efficiency
- Product Innovation Process

- Agile Project Management

Developing the "recipe for success" in the graphic communication industry requires a refinement of key processes such that there is a successful balance between meeting the specific needs of your customer while operationalizing the needs of all your customers. Process mastery is a careful balance of tradeoffs that are distilled into a winning set of replicable procedures that deliver what appears to be a custom result through an efficient process.

Value-added services in the graphic communications industry are built off of a technology platform that leverages these essential processes.

Operational Efficiency

We take a practical look at Lean manufacturing techniques and make specific adaptation for the graphic communication industry. Combining the principals of Lean manufacturing with the concepts of forward-constraint design (thinking back-to-front, from finished goods to product offering) can be a powerful approach to achieving an efficient and predictable production operation.

Product Innovation

We explore a refinement of the traditional product development process to include new upstream steps. This product innovation process is adapted to the graphic arts industry from companies you have delivered breakthrough products to. Before the product concept is finalized, the process requires immersive engagement with customers, and exploration of the market space and various business models.

Project Management

Developing the culture and process discipline to incorporate project management for all custom projects is essential to managing scarce resources effectively. All too often, project management efforts are cumbersome, and they prevent easy adoption and standardization. Developing a simple-to-understand and easy-to-use Agile Project Management process can help make your projects successful and profitable.

Each of the essential process management techniques is covered in the Process chapter and is integrated into the platform discipline.

Services

The Services chapter brings together the concepts of technology and process to establish a market engagement approach for services that can address the needs of the market while bringing acceptable profit margins to service providers. The Services chapter is all about a new approach to old business models, as well as the inclusion of new business models for certain types of work. These topics are discussed in the Services chapter:

- Jobs versus Projects
- Selling Services
- Customer Lifecycle
- Skills for Services

Jobs versus Projects

Fundamentally, the *UnSquaring the Wheel* approach considers a partitioning of work into two key segments with a unique business model and workflow tailored for each. Establishing a unique services delivery model around "jobs" and "projects" will be a liberating factor for graphic communication firms. This approach provides a way to optimize the entire engagement and delivery process independently for both types of work, while leveraging a common core infrastructure. Breakthrough companies in the graphic communication industry are masterful at employing this approach. This is one of the key reasons why some firms are delivering solid profits, while others are losing money doing, in some cases, the same work.

Selling Services

In addition to managing jobs and projects effectively, graphic communication firms need to develop an effective services-selling process that is aligned with both types of work. The sales process for commoditized jobs is different than the sales process for projects. The Services chapter provides insights into the sales process necessary to sell complex projects with profit margins never seen before in the printing industry.

Customer Lifecycle

The services-selling process is complemented with a section on lifecycle engagement that presents the components of delivering reoccurring campaigns throughout the lifecycle of a target population. Insights into the unique content needs of an customers throughout their lifecycle will equip service providers with a new approach to customer engagement. This lifecycle approach can produce more effective communication and results that can be measured.

Skills for Services

As graphic communication service providers move further upstream and the traditional print offering expands to include the deployment of all media, there is an increased demand for a more technical workforce. The Services chapter explores emerging needs for critical skills that can enable the delivery of new services. The most critical new skills are:

1. Strategy and Marketing
2. Data Processing and Content Management
3. Information Technology and Cyberinfrastructure
4. Cross-Media Channel Deployment (print plus, mobile, web, and social media)

Putting it All Together

The transformational success of *UnSquaring the Wheel* is built off of a platform discipline that can support your firm from all perspectives. Breakthrough companies have a well-established platform that is foundational to their firm. It is a platform that allows them to execute on the following key dimensions:

1. Uncover unique needs of customers through a consistent needs analysis discovery process.

2.   Scope and deliver customer-driven services programs that can be project managed.

3.   Integrate technology, processes, and services into a platform that can provide optimized services (that is, services that can be supported and scaled).

4.   Deliver and extract value (satisfied customers with high-profit margins) from the services engagements (product- and project-focused).

6

TECHNOLOGY

by Chris Bondy

The graphic arts industry is in a time of dramatic change. Some might say that it is a "perfect storm" of dramatic cultural, economic, and technological change — all creating a multiplier effect that is driving wholesale change for graphic communication service providers. The mandate for change in the graphic communications industry comes largely as a result of significant advancements in technology that are enabling new communication modes that threaten the historical print-centric business model.

When evaluating technology trends and their potential impacts, it is helpful to consider these two perspectives:

1. How easily will these technologies be assimilated into or adopted by the masses, and by the market segment you are focused on?

2. What technologies have the potential to change the way you function by making current tasks easier or by introducing new, previously unavailable, capabilities?

Technology Adoption

In *Crossing the Chasm*, Geoffrey Moore (1991) memorialized the Technology Adoption Lifecycle first characterized by Rogers (1962). *Diffusion of Innovations*. It suggests that technology adoption follows a bell curve distribution with innovators, early adopters, and early majority representing the first movers on new technology, together accounting for a 50% adoption rate.

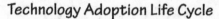
Technology Adoption Life Cycle

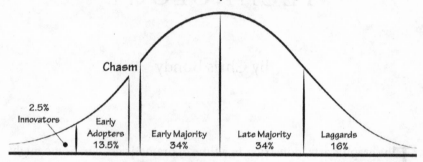

Keeping a close eye on early adopters provides insight into the maturity of a certain technologies and into how close they are to being assimilated into the mainstream. Following the flow of technology adoption from consumers to knowledge workers, and ultimately by enterprises, is also important when identifying technology trends.

Consumers are the most fleet-footed of the early adopters sector and provide an early view into potential trends. Identifying certain consumer products and habits that will roll over into the workplace can provide valuable insights into emerging trends. Early adopter consumers and early adopter knowledge workers tend to align on significant trends that ultimately have an impact on the way that enterprises function. In most cases, we need to look to the "technology geeks" to get a read on what technologies are emerging as potential points of leverage in the graphic communications space.

Look to fast-moving start-up firms as another point of validation when trying to read technology trends. New-entry companies into the market have the ability to leapfrog ahead of the mainstream with respect to technology because they have minimal infrastructure and are the most agile.

These firms can quickly adapt, integrate, or reject technology, and they can help shake down which technologies are ready for wide-scale use and which are not.

Let's take a look at cloud computing technologies in graphic communications as an example of technology adoption trends. Some form of cloud computing has been available for well over a decade. Early adopters in the consumer space accessed the Kodak Gallery web service (first launched by Ofoto 1999) for photo processing, and for creating photo albums and calendars. In today's market, most graphic arts service providers are using cloud computing for not only job submission, but also for all their software composition tools, such as Adobe Creative Cloud. The graphic communications industry will re-invent itself under cloud-computing architectures because these technologies provide a more cost-effective and streamlined business model.

Looking at the early adopters (consumers, knowledge workers/technology geeks, and enterprises/fast-moving start-ups) can help to determine whether a new technology is mature enough for wide-scale adoption. Observing technology adoption trends is essential for graphic communication service providers who are looking at expanding services offerings, keeping in stride with emerging demand.

Disruptive Shift in Demand

Consumers are looking for the best value, relevant content on any device, real-time access, and a pleasant experience. Knowledge workers carry similar requirements as consumers; yet their devices incorporate a variety of different functions that are driven from the specific needs associated with their job functions and the work they need to perform. Knowledge workers also want the right content at the right time and in the right media—all wrapped in a pleasant experience. Marketers, for example, are interested in building awareness across all media and the measurement of marketing programs (return on investment, or ROI) and the efficiency of the workflows that use. Publishers are interested in cross-media content, building communities, and measurement of the value of the content they produce and the relationship they create. Procurement managers are interested in cost savings, strategic sourcing, and reporting and au-

Shift in Customer Demand

Learn from Consumer trends"
1. Consumer
2. Knowledge Worker
3. Enterprise

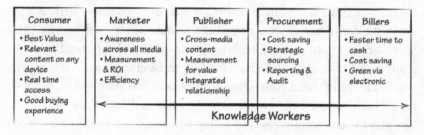

Consumer	Marketer	Publisher	Procurement	Billers
• Best Value • Relevant content on any device • Real time access • Good buying experience	• Awareness across all media • Measurement & ROI • Efficiency	• Cross-media content • Measurement for value • Integrated relationship	• Cost saving • Strategic sourcing • Reporting & Audit	• Faster time to cash • Cost saving • Green via electronic

←——————————————— Knowledge Workers ———————————————→

diting capabilities. Billers are interested in fast time-to-cash, cost savings, and going green via the use of electronic media.

The entire graphic communications ecosystem (i.e., all producers and consumers of traditional print) has had to stop and take notice of the dramatic shift in demand to electronic content, real-time access, and a pleasant user experience, making this shift one of the most significant and disruptive changes in demand since the introduction of the movable type and the printing press. (Gutenberg, 1440) More than any other force in many decades, the mass digitization and electronic distribution of content has been the most disruptive force on the traditional printing industry.

The second part of evaluating and recognizing technology trends is to determine whether a new technology has the potential to change the way we function by making current tasks easier or by introducing new, previously unavailable capabilities? In other words, does the technology have the potential to be disruptive?

Mass digitization and electronic distribution of content is a truly disruptive technology on the traditional printing and publishing industry. As such, it requires rethinking foundational business models with a mission to incorporate this disruptive technology into new revised business models, or for a service provider to exit the business.

"Disruptive innovation", a term coined by Harvard Business School professor Clayton Christensen (1997), "describes a process by which a product or service takes root initially in simple applications at the bottom of the market and then relentlessly moves up market, eventually displacing established competitors" (225-228).

Recent waves of technology, or disruptive innovation, have caused a domino effect on the historic printing and publishing markets in all developed nations. What key technologies enabled this wave of disruption? How do we develop a technology roadmap to ride this wave and proactively look for subsequent waves we can ride vs. being surprised and potentially capsized?

Chris Anderson, editor of *Wired Magazine,* and author of *The Long Tail, and Free,* (13) says we that a "technology triple play" is the disruptive force behind the mass digitization and electronic distribution of content. Fast computer chips, large capacity and low-cost memory/storage, coupled with high-speed untethered bandwidth has created a technology triple play that has enabled this current wave of mass global digitization of all content.

The seamless integration of fast chips, cheap storage, and unlimited bandwidth is the perfect technology storm, wreaking havoc on the graphic communications industry. How can we leverage this disruptive force and realign our graphic communication services to intercept this shift in demand?

The Next Wave:
Content, Data, and Cross-Media

Content is King

If we agree that all content that we watch, listen to, or read is (or will be) digitized, it stands to reason that there will be an increasing demand for services that complement this emerging need—namely, the management of collections. Taking a lesson from consumers, we can see that the management of digital content is extremely important. The skyrocketing prominence of iTunes and YouTube, among other cloud-based consumer digital asset management systems, validates the need to manage what we digitize. With the proliferation of digital content, consumers realized in mass that having real-time access to their full collection of music and videos has dramatically increased their quality of life. Having access to old tunes, new tunes, and the right tune at the right time, as well as family videos, favorite movies, training clips, etc., has changed our interaction with and reliance on digital content.

The management of digital collections now migrates to knowledge workers who want the same consumer experience with their digital assets at their work place. A tremendous opportunity exists for graphic communication service providers to offer a web portal for businesses to organize digital collections with the same ease that consumers enjoy while using iTunes. Digital asset management (DAM) technology has been around for decades. In fact, in highly regulated industries like the pharmaceutical industry, solutions (such as EMC's Documentum) have been a big success. The time is right for DAM technologies to make their way into mainstream business and into marketing departments.

The technology is aligned like never before for low-cost ease-of-entry programs in the area of DAM. In the same way that the web storefronts have evened the playing field for small-medium business with the large enterprises, next generation cloud-based DAM technologies are viable— no matter what the size of your business. The latest DAM technologies also provide "white-label" capability, which will allow service providers to rebrand the service as their own.

Managing collections is a consumer trend that will permeate the business world since the technology has come of age. It is easy to use, storing content is relatively inexpensive, adding meta-data (information about the information) is easy, and system performance is acceptable. Graphic communication service providers that offer branded DAM services will have the same control of client content as printers did in the day when storage and control of the negatives used to make printing plates was a coveted asset that printers guarded with their lives.

Data is King, Too!

Parallel to the trends in digital asset management, and equally as important, is the wide-scale demand for data in the business world. Since the recession of 2007-09, many sectors of the graphic communications industry have had a heightened interest in data. Marketers and publishers are charged with the measurement and quantification of all campaigns and publications, and operational managers find it necessary to ensure operational efficiency though measured process improvement.

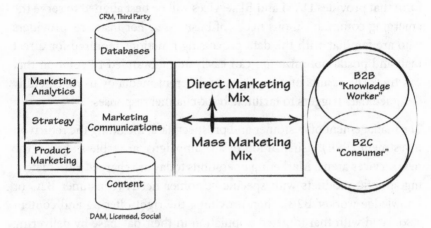

Today, agile marketing operations are a necessity with a tight integration of product marketing, marketing communications/ business development, and marketing analytics. These three marketing disciplines are hinged together by marketing strategy. A constant flow of data is needed—from product marketing regarding the acceptance level of the product by customers, and from marketing communications regarding the adoption of program offers to customers and prospects. The need for real-time access and visualization of these business activities has opened the door for a new set of services to be offered by graphic communication service providers.

Publishers have the same needs as marketers—to provide fresh, relevant, and targeted content in the right media, at the right time. Consider that marketers and publishers are both focused on a targeted audience (data) trying to communicate meaningful content to that audience. Their needs are very similar from a technology perspective.

The fast-growing world of business intelligence (BI) software solutions is now ready for adoption by service providers who can integrate data analytics services into their offering. Much like cloud-based DAM solutions, cloud-based BI solutions provide a tremendous opportunity for service providers to deliver integrated and closed-loop data services.

Service providers who lead with the strategic development of campaigns and publishing programs that are enabled through a technology platform that provides DAM and BI services will be best aligned to serve the emerging communications needs of businesses. For instance, providers who are familiar with the data processing functions required for direct mail and postal optimization can easily add a branded BI solution that can track the results of campaigns in different media by using carefully designed data triggers to facilitate back-channel responses.

The management of customer and prospect data, including the return on investment (ROI) visualization of all campaigns, are table stakes in the new services arena. Marketing operations today are charged with matching specific products with specific customer needs (consumer B2C or knowledge worker B2B), then providing the right offering and content associated with that targeted population in their database by delivering cross-media campaigns that need to be measured and tracked. Service providers that can deliver integrated DAM and data analytic services, along with their traditional graphic communication services, will be well aligned with needs of marketers.

BI solutions represented in Gartner's Magic Quadrant (source) (such as Tableau, Sisense, Tibco, Kipfolio, and others) leverage the similar cloud-based architecture as DAM systems do and provide an easy point of entry for traditional graphic communication service providers who wish to compliment their services with a branded BI solution, including a marketing analytics dashboard. The addition of integrated DAM and BI services provides the technology foundation for better upstream management of content and data, as well as downstream management and reporting of results. Both are strategic ways for service provider to extend their relevance with the market.

It is important to note that the use of data in the graphic communications industry has an extremely important operational component, as well as an emerging services opportunity. The drive to eliminate cost and reduce cycle-time in the graphic communications industry places a mounting demand for operational leaders to be able to track, measure, and analyze the complete production value chain. Innovative techniques in process automation and lean manufacturing from mainstream manufacturing are driving precision in print and in publishing. The streamlined integration of all tasks in a production workflow and the real-time tracking of each step in the process are operational table stakes.

Print - Management Information Systems (MIS) (by EFI, Avanti, HiFlex, PrintVis, PressWise, among others) have more device data than ever before, making it much easier to monitor the time and movement of a specific job through the production workflow. Other process tracking and reporting software (through companies such as SpencerLabs' Spencer-Metrics) are designed to capture real-time production data and provide a variety of reports, including an interactive productivity dashboard to better track and report production. Operations managers are able to use data to analyze the operations with a focus on reducing waste and cycle-time.

The use of data analytics is as important in the operations of graphic communication service providers as it is as an emerging service. More specifics regarding the use of data as a service and data in operational processes will be covered in their respective chapters.

Integrated Cross-Media Communications

Marketers and publishers continue to transition their focus from mass distribution of static information to targeted distribution of personalized content. The trend from traditional static communications to personalized and customized printed material, websites, e-mail campaigns, and social media is being further propelled by the maturity and robustness of cloud computing.

Integrated cross-media communications will be the prevailing workflow that is revolutionizing the graphic communications industry. Cross-media technologies are designed to leverage new capabilities in cyber-infrastructure that both enable the technology and provide an attractive deployment model. This expanded cross-media terrain has attracted solution providers from several fronts: evolving composition solutions, new media entrants looking to add print to the mix, and CRM (customer relationship marketing) solution providers that are familiar with managing cross-media campaigns.

Some leading composition solution suppliers in this space evolved from the natural migration of compositions systems upstream in search of a more strategic connection with content and data sources, and downstream to integrate better with the deployment of all relevant media channels. These companies are an advantage for the print channel since they have already developed highly functional VDP creations tools that are optimized for the leading digital printing systems. Variable Data Printing (VDP) solution providers (such as XMPie, MarComCentral, GMC Software Technology, PageFlex, among others) are expanding their offering to include simultaneously deployment to print and the Web, as well more robust campaign management capability.

Solution suppliers with offerings in "new media", such as personalized website production and email campaigns (including EasyPURL and MindFire) are expanding to provide more complete campaign management capability. And providers of Web-to-Print solutions (such as EFI's Digital StoreFront, among others) are embedding more robust VDP composition engines in their platform to compose personalized campaigns for print and the Web.

Finally, there are a number of new entrants into this space that are coming from the campaign management perspective. Konica Minolta teamed up with SK+G Lab to launch X-Media Engage IT with a new cloud-based cross-media solution design by direct marketing professionals to stitch together all the elements of the cross-media value chain under one integrated application.

SK+G Lab is a large direct marketing agency in Las Vegas with an impressive client list that includes top casinos, and medical, and non-profit organizations. In this scenario, we have an agency-turned-developer to build cross-media solution that more completely meets their needs of their clients.

Needless to say, there is a lot of activity in this space; these and many other solutions all have merit, depending on the detailed requirements that your customers and business plan dictates. The first step to understanding and leveraging technology is to understand the critical trends, and then develop the technology platform that will enable your to offer the vital services your customers are looking for.

There is tremendous technology alignment with respect to cyberinfrastructure and the integrated cross-media communications opportunity for graphic communication service providers. We have mentioned previously that fast chips, cheap memory, and increasingly more wireless bandwidth have enabled this new wave of software applications. The truth is that there has been significant and positive movement across all the elements in the value chain.

Workflows that were once difficult to conceptualize and very customized to implement are becoming more modular. Interfaces and standards are better defined, and obvious bottlenecks and workarounds have been addressed. Of course, the workflows are much more complicated with the need to address data and content management, cross-media deployment, integrating MIS systems, and establishing a closed-loop communication process that fuels the process. A closer look at the following model of the cross-media value chain will help to visualize this new workflow with an eye to determine what is new and what can be leveraged from your existing operation.

Cross-Media Communications Value Chain

The cross-media communications value chain pictured above provides a process view of the workflow and the significant way that the workflow has changed for graphic communication service providers. In order to accommodate customers who require results-driven cross-media communications and reporting, it is essential that the process begin first with data and content.

Whether it is a publishing, promotional, or transactional workflow at a macro-level, a cross-media communications workflow requires a solid

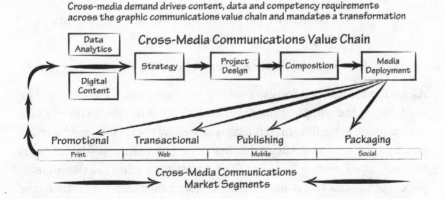

Cross-media demand drives content, data and competency requirements across the graphic communications value chain and mandates a transformation

understanding of the target audience (data), and the specific content and participation necessary for a specific project. A more comprehensive understanding of the target audience will enable a more focused the deployment of the content. Marketers and publishers today are interested in a deep dive into the needs of each individual in their targeted audience. What content do they want or need? In what specific media and at what time? When this type of demographic and psychographic data is understood, the content can be assembled in a more strategic way.

When the content needs of the targeted audience have been well established, the next natural step in the workflow is to determine "strategy". This is a tough one for traditional graphic communication service providers, yet it is the most critical step that ties together the purpose of the project. Determining the strategic objectives for cross-media projects is as important as a developing a trip plan for a long journey. Without having a strategic map for the cross-media project, you will be unable to execute the project and deliver results that can be measured. In the *Process* chapter, we will provide details regarding the steps necessary to develop strategies for cross-media campaigns that include built-in triggers that will facilitate closed-loop measurement.

Assuming that the project has a well-defined target audience with a strategic plan for deployment of cross-media content, we now move into the part of the workflow that more closely resembles the historic graphic communications workflow: the composition stage. In this segment of the workflow, three key elements come together:

1. Project design (look and feel of the deployment in all media formats),

2. All the content in its various target formats and resolutions (images, graphics, text, video, etc.), and

3. The target database representing the audience for the project.

As we mentioned previously, a variety of composition engines may be used during the composition stage. The selection of which composition engine to use is significant. it is largely driven by the specific media channels that the project strategy dictates. It is very common for designers to use Adobe Creative Suite or QuarkXpress to develop the design templates for various target media channels, and then move directly to the channel or bring the template into another composition system that supports a unique media channel via a PDF file.

For example, a designer might design the project templates in InDesign. Then, the project may be recomposed with the variable content in a variety of other composition systems, such as XMPie (PersonalEffect), MarComCentral (FusionPro), GMC Software Technology (Inspire), PageFlex, EFI (Digital StoreFront), MindFire (LookWho'sClicking), among others.

Remember that this cross-media composition space is very complex, with many competing and converging technologies, as mentioned previously. Determining the appropriate workflow at this juncture in the workflow is critical and has everything to do with the types of customers you intend to serve. Later in this chapter, we will investigate the keys to technology adoption and developing an extensible technology platform that will meet your short-term and long-term needs.

The next step in the cross-media communications workflow is the project deployment step. In this step, we execute the deployment of content across each selected media channel and in the predetermined sequence to the target audience. The project may entail an email blast linked to a personal URL (pURL) for an electronic survey, followed by a customized printed piece that is reflects responses in the survey. Following the printed piece, there may be a link or code to join a social media forum and receive some meaningful promotion for joining. Each of the specific channel engagement efforts is defined in the project strategy and composition phase, and is designed with a specific measureable objective in mind.

The final step in the workflow is closing the loop, signified by the return arrow that brings the workflow back to the very start once again. In this step, all the interaction with the target audience is monitored, followed up, and measured accordingly. This is when the various call-to-action engagement efforts with the target audience are recorded and responded to as necessary. The live data feed from the project provides updated information to the target audience database, as well as project results data that can be represented in a BI dashboard for reporting and analysis. The constant monitoring of each project provides a continuous flow to the effort that makes the workflow much more circular in nature that a linear workflow would be. The model below is the same workflow that we just described, but now portrayed in a circular workflow where there is constant iteration throughout the process.

A clear understanding of the significant trends affecting the graphic communications industry and how these trends integrate into the cross-media communications value chain provides the right backdrop to investigate the implications of technology further. An understanding of *how* to develop the appropriate technology platform and *what* is necessary to deliver services in this expanded cross-media space is essential.

The Cross-Media Technology Platform Reference Model

Transformation from a traditional printing or publishing company to an integrated cross-media communications company comes, in part, from the careful selection and integration of information technology and print technology. Technology selection should be in direct response to two key driving forces: support of the needs of your current customers, and support of the anticipated needs of the customers you aim to serve in the future.

If we assume that the digital adoption trends of consumers, knowledge workers, and enterprises are reasonably accurate (as described earlier in this chapter), we are basically shifting from a print platform to a print-plus platform—in other words, print + the other non-print media (Web, mobile, social media, etc.).

The graphic communications industry has a historic and meaningful heritage as an industry that can string together a wide variety of disparate technologies and processes into a workflow that delivers high-quality and repeatable results. Throughout the years, printers, publishers, typesetters, mailers, and bindery/finishing firms have mirrored each technology revolution with their workflows. From analog to digital, to networked systems, to interactive digital and social/mobile interactive platforms of today, the graphic communication industry is a manufacturing test bed for new information technology.

Today extensive skill sets in information technology (including the internet, broadband and wireless services, software development, database development, data analytics, and networking coupled with print technology) are the foundation of building blocks for an integrated cross-media communications platform.

Graphic arts service providers are charged with understanding information technologies and printing technologies (traditional and digital), while simultaneously being adept at leading manufacturing processes that employ rapid customized, Just-in-Time (JIT) processes that deliver consistent product with minimal waste (lean). The cross-media communications value chain is, indeed, the future mass-customization workflow for future graphic communication service providers (Mass Customization: The New Frontier in Business Competition, B. Joseph Pine, 1999).

Technology selection is a complex conversation since there are several variables to consider. Our goal is to identify the variables and some viable approaches we have seen used by successful companies with hope that you can adapt these principals for use in your firm.

To build a technology platform, we need to not only consider our current customer/future customer needs, we also have to consider our point of entry. For this conversation, we will begin with the assumption that we are looking to transform a traditional printing/publishing company to a cross-media communication firm. Later, we will discuss the approach for new entrants that do not have the traditional printing/publishing operation.

In the information technology arena, it is commonplace to discuss technology in terms of a "stack", or series of layers, that represent the resident equipment (hardware and software) through the virtual software applications that are cloud-based. Reference models, such as SaaS (Software as a Service), typically follow this type of visualization.

Technology Layer	Example
Application	Email, Word Processor
Platform	Database, DAM
Infrastructure	Servers, Storage Devices
Technology	Computers, Printers

For the purposes of this book, we have created a cross-media Technology Platform Reference Model to bridge the world of information technology and graphic communications. This reference model is designed to help illuminate the somewhat abstract world of information technology and to establish some baseline terminology that will help to identify how to design a platform and to determine where to start.

It may be easier to follow the framework for the cross-media reference model by starting the discussion from a familiar place, the production floor. We will construct the cross-media platform reference model from the shop floor through the systems and software, and ultimately to the customer.

At the base level of the model, we consider the physical or resident hardware, software, and systems (physical assets) that we acquire and configure into an efficient workflow across the production floor. The production layer in the model begins with processes that move a project from the collection of components (art, copy, images, and a design) though composition and preparation through deployment (as shown in the diagram below). For this cross-media reference model, we define deployment as the final execution of a project in the various targeted media channels. This could be a combination of traditional print/digital print, Web, mobile, or social media.

The production layer is the "wheelhouse" for graphic communication service providers and, for most operations, represents a position of strength with a tightly integrated mix of technology, process, and crafts-manship. The techniques and service-levels established in the production layer, combined with the careful integration of technology, has provided foundational set of practices that are unique in the services arena and are a solid point of leverage for expanded services opportunity.

The next level in the model is the Process Management layer (as shown in the diagram below). In this layer, we are concerned with the dynamics of job processing—from the inception of a job in the system, the pro-duction schedule, the movement and tracking of the job throughout the workflow, and the reporting of the job in terms of cost, quality, and time.

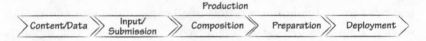

The process management layer is typically managed by a print man-agement information system (MIS) offered by companies such as EFI, Avanti, HiFlex, PrintVis, PressWise, among others. In this layer, not only are jobs/projects scheduled, but they are also cost-accounted and tracked from a financial perspective to identify whether the project is profitable or not. The MIS system also typically provides the original project esti-mate, tracks inventory, and either produces a billing statement or is inte-grated with an accounting system that manages accounts receivable and payable transactions.

The process management layer, or MIS, has a few challenges (identified in light red in the diagram): tracking of non-print components of the project and providing closed-loop feedback to the firm regarding results data associated with the project. Most MIS systems are designed with print in mind (traditional print, including offset, flexo, gravure, screen, etc. or digital print, including electrophotography, inkjet, etc.), or with new media in mind (email, pURL's social media, blogs, etc.). Not all MIS systems provide a path for service providers to manage the estimating, scheduling, tracking, and reporting of a project with integrated deploy-ment across all media channels. Many graphic communication service providers are using several systems to manage the processes of two work-flows and stitch together the billing efforts at the end when the project is ready to be delivered.

Service providers need to comprehend the entire cross-media reference model with respect to the services offering and determine an MIS technology strategy that will incorporate the integration of traditional services offering with the new media services that customers demand in an integrated offering. Processing components in a separate MIS system in stringing together an invoice at the end of the job is not a long-term solution. This is a costly and time-consuming approach that does not provide visibility to the production management processes.

Further complicating this layer is the growing need for everyone in the graphic communications ecosystem to track and report results data regarding various projects. Whether the projects are promotional, publishing, or transactional, marketers, publishers, enterprise executives want and need to see the business results of all communications efforts. The service companies that can design a technology platform that supports programs with embedded closed-loop triggers into the cross-media projects will have a competitive advantage in the future. If there is a call to action or participation that can be tracked, incorporating that tracking mechanism at the process management level of the workflow is key to a streamlined data feed to the business intelligence layers that we will discuss coming up.

The Production and Process Management layers combined are an extremely important point of leverage for traditional graphic communication service providers. These layers are a source of strength and differentiation for traditional printers; there are no other service providers that possess the job and project management competencies that printing companies have historically mastered regarding this complex manufacturing process. The most successful graphic communication service providers are companies that have proven experience in these layers, coupled with tight integration of the next two layers in the model.

The Business and Information Management layer (shown below) is a complex layer, which presents the most difficult set of technology integration issues in the entire reference model. This is the layer, which includes the management of traditional business operations, such as estimating; order processing, financial (AR/AP), inventory management, etc. The business functions of this layer are either embedded in the MIS system or the MIS integrates with accounting systems to provide the link between production management and business management.

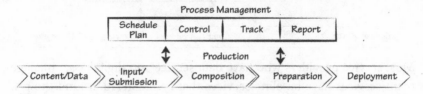

As we mentioned previously, this is well and good for print-related projects. The problem becomes how are non-print projects and work efforts estimated, tracked, and billed. When a graphic service provider incorporates expanded services in the areas of copy writing, design, Web development, training, non-print project deployment (Web, mobile, social media, etc.), how are these components integrated? Clients want an integrated estimate/proposal and billing statement. Service providers want and need to track the job status and cost throughout the production process.

MIS technology providers are working to build flexibility into their products to address the changing and increasing need to incorporate a wide range of print and non-print services into their MIS systems. Careful selection of a MIS system that enables integration of all components in the cross-media value chain is critical. In most cases, the service provider will also need a resident system integration expert who is familiar with software integration and workflow in order to harmonize the MIS system with the subtle nuances that are evident in each service provider's operation.

Next in the Business and Information Management layer is a series of capabilities that is highlighted in light red above. For years, many service providers have understood the importance of managing data and content. In fact, some companies already have customer-facing digital asset management systems, and most direct mail/marketing companies are already processing data. This is a good start, yet the technology requirements for effectively managing data and content are expanding and could be the difference maker for success in the future.

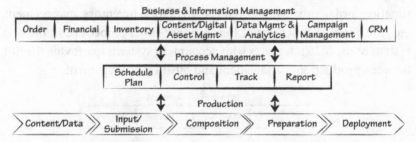

Most service providers who have data service and digital asset management services have baseline services that are centered around the production of a project—not the customer-facing management of a comprehensive data or content management service. Clients are looking for secure cloud-based solution for management of all their digital assets and data. Some progressive enterprises are already there and have established a corporate-wide data warehouse and asset management platform from a leading IT supplier.

Service providers will need to plug into their platform with a fluid and secure exchange. Many companies have not yet moved on a solution for their data and content, and this will prove to be a very fertile place for savvy service providers who seek to expand in this area. Involving an expert in the selection of data and content management systems is very important to make certain that the offering integrates well with your environment and, of course, your customers.

The next two items in the Business and Information Management layer are campaign management and customer relationship marketing (CRM). These systems involve the end-to-end orchestration of cross-media projects. Campaign management is concerned with the management of a cross-media project (or projects) and the timing of each component in the project (i.e., how the project unfold and cascades from beginning to end, including collection of campaign results, if possible).

CRM is a client-facing service that provides insights into the lifecycle activities of your customers' customer. CRM provides feedback to the enterprise on how prospects and customers are responding to content, promotion, and participation with the various communications they receive. Service providers typically do not need a CRM system; they only need to know how to tap into their client's CRM system to harvest the important information regarding the activities of their customers.

Again, some leading service providers have chosen to incorporate a CRM service into their platform and brand instances of that CRM service to their customers to more fully support the results-tracking efforts required by some customers. At a minimum, service providers need to know how to connect with CRM systems and, most importantly, how to incorporate CRM data into their business analytics services.

Next in the cross-media reference model is an important strategic area, the Partners layer (as shown in the diagram below). This layer involves the strategic and technical integration of all the partners that you will incorporate into your platform that address the "buy" side of the "make-buy" decision for your operation. It is more apparent than ever before that "you can't go it alone". In fact, we devote an entire chapter to Alliances since we understand that service providers of the future need expanded relationships with partners and suppliers who can fulfill the key services that need to be integrated seamlessly into the platform.

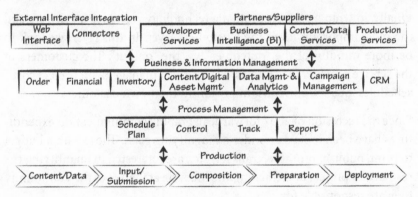

The Partners layer includes traditional suppliers who provide "buy-out" services, as well as embedded providers who provide white-label technology components that service providers will integrate, brand, and offer as their own service.

With the mature nature of cyberinfrastructure and success of cloud-based hosted software solutions, there are tremendous opportunities for service providers to add new capability with key technology partners. Prerequisite to the addition of data analytics, content managements, and other services is the expansion of the resident skills in project management, systems integration, and software development.

Leading graphic communication service providers have added in-house expertise in this area to operationalize new partner technologies and to provide expert customer services for onboarding customers' content and data. Selecting the appropriate technology that provides a secure and flexible integration is key, and it comes as a direct result of determining your future customer needs. Expert advice is needed in this space to determine the right technology that will complement the services offering and business model.

The Partners layer is a pivotal layer that can be expanded with a manageable effort and, if done correctly, can be a strategic differentiator for the future. It is difficult to make sweeping recommendations at this level; this layer is really a needs-driven layer that reflects gaps that need to be filled in order to deliver a complete integrated services offering to your customers. The offering may be a mix of technology, buy-outs, and even an acquisition.

Finally, to wrap up the cross-media technology reference model, we add the most important layer, the Customers layer. In this layer, we look to be more mindful of the "outcomes" vs. the "output". The customers of the service providers are interested in project management, project costs, schedules, quality, and most importantly, their own customers.

Since the recession of 2007 forward, all graphic communication expenditures have been looked at under a magnifying glass. Those with a budget to print, publish, promote, transact, etc., are interested in quantifying the results of a project and tracking the lifecycle activities of the community they are responsible for.

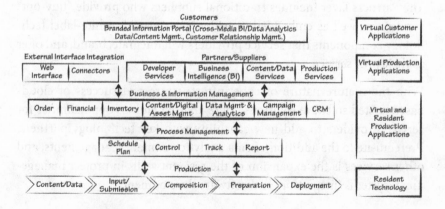

Service providers will need to provide a portal or dashboard that provides insights into the business aspects of the cross-media communications programs. These types of services can be offered in a more seamless way than ever before through cloud-based services that can be tailored to the needs of various types of customers.

Business and marketing customers need results-data and CRM information. Procurement customers need production status and costing data. Service providers need to be able to harvest the information in their MIS, BI, CRM, DAM systems in order to provide an integrated dashboard that can be customized to address the unique needs of each individual customer.

Decomposing the technology requirements in the cross-media value chain into a technology reference model can be helpful to identify where you are with respect to the model, and how various complimentary and disruptive technologies will fit within your framework. Next we will discuss how successful service providers are making the technology transformation.

Building a Technology Platform: Assessing Where You Are

One of the most difficult aspects of managing technology is determining what new technologies to select. Successful technology acquisitions should provide an improved offering to your customers and a more optimized workflow that reduces time and cost.

The stakes regarding technology selection are high for many reasons. It is impossible to invest in every new technology that comes along; yet technology investments need to provide a firm with new services, better differentiation, and reduced cycle time. It is best, of course, that a new technology acquisition delivers on all these goals. But how do you make sure you pick a winner and minimize your risk?

There are two critical aspects to consider when building your cross-media communication technology platform:

1. Determine your current-state platform model as it relates to the cross-media technology reference model.

2. Define what new services your customers want and are willing to pay for that are within your current core competency to deliver.

Let's begin by looking at the first question, assessing where you are with your current platform. It is important to take the time, do the inventory, and construct a platform reference model of the current set of technologies you have. This exercise will bring together the technology, operations, and sales teams to do a thorough snapshot of what you currently have with respect to a technology platform.

You may feel that you cannot complete the entire framework. That's not surprising since this is very expansive, and it is doubtful that any one company has a leadership position with respect to all aspects of this framework. The key point is to do the assessment and take an accurate snapshot of where you are today. If you don't know where you are, it is very difficult to define where you should be going.

During this assessment effort, it is good idea to characterize the maturity of each technology into three categories: emerging, developed, or innovative. If you are just beginning with a technology and you are still incorporating it into your operation, you would classify it as "emerging". If the technology is mature and there is good balance between your ability to sell and to deliver services using this technology, it is "developed". Finally, if the technology is unique to your firm (either the core technology or its specific implementation) such that you have a unique and competitive offering, it is "innovative".

A personalized sketch of the cross-media technology reference model will help you to visualize where you are today, where strategic points of leverage exist, and most importantly, where the gaps are that need to be filled. The next step in the assessment process is to characterize your core competencies in four key areas: Development, Integration, Technology Selection, and Project Management. A simple 0-5 scale (where 0 = poor and 5 = excellent) will work for assessing your firm's core competencies in the technology arena.

For Development, determine your firm's ability to deliver custom solutions to your customers. Is your firm able to evaluate needs, determine a plan, and implement a custom solution routinely with all your customers? Are you able to deliver solutions that are tailored to each customer, but are delivered from a common set of technologies? Companies that possess a development core competency are leaders in this area and have integrated technology, processes, and services into a predictable and scalable business model.

With respect to Integration, evaluate how mature your capability is to integrate disparate systems into your targeted workflow. Is your firm able to identify strategic gaps in the workflow, investigate leading technologies that can fill the gap, and acquire and integrate the technology into the workflow in a seamless and efficient manner? Firms that exhibit a strong core competency in integration are comfortable with adding and incorporating new technologies into their operation.

The third aspect of your core competency evaluation is Technology Selection. For this core competency dimension, you will determine how proficient your firm is at assessing and acquiring technology. Does your firm have a process to evaluate technology that involves all key departmental stakeholders? Do empowered committees work efficiently and cooperatively to refine the requirements, operational, and financial impact of a selected technology and provide a unified recommendation in a timely manner? Companies with a strong technology selection core competency are masterful at evaluating and selecting technology by eliminating unnecessary politics and by adhering to a consistent selection process.

Finally, how does your firm rate with respect to Project Management competency? With the increased role information technology plays in the graphic communication industry, firms that possess advanced skills in project management have a leadership position. Does your firm have the ability to project manage complex internal and customer-facing projects from beginning to end? Firms with a strong core competency in project management use a consistent process/system to initiate, track, and deliver projects, allowing them to engage in more complex, high-margin work.

- Completing a comprehensive assessment of the current-state of your technology platform and the rating of your firms core competencies can provide an extremely valuable view of where you currently are with respect to technology. From this exercise, you will be able to confirm a view of the technology prowess of your firm. Is your firm an ad hoc organization that builds technology as needed in response

to today's business, or is your firm a strategic and innovative company that designs and integrates new technology to form a competitive
advantage? There is quite a continuum in the graphic communication industry; yet "breakthrough" firms are those who possess strong
core competencies across all these strategic dimensions mentioned.
No one firm has it all. However, knowing where you are is the beginning of setting a new strategic direction.

- Now let's consider an approach to determine the highest priority
  technologies that are most important for your business growth.

Building a Technology Platform: Iterative, Customer-driven

It is important to establish an anchor-point with your customer whenever having a technology discussion. Adding new technology because
you believe that it is what your customer wants without confirmation is a
recipe for disaster in graphic communications. Every company has a war
story of a special project that occupied a lot of company resources, yet
never delivered a dime to the bottom line.

"Technology push" is a dangerous way to approach technology selection.
Successful firms establish an immersive technology process to simultaneously engage customers while mindfully building out their technology
platform. These breakthrough firms are able to test customer needs and
reconcile these needs with offerings that meet their needs which they
are willing to pay for. In the *Process* chapter, we will discuss in detail a
product development process that is designed to support this iterative
development with customers.

For the Technology section, we are concerned with how to determine
what leading technologies to acquire and with integrating these technologies into the technology platform.

Most graphic communication service providers provide two types of
work products – jobs and projects. For purposes of this discussion, we
will define a "job" as a work request for an item that can be delivered in
a routine manner with pre-defined procedures. We define a "project" as
a unique request that involves a variety of skills and resources that are
applied in a custom way for each project.

Graphic communications service providers respond to a mix of jobs that they can design a streamlined manufacturing process for and projects that they need to respond to in a more individualize manner. Service providers have historically been brilliant at responding to the job demand because this type of work requires a reoccurring workflow that is optimized through volume and repetition. Custom projects have been a source of lost income for many service providers.

The breakthrough service providers, however, have embraced custom projects. They use projects as a means of distilling advanced customer needs and, most importantly, getting early adopters to pay for technology acquisition. These advanced service providers do this by using a well-planned out technology platform, leveraging their core competencies. They also incorporate a project methodology that tames the risk of custom projects.

If we can consider project work as a strategic way to have our customer lead us down the technology selection path and to bankroll the effort, we will have a more fond appreciation for projects and for how they are truly a foundation to expanded service provider growth.

The diagram below provides a view of the custom project delivery process in response to customer needs, or "customer pull". If completing the technology assessment work described earlier in this chapter leads you to a conclusion that you have a gap in your technology platform, then the gap is substantiated by real customer demand, and the request aligns with your core competencies, you are ready to engage.

Find a customer with a somewhat flexible schedule, with whom you have a good relationship, and approach that customer about meeting his or her need with a new service. Assuming you have done your work and have a technology selected to develop or integrate, you will need to develop a project plan that comprehends all the details of the project. (Project Management will be discussed in detail in the *Process* chapter.)

You are now engaging in a customer-driven customization (CDC), which you can harvest after iterating with several customers as a key component of your technology platform.

Establishing a consistent way to engage lead customers with custom projects is the most realistic and proven way to advance technology in

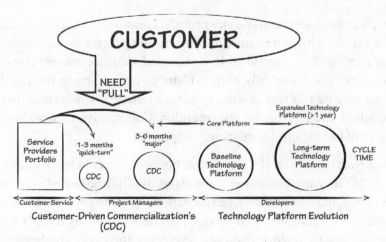

Customer-Driven Commercialization's (CDC)   Technology Platform Evolution

your graphic communication service provider company (need citation). It minimizes risk, creates an inextricable bond between you and you customers, expands your core competencies, and creates major differentiation between you and your competitors.

The technology space will continue to be a challenge for all service providers. Cost and complexity will always be factors of technology adoption in the services business. Without a way to engage the market in real-time and to evolve your technology platform as you proceed, you will never be able to keep up with technology, nor fund it appropriately to meet your customer needs. If you engage in an iterative engagement process that compliments your mainstream business, you will not loose ground to the completion, and you will emerge with an enviable cross-media technology platform.

References

Anderson, Chris. 2008. *The Long Tail: Why the Future of Business is Selling Less of More.* New York; Hyperion Books.

Anderson, Chris. 2009. *Free: How Today's Smartest Businesses Profit by Giving Something for Nothing.* New York; Random House.

Christensen, C. *The Innovator's Dilemma.* 1997. Boston: Harvard Business School Press.

Moore, Geoffrey. *Crossing the Chasm.* 1991. New York: Harper Collins.

Rogers, Everett M. (1962). *Diffusion of Innovations,* Glencoe: Free Press.

7

PROCESSES

By Chris Bondy

Making the right technology selections is essential to developing an effective platform. So is the ability to operationalize technology through the adoption of a well-defined and repeatable processes.

For *UnSquaring the Wheel*, we define "process" as a fusion of traditional Deming-like thinking with the present-day nature of Agile development used in software development.

William Edwards Deming is best known for his influence on the miraculous economic rise of Japan after World War II. Japan rose from the ashes to become the second most powerful economy in the world in less than a decade. This economic recovery was in good part due to the strategic influence of Deming's principles of Statistical Process Control, which contributes to reduced waste and increased quality. (Deming 2000) Establishing a foundational set of finely tuned processes across the organization is critical to wringing out the full value that new technology can provide, and is an essential component of a platform.

We often find that the complete benefit of any technology has a hard time making it from the demo to the production environment. Why is this? A fundamental lack of discipline with respect to process is often a significant reason for the inability or organizations to extract the full value of technology is rooted in.

While systemic process optimization is essential to repeatability and profitability in graphic communication firms, the commitment to process requires a complementary component of flexibility. Production flexibility is a historic attribute of the graphic communication industry, and most specifically, of the general commercial printer. Traditional commercial printers are known for their ability to string together a series of disparate production processes to deliver to a unique customer requirement.

Building on this production versatility, graphic communication firms can establish a process regimen that anticipates a wider range of requirements. One way to do this is to introduce process techniques, such as Agile software development (ASD), which is used by software developers. (Mathis) Agile software development is a methodology that anticipates the creative process and iterative nature of collaborative works. It concentrates on keeping the software code very simple, testing often, and delivering segments of the codes in pieces along the way—all leading up to the complete deliverable.

The careful integration of rigorous statistical process control methods balanced with the fluidity of Agile development provides a foundation for the process discussion. Striking a harmony between thorough processes that are streamlined and customer responsive is foundational to building a platform that will support transformation to integrated cross-media communications services.

Let's explore the Process vector, including the best practices, tacit knowledge, and procedures that link people and technology together for the purpose of delivering graphic communication products and services that customers demand.

What is Process and Why Do I Care?

At a fundamental level, a process is a "series of actions or operations conducting to an end". (Merriam-Webster Online) An apple pie recipe is a process. It links together materials (apples, cinnamon, flour, etc.), technology (blender, over, etc.), and know-how (functional knowledge of measurement, basic kitchen operations, etc.) into a procedure that has a predictable end result—an apple pie.

There are many ways to make an apple pie. Some approaches deliver delicious results, while some approaches deliver an efficient process. The key to success in any business, however, is to deliver a product that your target customers wants – at a price that allows you to make an acceptable profit, and in product cycle time that is realistic.

Developing the "recipe for success" in the graphic communication industry requires a refinement of key processes such that there is a successful balance between meeting the specific needs of a customer while operationalizing the needs of all your customers. Process mastery is a careful balance of tradeoffs that are distilled into a winning set of replicable procedures that deliver what appears to be a custom result through an efficient process.

Successful process optimization can provide two key business benefits: (1) operational efficiency and (2) product innovation. Process improvement efforts that reduce cost and cycle time provide operational efficiency, which allows more work to get done in less time. This has a direct impact on profit and productivity. Process improvement that delivers new product innovation provides incremental product capability and features that allow a firm to offer new and differentiated products with potentially higher profit margins. Process improvement that drives product innovation drives "top-line" revenue growth (sales), and operational efficiency drives profit through reduction in cost.

When these two operational process improvement efforts are combined, the best possible business result occurs: incremental sales growth with high-profit margin. Exploring process improvement simultaneously from an operational efficiency perspective and from a product innovation perspective is core to the principles of *UnSquaring the Wheel*.

Additionally, process improvements in operational efficiency and product innovation can be greatly enhanced by process proficiency in project management. Establishing a core competency in project management is essential to linking together the dynamic needs of your customers in a changing marketplace and your plan to meet their needs. The ability to form responsive Agile teams to quickly and efficiently solve real-time problems is instrumental to balancing product innovation and operational efficiency. It is the project management processes that become the hinge point between creative solutions that can be implemented practically.

In this Process section, we will explore process elements of (1) operational efficiency, (2) product innovation, and (3) project management. When these three core processes are well defined and harmonized to work together, they can provide the most effective operational and competitive differentiation for graphic communication service providers.

1. Operational Efficiency: Lean-Constraint Production Management

Operational efficiency involves the refinement and rebuilding of key operational processes into more streamlined and efficient workflows. This process enhancement concentrates on the elimination non-value-added activities (waste), with the objective of reducing cycle time and costs while maintaining quality.

Investing in operational efficiencies provides a path to process automation with many benefits for the transformed graphic communications firm. Increased efficiency enables graphic communication service providers to optimize capital equipment and labor resources to deliver the best possible return-on-investment (ROI). Increased automation provides opportunity to produce current products more cost effectively, while opening the door to incorporate new products into the operation.

Two key principles can be exercised to drive operational efficiency in a complementary manner from two unique perspectives. In this Process section, we will explore the process improvement approach and benefits from the combination of (1) Lean manufacturing and (2) forward-constraint design.

Keeping it Lean

Effective workflow design for graphic communications requires a "lean" process discipline similar to the principles deployed in successful automated Lean manufacturing operations in other industries. Establishing a Lean mind-set is important. It is built on the premise that your graphic communications firm is a "manufacturer" of communications products. Every "product" needs to have an established manufacturing process that is designed to optimize all resources for the efficient production of that product. Letting your operation run in an ad hoc manner is like leaving the water running. It will ultimately flush your profits down the drain.

In this Process section, we will discuss the essential elements of Lean manufacturing as they relate to operational efficiency in graphic communications.

For this book, we assume a basic understanding of Lean. For a more comprehensive understanding of Lean manufacturing, we can suggest *The Lean Six SIGMA Pocket ToolBook* (George et. al 2004) or various other Lean six SIGMA manufacturing experts (such as JD McCormick & Associates, Brookfield, WI) who focus on graphic communications.

Traditional manufacturing is arranged in departments, while Lean manufacturing is arranged in cells in order to provide complete products to an internal customer (another cell) or to an external customer. The cell is a focused team of employees who are empowered to provide products in the quantity, quality, and time frame that the customer wants. Product goes from raw material to finished assembly with a very short cycle time.

The Lean operation is focused on a well-defined set of customer requirements and on cost associated with meeting those requirements. The Lean manufacturing approach begins with an enterprise-wide focus on the Customer, Cost, Flow, and Resources.

Focus on the Customer

The focus on the customer requires a deep understanding of value. Value can easily be summed up as "what the customer is willing to pay for." The term, value-added, has a very specific meaning for the Lean enterprise. It is any product that is perceived as valuable by your customer and that they are willing to pay for. All other activities in your firm are considered non-value-added. This is not to say that they are not important. It's just that they are not activities that your customer pays for. These activities may be embedded in the price or may be candidate activities for further efficiency.

An example of a value-add is the printing of a customer's brochure. This is the value-added activity that the customer is paying for. Non-value-added activities are virtually everything else: plating, make-ready, wash-up, meetings, finding tools, etc.

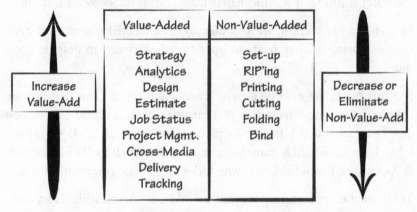

Value-Added	Non-Value-Added
Strategy	Set-up
Analytics	RIP'ing
Design	Printing
Estimate	Cutting
Job Status	Folding
Project Mgmt.	Bind
Cross-Media	
Delivery	
Tracking	

Increase Value-Add

Decrease or Eliminate Non-Value-Add

Source: PRIMIR 2011 study "Transformative Workflow Strategies for Print Applications" by Info Trends.

The next chapter is Services. Here we will discuss the services engagement process that begins with "discovery" and a focus on determining a better understanding of the needs and desired outcomes of a communications program. Suffice it to say—the primary driver in the Lean manufacturing process is complete alignment of what the customer will pay for and how they will measure the success of the communication project.

UnSquaring the Wheel has foundational emphasis in a customer-driven transformational business model—so much so that we have devoted an entire three-chapter discipline customer-facing mindset with respect to the repositioning of your business model. Several other chapters round out our customer-centric approach with a consistent premise that all insight for the business begins with a deep and iterative understanding of customer needs. And this deep understanding comes in advance of other activities and becomes a compass setting for your future direction and priority.

The time spent to investigate, document, and confirm the specific requirements of your customers will not only have payout on a specific project. This customer insight will also drive the overall direction of your operation. Tightly connecting the real-time needs of your customers with the process efficiencies in manufacturing is core to the refinement of the operation and ultimately profitability.

Organizations need to establish a way to aggregate the specific requirements by individual customers into a superset of requirements that define the production workflow. This will help operationalize reoccurring needs and flag unique needs that may be better served as a buy-out.

Graphic communication firms with mature Lean manufacturing processes are able to define a general set of offerings based on proven efficiencies, while providing specific areas of customization that are known to be value-added and are within the capability of the operation. The delicate balance between standard and custom offering is a key indicator of the operational maturity of an organization. The only way this balance can be achieved is through a well-defined process that captures customer requirements at a micro and macro level, then distills those requirements for both immediate production and for continuous improvement.

A good place to operationalize the customer focus for Lean manufacturing is through the MIS system. Begin by analyzing the highest margin activities in your operation, then compare these activities to the requirements of your top customers. The MIS system should provide a constant flow of the winners and losers with respect to operational efficiency. When a firm has tuned high-demand activities into the most efficient processes, the result is the best possible profit scenario.

Customer focus in Lean manufacturing is harmonizing value-added customer requirements with efficient manufacturing processes. Establishing regular dialog and information flow between customers and operations is vital to success in Lean. It can be facilitated through sales and customer service staff and reporting through your MIS system.

Focus on the Cost

Lean manufacturing principles attack operational inefficiencies with a focus on cost analysis in search of waste throughout the operation.

If the objective of your firm is to deliver quality services to your customers, while simultaneously delivering an attractive profit margin, then attacking operational cost through Lean is essential. Ultimately, your efforts in Lean are an effort in cost reduction by eliminating waste.

Identifying cost throughout your operation is an important activity and at the root of knowing what really is value-add/non-value-add in your operation. Simply put, cost is associated with the totality of all expenses incurred during the production and delivery of the product to the customer. Cost it is not just the cost of labor and inventory. True product cost includes the amortized overhead expense of all systems, materials, and individuals involved in the manufacturing process from creation through payment. This is known as order to cash.

Cost analysis includes costs that may not seem directly connected to the production process. These costs include utilities, maintenance agreements, software licenses, training, support resources (accounting, delivery drivers, etc.) quality control, and many other somewhat transparent expenses that must be considered.

Once all the costs are identified, Lean exercises determine and eliminate waste can be applied to the largest and most problematic cost areas. Taking this approach will ensure the best result for your time spent.

Make sure to target these specific areas in your operation:

- Waste caused by defects – Does product does not meet the quality level acceptable by the customer?

- Non-value-add activities and materials – Which processes and activities are used to support the production of the customer deliverable? Determining which activities are necessary and which are unnecessary is key.

- Overproduction– Are products produced coincident with need, or are they produced in advance and are waiting at a cost to you?

- Extra processing – Are additional processes needed to meet the requirement on a certain project that are in addition to typical requests, and is there coverage for the cost?

Focus on Flow

Flow of information or material (data storage, inventory, transportation, etc.) is critical in the fast-paced operations of a cross-media communication firm. Developing systems to identify and track the processes that run the operation is important when streamlining operations.

The goal of Lean is for the "systems to run the operation and the people to run the systems." The following elements influence how fluidly information and material can flow through the operation.

- Inventory – Is there synchronization between the inventories on hand to deliver the work-in-progress (WIP), or are special orders needed to meet demand? Are finished goods in inventory awaiting demand?

- Transportation – Is there unplanned movement of paper, supplies, information, and people that is not orchestrated in the routine processing of the work?

- Data and Job Instructions – Is the information required to process the job at each juncture of the workflow available on time and in the appropriate format? Is the recording of time-spent and job status conveyed in real-time regarding the job status?

Focus on Resources

The *UnSquaring the Wheel* approach to transformation is completely aligned with the traditional Lean focus on resources. In fact, two of the three chapters on Resources are dedicated to People and Alliances. Both are core to the principles of Lean manufacturing resources.

Recruiting, training, and nurturing a well-integrated operational team are essential to the objectives of Lean manufacturing. Lean operational leaders are focused on empowering teams with the ability to (1) solve problems, (2) probe with open-ended questions, and (3) manage their operational unit (cell) by observation, also known as *management by walking around*.

The Lean operational team is fully trained, cross-trained, and empowered to make the operational unit work as an autonomous cell that is also tightly integrated with the rest of the operation.

The time investment in mentoring internal and external resources with appropriate training and operating procedures is well spent when the Lean culture drives consistent cost and quality conscious behavior of the team. As more of the graphic communications workflow becomes digital and some of the work products also become digital, the crisp definition of all processes becomes essential to drive swift and accurate movement of instructions and job content through each stage of production.

Each of the areas of waste listed above can be addressed with a comprehensive Lean manufacturing plan. Since many costs and wastes are hidden, there are a variety of Lean manufacturing tools developed to help better understand and isolate waste, and to determine the best process approach to eliminate waste.

Lean Tools

The Lean manufacturing processes makes use of specific tools that help to identify and eliminate waste, and to streamline the manufacturing process.

The following list describes several of the key tools used in Lean manufacturing. For a complete list reference, see The Lean Six SIGMA Pocket ToolBook (George et. al 2004) or other Lean manufacturing reference books.

- **Spaghetti Diagram** – Traces the time-motion activities in a particular workflow.

- **Value Stream Mapping** – Identifies the input process and output of every step in a specific workflow (activities, materials, people, and information) from order to cash. The Value Stream Map becomes the blueprint for the current, or "as-is", state of the workflow and provides a visualization of target areas for improvement.

- **Kaizen** – Is the continuous improvement process that incorporates a "plan-do-check-act" analysis of the workflow with the goal of eliminating waste in the value stream.

- **5S+** – Are Lean terms used as a checklist to migrate the workflow to an environment of safety and order, making it easier to identify waste. The five "S+" stands for: sort, straighten, scrub, systemize, and standardize, while eliminating any safety concerns.

- **Kanban** – Is a production scheduling system that manages the upper and lower levels of materials in a cell, such that the system is loaded to the appropriate levels, with the right resources at the right time in the right quantity.

- **Reward for Knowledge** – Is a Lean management principal rewards employees that exhibit behavior and action that helps to drive Lean process. It is customer focused. It focuses on waste elimination and quality, and on effective problem solving.

Integrating Lean principles into your operation can dramatically improve your operational efficiency. Lean can build a operational culture that is focused on the customer, is in support of the empowered team, and has a penchant for continuous improvement and the elimination of waste.

Incorporating Lean processes into your operations can be accomplished by following these 10 basic steps of Lean manufacturing success:

1. Create a Value Stream Map of a specific workflow (order to cash).

2. Develop a spaghetti diagram of the key processes in the value stream.

3. Rearrange the workflow into productive cells.

4. Apply the 5S+ to each cell such that each cell is tightly organized.

5. Establish a Kanban scheduling system for resources to and from the cell.

6. Develop a Kaizen (project plan) for the process.

7. Document each major step in the value stream and build a manual of best practices

8. Establish an employee reward system that encourages proper Lean behavior.

9. Establish empowered teams by cell.

10. Create an interactive link between your sales/customer service teams and the production/operational teams to convey

and refine customer requirements and value-added activities.

Forward-Constraint Design (FCD)

The second component of effective workflow transformation is forward-constraint design (FCD). This manufacturing approach involves thinking of your workflow processes from back to front. Forward-constraint design requires a restricting of your services offering around production processes that balance features and manufacturability.

We refer to forward-constraint design as "managing your sandbox." If the "sandbox" is your manufacturing operation, and the sales team is in sync selling services that the manufacturing plant can't deliver, we have ciaos. How often have we heard war stories of sales folks selling what is difficult, if not impossible, for the plant to produce?

Better synchronization between the sales offering and the ability of the plant to produce efficient results provides a much more profitable and smoothly running graphic communications firm.

FDC is a concept easy to understand, yet very difficult to implement. Until the recent wave of web-to-print technology became widely available to firms, the concepts of FCD were not widely understood or utilized in the graphic communication industry, even though there is some evidence of FCD being utilized in the gravure printing of flooring material.

If we continue with the flooring example, let's consider going into Lowes or Home Depot. You ask the sales associate to match a laminate floor sample to a piece of wood that is the front of a cabinet drawer. The sales associate will go to the laminate manufacturers product brochure and help you select the sample floor that best matches the door. The sales associate does not take a sample of the cabinet drawer and ask Pergo to develop a special laminate floor that matches the cabinet. That would be a ridiculous request and extremely price-prohibitive.

This is an example of forward-constraint design. The manufacturing process involved in producing laminate floors can only accommodate a refined list of floor types. These flooring types are pre-manufactured and made available for customers to choose. The process is constrained according to the demand of the various samples and does not permit customized request.

Taking a lesson from more restrictive print processes (such as the flooring example) can provide a valuable tool to help drive efficiency in graphic communications by minimizing the choices to a viable set of options that provide flexibility, while also supporting cost-effective manufacturability.

It is imperative that there is alignment between the production offering the various services, programs, and products that a service provider offers and production's capability to deliver those goods and services. This includes the people, process, culture, and technology that are aligned in the manufacturing plant to deliver the products and services.

FCD involves looking at the capability of your plant from back to front to determine what types of capabilities it can do successfully, efficiently, and profitably. Then you step back once again to determine what types of production capability are viable to deliver integrated cross-media services, including strategy, design, and composition. These capabilities are what should drive specific order processing to give the right instructions to the operational cells in the plant.

With appropriate forward-constraint design planning, the sales and marketing arm of your graphic communications firm can be directly in

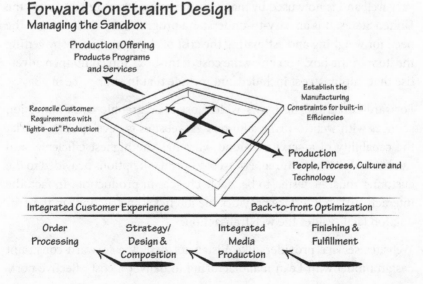

Forward Constraint Design
Managing the Sandbox

sync with the manufacturing or production. Sales and operations can be working in harmony such that products, programs, and services offered by sales and marketing are aligned with what operations and production can produce efficiently.

Another example of forward-constraint design is seen in the Priority Mail program of the United States Postal Service (USPS). It set out to organize priority mail in response to people around the country who are using web storefronts like eBay and Amazon to ship goods.

If we understand eBay sales, for example, people wishing to buy and sell goods using eBay want to know the shipping cost. And they want to understand that shipping is included in the sales price of the particular product being sold on eBay. That consumer need led the USPS to develop their Priority One program that states, "If It Fits, It Ships".

This program provides a series of flat-rate envelopes, as well as small, medium, large, and very large sized boxes that were pre-defined with a set fixed-rate fees for shipping anywhere in the United States. By establishing pre-defined box sizes and the set rates, the USPS employed the forward-constraint design approach, allowing their customers to comprehend the cost involved with shipping before anything had been shipped.

If customers could fit the item in the box, it would ship for the pre-determined price. This was a successful program for the USPS that worked very well and is now used by many businesses and consumers across the United States. It is an easy-to-understand program, and it eliminated the need for weighing and estimating the cost of shipping. Simply by getting the item in the box, you knew the cost of the box. You could then advertise that shipping cost included and include that in your price in eBay.

Forward-constraint design is widely used for graphic communication services with web-to-print solutions. A websites is developed to restrict the capability of a service around what has the highest efficiency and can be easily manufactured. For web-to-print, all options provided to the customer must be tested to be viable choices in production. In fact, the interactive Web interface provides the job ticket instructions to the production facility after the web transaction.

Websites service providers like Vistaprint deploy a forward-constraint design model with Lean manufacturing to deliver a cost-effective portfolio of products. The Vistaprint manufacturing operation designs the products in the most optimized manner that are offered through their web-to-print portal.

Natural areas for efficiency using forward-constraint design are offerings like standard "house" sheets for targeted paper stocks, or select paper sizes and bindery and finishing treatments that run efficiently. By involving the customer in the order process effort, the customer can provide accurate job specifications, and the service provider can provide options that are efficient.

Companies such as Smarter Agent and Constant Contact provide other examples of forward-constraint design web-to-print solutions that dramatically reduced the cycle time in the upstream order processing and help service providers to streamline workflow with very specific production intent.

Forward constraint design refines the choices to only those that can be delivered in a productive manner. It streamlines the offering, inventory, and variables for better efficiency and simplifies the process and makes it easy to use.

Combining forward-constraint design with Lean manufacturing principles enables graphic communication service providers with the tools necessary to develop efficient production workflow processes. A frequent audit of the production value chain will provide areas for continuous improvement and opportunities to incorporate the techniques discussed in the segment.

2. Product Innovation Process

The second "process" concentration in *UnSquaring the Wheel* looks beyond operational efficiency and into processes that promote product innovation through a revised product development process.

The traditional product development process moves quickly from strategy exploration to a product specific focus with assumptions that the future view of technology, products, and market conditions support the ideas for the product. Some companies perform other strategic functions in advance of the product development process that provide the strategic framework for their product developments initiatives.

Efforts such as competitive benchmarking, market analysis, business model analysis, assessment of technology trends, etc., for many companies are included in the company's strategic plan or the market and strategy map for a particular division. These efforts are all very critical to the success of a product development initiative, yet they need to be much more tightly linked with the product development effort, and not be a separate and de-coupled process or activity.

Breakthrough products require a different product planning approach than do the traditional product development process, which is somewhat serial in nature. The traditional product development process is structured to be more of one-time-through-the-process approach, or a "pipeline," that has limited commitment to iteration prototyping. This approach also usually offers a much too limited engagement with the target customer.

With the traditional product development process, multiple studies have shown that firms are ineffective at capturing and interpreting the Voice of the Customer (VOC), and with reflecting true customer needs in their new products [8].

Breakthrough products and services that have had success in recent years deploy an expanded view of the traditional product development process. In the early stages of product planning, they add a couple of other phases to the ideations phase where the concept of the product or solution is being defined [9].

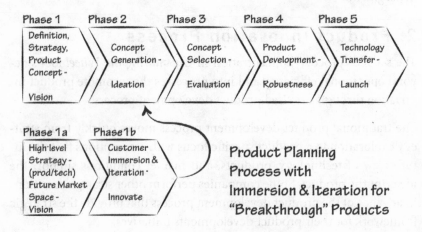

Product Planning Process with Immersion & Iteration for "Breakthrough" Products

First, they expand heavily in the high-level strategy and definition of the future market space with a vision that defines the environment, the conditions, and the usage of the particular product concept that they have in mind. Second, the ideation phase incorporates a comprehensive customer immersion and iteration step. In this customer emersion step, much attention is spent on studying the way people work.

The way work gets done, the way work is conceptualized, how people go through their current work process, and where there are potentials for unmet and unspoken needs— it's all evaluated. (Christensen et. al 2007) As the company takes the time to document this ethnographic data and become emerged in the very specific customer issues, it is able to uncover innovative ways that the product can be used as a catalyst to deliver on unmet and unspoken needs.

The **High-Level Strategy** stage includes a process of discovery and assessment at all relevant data sources. A thorough analysis in the following areas will help uncover the overall market potential for the product, as well as your best opportunity for success in this new product endeavor.

Make sure to discover and assess each of these areas:

- Business/Market
- Customer
- Competition
- Technology
- Product Portfolio
- Core Competency

During the strategy stage, the view should be open and all-encompassing. Explore all good ideas and sources of input and feedback. The diagram below represents the strategy stage as a wide funnel, bringing in all potential ideas and data to come to bear on a comprehensive view of the space. Ideas can filter out in time. In this step, it is important to consider all inputs.

The Customer Immersion and Iteration stage combines the strategy effort in the previous stage with a first-hand immersion engagement with

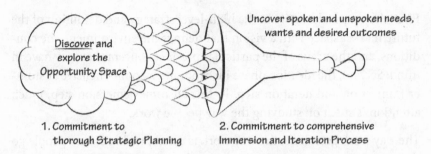

1. Commitment to   2. Commitment to comprehensive
   thorough Strategic Planning   Immersion and Iteration Process

the customer at their site to uncover unmet and unspoken needs and wants.

The steps below provide the immersive sequence that will allow your customer to open up and share information that may be extremely valuable to you. This discovery process may take place though a work practice study of a process that is problematic for your customer. It may take place in a collaborative effort to develop a prototype solution to a problem that the customer is facing.

The bottom line is that, if you don't explore, you will never know. Developing product offerings for customers without walking in their shoes is a recipe for disaster. It's the reason why many products do not meet customer needs. If customers are not intimately involved in the planning process, it is highly unlikely that the product with resonate with them the same way that breakthrough products do.

Customer Immersive and Iteration Steps:

- Select

- Observe/Engage

- Iterate & Prototype

- Analyze

- Recommend

The product planning process with immersion and iteration is essential to creating breakthrough products. Adding this thinking to your product development department efforts will put you on the road to delivering breakthrough products and transforming your company to be aligned with the emerging market needs.

Breakthrough products delight customers, deliver unmet wants and needs, and provide an emotional connection. The upside for firms that develop and deliver breakthrough products is a sustained competitive advantage, increased market share, and revenue growth.

Graphic communication service providers can benefit from a refinement in the product development processes to be more in sync with the marketplace. Pushing technology and unique offerings on the market provides you with less traction than does establishing a good process for iterating with your customers and gaining first-hand knowledge about their specific needs. This customer information can be a valuable driver in the shaping of your future product offering.

Immersive customer discovery is also aligned with Lean manufacturing and forward-constraint design methods. Better synchronization with your target customer provides the best compass setting for new product development.

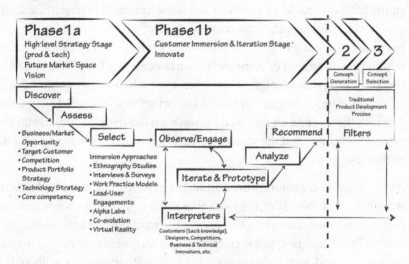

3. Agile Project Management

The third major process focus for *UnSquaring the Wheel* is developing a core competence in project management. Understanding how to scope, plan, set expectations, schedule, orchestrate, budget, deliver, and complete projects is a critical skill set for graphic communication service providers.

From a simplistic perspective, all work that you encounter as a service provider can be placed into two basic buckets. One type of work is routinely produced that has a standard well-known sequence of tasks that is understood inside your operation and can be produced with relative ease. For this discussion, we will call that work a "job." Jobs can be automatically estimated from a price list, web-to-print systems, or MIS systems. Jobs are initiated with a job ticket and associated work order. All other types of work are projects. For this section, we are interested in managing projects.

Establishing a predictable project management discipline will allow you to conduct a variety of internal and customer facing projects that will provide you with a unique competitive advantage. Mastery in project management is a table stakes competency with respect to consultative sales and will ensure success with high-margin programs.

What makes a "projects" unique from our previous definition of "jobs"? At the fundamental level, a project has some unique characteristics. Projects typically involve the collection of a variety of resources for the sole purpose of the project goals or outcomes. Projects are custom in nature, but they leverage a set of common resources or a "platform" (discussed in the Technology chapter). Projects have a set schedule (a beginning and an ending date), a budget, and most importantly, a Project Manager. For projects, there is one empowered person who has the authority to run the project and command the various resources towards the shared goals and outcomes.

As the graphic communications industry expands upstream and downstream, the complexity of the work that service providers do has become increasingly more complex. Not only is the workflow and range of deliverables more complex, but service provider customers are also demanding more closed-loop information about the outcomes and results of the various programs (promotional, transaction, and publishing programs).

The complexity of the work and the need for more results information has created an expanded opportunity for service providers to become more consultative in their customer engagements. Approaching customers with consultative sales has plenty of up-side margins, relationship building, and long-term reoccurring programs. However, without a consistent project management process, this business model is high-risk.

Agile Attitude

There are many approaches, tools, and techniques used for project management. Yet, not all are right for fast-paced cross-media graphic communications service providers. Over many years of experience running both successful and unsuccessful projects, we have distilled the project management mindset for service providers down to two key elements that work very well together, "Agile" and the "One Page Project Manager".

First, lets discuss Agile, and why the Agile Attitude is essential for your success with offering more complex programs to your customers. The Agile Attitude has roots in the area of software development and as such has many of the same demands as do the graphic communications industry. Customers with a need for software typically need a custom project (built off of a platform), have limited time and money, and have little know-how regarding the details of how code gets written. Sounds like the same industry—right?

Agile software developers were searching for a better way to iterate with customers to meet their needs while continuing to grow a development platform that can be instantiated in variety of ways to solve different customer problems. Agile development is also a very Lean approach. It concentrates on value-adds and not so much on costly processes that have no value to customers.

The following Agile Development principles are provided from *The Agile Manifesto* (Mathis) (http://agilemanifesto.org). Their best practices in project management in graphic communications make much sense.

Agile Attitude includes these principles:

- Doing more with less
- Individuals and interactions over processes and tools
- Working software (completed projects) over comprehensive documentation
- Customer collaboration over contract negotiation
- Responding to change over following a plan

Taking a lesson from Agile development and applying the approach to project management in graphic communications can go a long way to making projects successful for both your customer and your bottom line. To compliment the Agile Attitude, there needs to be some formal project management processes that allow you to approach projects in a consistent manner. Next we will look at the One Page Project Manager.

Project Management on a Single Page!

Through our various project management experiences, we found that the *One Page Project Manager* (*OPPM*) (Campbell & Campbell 2012) is an excellent tool for managing all projects in a consistent, easy-to-use template. The *OPPM* provides a way to identify the major tasks, the project completion dates, and the owners of the various tasks in the project. *OPPM* allows you to monitor these tasks and objectives against the schedule and the budget with summary information—all in a single-page MS Excel spreadsheet.

Many project management tools are complex. They require specific software and training, but not *OPPM*. It provides a printed book, or an eBook with downloadable templates, that you can adapt and customize. In a very short period of time, you can be up and running with *OPPM*. (Campbell & Campbell 2012)

OPPM templates can be adapted for complex traditional project management efforts with comprehensive references to the *Project Management Book of Knowledge* (PIMBOK) for experienced Project Management Professionals (PMPs) (PMBOK 2012), for or an individual with no project management experience. There is even a section on Agile Project Management that provides further insights into this very relevant approach for the graphic communications project management.

Project management is a critical component of the processes necessary to bring together the more complicated program-like needs of your customers and the valuable resources of your operational team. All "work" in your operation needs to have a work-order (job) or a project plan. Everything else is not work. Even internal skunk works, need a project plan! Developing a consistent approach to engage your customers will be discussed in detail in the next chapter on "Services" and assumes that you have a core competency in project management.

Putting it All Together

Value-added services in the graphic communications industry are built off of a technology platform that leverages the essential processes we have discussed, including Operational Efficiency (Lean and Forward-Constraint Design), Product Innovation Process, and Project Management.

To determine where your firm is as it relates to the various processes we have discussed, it is useful to assess your capabilities based on some key dimensions. The overarching approach of *UnSquaring the Wheel* begins with a self-evaluation that will allow you to observe and document your current state status as it relates to characteristics of transformed companies.

Of particular interest are four (4) key areas that, through our research, we know provide a solid assessment of the process maturity of a graphic communications firms. Transformed graphic communication firms are accomplished in the following areas: Workflow Innovation, Continuous Improvement, Process Engineering, and Customer Needs Assessment.

UnSquaring the Wheel – Business Transformation Assessment (BTA) provides a mechanism to help you determine how far evolved or mature your firm is along each of these dimensions. A firm can be very basic in its processes and have an ad hoc approach, or they can be on the other side of the scale developing innovative processes that transform their customers business models. The point is that all companies have processes. Some process are stronger than others. Our objective is to help you determine where you are and where you need to go with insights on how to get there.

Contemplate where is your maturity for each of the "process" dimensions and consider where you would like to be. Ask yourself: Do you have a core competency in "workflow innovation"? Can your firm easily understand process issues in you and your customers operation? Can you suggest and implement changes that show measurable improvement? Is "continuous improvement" a way of life in your firm? Do employee, customer, and vendor feedback get integrated into the operational changes that your firm makes?

Does your operational team have the ability to quickly implement a new work process or modify an old work process and bring that process operational so a regular production team can successfully execute? Do the employees have the ability to distill "customer requirements" in real-time from all sources of feedback into actionable projects that can be delivered?

These questions and others are foundational to building a core competency in the area of process. No single operation does everything well. However, if you are able to evaluate progress in specific areas of your business and work on continuous improvement initiatives, you can transform!

References

Agilemanifesto.org. *The Agile Manifesto.* http://www.agilemanifesto.org.

Bondy, Christopher, Rahill, John, &Povio, Michael. 2007. *Immersion & Iteration: Leading Edge Approaches for Early Stage Product Planning.* Rochester, NY: Rochester Institute of Technology.

Campbell, C. & Campbell, M. 2012. *The New One-Page Project Manager.* Hoboken, NJ: Wiley.

Christensen, C., Anthony, S., Berstell, G., & Nitterhouse, D. 2007. "Finding the Right Job for Your Product." *MIT Sloan Management Review,* 48(3), 38-47.

Cooper, Robert & Edgett, Scott. 2007. *Generating Breakthrough Product Ideas: Feeding the Innovation Funnel.* Ancaster, ON, Canada: Product Development Institute.

Deming, W. Edwards. 2000. *Out of the Crisis.* 88. Cambridge, MA: MIT Press.

George, M., Maxey, J., Rowlands, D., Upton, M., & Jaminet, P. 2004. *The Lean Six SIGMA Pocket ToolBook: A Quick Reference Guide.* New York: McGraw-Hill Professional Publishing.

Mathis, Bryan. (nd) *Agile Project Management for Beginners Mastering the Basics.* http://www.thetruemanager.com/ Bryanmathis.

Merriam-Webster Online. http://www.merriam-webster.com/info/copyright.htm

PMBOK (Project Management Book of Knowledge). 2012. Newtown Square, PA: Project Management Institute.

8

SERVICES

By Chris Bondy

As the graphic communications industry expands both upstream and downstream, so does the complexity of cross-media communication projects also expands. In this chapter, we explore the "services" opportunity and how you'll need fundamental changes in your business model in order to support services-oriented engagements.

We'll build on the work segmentation introduced in the Process chapter. You'll recall that we divided the types of graphic communications work into two key buckets – Jobs and Projects. We'll concentrate on the services opportunity as it relates to jobs and projects.

A Case for Services

Recent economic conditions, coupled with advances in technology (discussed in the Technology chapter) have combined to create a multiplier-effect, or "perfect storm", for the graphic communications industry. Consumers, knowledge-workers, and enterprises have all reacted to these changes and are re-adjusting to them in hopes of better alignment.

From an economic perspective, the printing industry has endured several difficult recessionary periods. In the late 2001-2002, there was a recession; NAICS (2010) stated the US printing revenues during that period to be $104.2 billion. By 2003, revenues declined to $92 billion, and then by 2007, they stepped back up, almost recovering from that recessionary period to $103.4 billion. The most recent recessionary period of 2008 to 2010 reports a substantial loss of volume in the printing industry. From

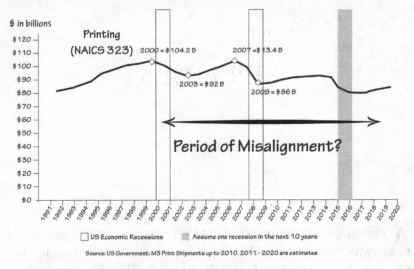

2007 to 2009, US printing revenues went down to $89 billion and in the years following we've been slowly recovering but never to the top level of revenues exhibited in year 2000.

Economists characterize the printing industry as an industry in precipitous decline. The overall decline is projected to be 3-5% per year. However, some segments (such as digital printing, packaging, and security printing) will actually increase.

Co-author Dr. Joe Webb's analysis indicates that in 1972, the average per person consumption of US commercial printing was $366 after inflation. Because of technological improvements and economic growth, by 1995 that peaked at $549. By 2015, it has dropped more than half, to $269.

Since 2000, US shipments of commercial printing are down by almost half, and industry profits are down by 75%. Industry shipments peaked in 1995, and are down more than 50% since then.

After all these years, it was only in late 2014 and in 2015 that industry shipments stabilized for more than a year. Gone are the companies that denied the effects of digital media on the way consumers and businesses use information.

The thriving printing companies that remain are not the ones consolidating failed printing businesses. The businesses that downsize and hunker down are clinging to hopes that the old market for print will return. The companies on the upswing are new and revitalized. They saw what happened to their peers. They have not just made investments in digital printing and workflow technologies, but they have re-thought their entire business models to understand communications and their client's objectives. They become a valued resource for their clients in a confusing communications marketplace with unprecedented demands for accountability. Printing is not their product. Client objectives drive their offerings.

History will repeat itself. There is an ebb and flow to growth periods and recessionary periods in the industry. Service providers need to be conscious of market conditions, and they need to understand how to use their scarce resources and technology to best respond to the changing needs of the marketplace.

During non-recessionary periods and periods of growth, companies move along with incremental changes in their offering in sync with minor market fluctuations. In recessionary periods, the gap between the offering and the market needs widens. Firms that are caught off-guard by a recession usually have a misalignment in their interpretation of market needs, as reflected in their offering and ability to respond to the changing market conditions. The gap typically comes from economic and technologic changes that shift the needs and priorities of the market.

Once the company becomes aware of this misalignment, they are confronted with a fork in the road. They can transform their business with a new set of products and services that are aligned with the changing marketplace and market conditions. Or, they can work a downsizing plan and ride the current set of services and products as long as possible, reducing cost and slowly winding down the business commensurate with the demand.

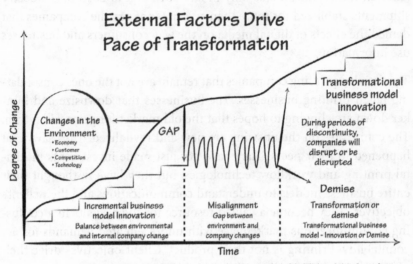

Source: IBM Business Model Transformation, adapted from Gerry Johnson, Kevin Scholes, Richard WHittington, Exploring Corporate Strategy, 7th Edition © 2005 Prentice Hall, Pearson Educations Limited

In some cases, companies cannot respond to the changing market conditions. They are under-capitalized, or they don't have a strategic point of leverage going forward and they fail. They go out of business, or they are able to sell, or they lose money and go bankrupt. Other companies, who are able to adjust, leverage their existing capabilities until they can synchronize with the changes in the market. These companies transform themselves with an updated offering that is aligned with the market, so they flourish going forward.

Recent economic, cultural, and technology changes mandate that graphic communication service providers look for disruptive ways to offer new compelling services to survive. In *The Innovators' Dilemma*, Clayton Christensen (1997) describes "disruptive technologies" as technologies that have a reduced time-to-market. They also have a different, more elaborate, value proposition or set of performance factors that make this product and service compelling to the marketplace.

In order to drive transformation (in other words, to meet the changing needs of the marketplace), service providers need disruptive technology. In the Technology chapter, we explored how the disruptive technologies of data, content, cloud computing, and integrated cross-media communications can be leveraged in the graphic communication industry in the future. Now, let's explore some of the emerging services that complement the traditional graphic communications service provider offering and pave the way for high-value, high-margin program work.

The graphic arts services transformation follows a progressive adoption cycle. It typically starts with a traditional offset printing company migrating upstream to use digital printing technology for short-run print-on-demand jobs. The company then further expands to develop some web-to-print capability using the Internet with some level of personalization. Expanding further, they move to provide marketing services that integrate a custom engagement with fully personalized print communications. Finally, the traditional printing company evolves to an integrated cross-media service provider offering a comprehensive range of integrated cross-media communications services, including print mobile, social media, database, analytics, and digital content management.

It is important to know where you are in the transformation process in order to determine the next viable steps for you to make. The *UnSquaring the Wheel* Business Transformation Assessment system (BTA) is a helpful tool to aid you and your management team in the evaluation of your transformational progress. The evolution to cross-media communications takes place by moving your focus and resources from a paradigm of a single message to the masses to a mass personalized communications across a variety of different media channels.

Services-Oriented Business Model

Making the adjustments towards a services-oriented business model requires significant changes across all aspects of the business. It is very important to note that we do not advocate an all-or-nothing approach here. There continues to be a significant demand for traditional graphic communication print jobs. Remember, print is still an $80 billion market. Print jobs are table-stakes and as such should move into a fully automated (web-to-print) context with minimal intervention from anyone in the operation. Automation from order through cash is essential in order provide a competitive price that still delivers an acceptable profit margin for print jobs.

Print jobs (whether digital or traditional) also provide critical basis work that is necessary to underwrite your core capital equipment and operational staff. For our discussion, we like to look at the services opportunity as incremental and complementary to the existing business offering.

In order to deliver services, however, your entire business model needs to be revised. You'll need to define a comprehensive services-oriented business model, including your offering, skills required, selling methodology, and program engagement model. In the balance of this chapter, we'll discuss will these critical elements of the services-oriented business model: your services offering, the cross-media lifecycle engagement model, how expanded services equal an expanded skill set, and the selling of program-focused services.

Your Services Offering

Graphic communication services can be categorized into two distinct service-types: *product-focused services* that are embedded or integrated into your standard offering, and *program-focused services* that are delivered through your consultative customer engagement. The transformed cross-media service provider clearly understands the unique operational treatment of these two service types.

Product-focused services should be centered on an automated, lean, forward-constraint design workflow. All options should be considered, tested, optimized, such that minimal human intervention is required—allowing the low-cost, short cycle time product delivery.

Program-focused services are centered on a discovery process that defines the strategy and measurement of an integrated communications initiative that is targeted to solve a specific business problem. Both service types are important, and both are essential to the livelihood of the service provider.

Product-focused services provide a solid reoccurring basis work that helps to cover the foundational operating expenses of the service provider. These types of jobs are table stakes to the operation. They provide a constant flow of work that helps to cover the operational costs of facilities, core employees, and equipment. Product-focused jobs have low margins, yet they should be simple enough to be produced without major human intervention.

Program-focused services require the expertise of your most advanced staff members and a highly interactive exchange with your customer. These programs, are very time-consuming. Yet they have very high margins if they are sold in a manner that properly represents the value-added nature of the project management and program outcomes.

Businesses today are in search of service providers who can provide a strategic roadmap for efficient and effective communication with their customers. This means the right content to the right person, at the right time, and in the right media—a very tall order!

Product-Focused Services

Product-focused services are most closely aligned with traditional print offerings in that they are embedded or adjacent to the tangible print products. For example, as print offerings become more personalized, and they are delivered directly to the target recipient, there is need for a host of data services that structure the customer data files for postal optimization. Embedding data processing fees per record into the integrated or bundled print cost for a direct mail project would be a natural product-focused service.

When embedding additional capability into your product-focused services, you should implement several of the techniques discussed in the Process chapter. Operationally, all product-focused offerings should be optimized with lean manufacturing and forward-constraint design workflow management. You can successfully implement product-focused services using web-to-print solutions that streamline the order processing steps. These solutions also provide discrete, predictable work orders into production for products that can be delivered with standard operating procedures. Work can also be normalized in product type batches to gain further optimization of the actual print and finishing stages of production.

Product-focused service providers concentrate on a very specific product offering that is fine-tuned with an efficient manufacturing process around delivering a particular product set to the broad market. Vistaprint and Shutterfly are two such product-focused service providers.

Vistaprint initially entered the market in 2001, leveraging web-to-print workflow offering a streamlined and cost-effective way to order business cards. Vistaprint's earnings from 2001 to 2010 were exponential. In 2010, their revenue grew to 194.6 million (a 40% increase over revenue the previous year). They also delivered a gross margin that was 65%, compared to 63% in that previous year—all in the middle of the recession! Shutterfly has enjoyed similar success with a product-focus on photo books.

These product-focused success stories begin with identifying a general product need, and then developing a manufacturing process that optimizes the production of this product. The final launch of the product takes place through a web-to-print portal, but only when the entire production process with all viable options are considered and tested are fully operational.

Product-focused services can be delivered to a local or regional market, and they can be specific to a single customer or a vertical market. The key ingredient to success with product-focused services is an offering that is as close to "lights-out" as possible. The business model for these types of services does not warrant a high-touch interaction of your team with the customer. If a high-touch interaction and customized approach is what your customers are looking for, they should be immediately transitioned to a program-focused services approach. Remember that transformed service providers are very good at segmenting their work between these two services types. They maintain the discipline of running their operation aimed at this unique approach to these two types of work.

Program-Focused Services

Let's continue on with the direct mail example and explore what the expanded services offering might be for program-focused services. Direct marketing program-focused services might include data analytics of the target customer database, a strategy plan for the measurable project outcomes, acquisition and appending of additional data fields and additional prospective customers, and response triggers designed for closed-loop response reporting. These program-focused services are delivered in an integrated fashion directly in response to the overarching objectives of the program versus a specific print product.

For a program-focus business model, service providers look at key vertical markets and the general needs and requirements of those markets at a macro-level. They then look for unique ways to differentiate and add value in each target market. Beyond the macro market requirements, service providers need to consider the lifecycle needs of the customers'-customer in order to uncover the subtle needs that will reinforce a solid services offering.

Examples of program-focused target market opportunities are business-to-consumer loyalty programs for firms such as dentists, auto dealerships, credit unions, and nonprofit organizations. Each of these firms have unique requirements at a macro-level that are distinct to the industry. In addition, at a micro-level, there are very specific requirements that are aligned to drive the acquisition of new customers and retention of existing customers throughout their lifecycle.

Service providers such as Direct Marketing Express (DME) have developed a broad services offering, or "platform", that takes into account the holistic needs of customers in a vertical market. They then engage the market through a consultative discovery process that defines the strategic intent of each engagement or "program". The program is developed (with measurement in mind), rolled out with a market test, adjusted as necessary, and then scaled.

DME has had success, for example, in the auto industry providing lifecycle cross-media communication programs for dealers who wish to have an ongoing dialog with their car customers. From the purchase of a new car, through each service interval, and on to a possible trade-in and re-purchase, each communication touch point is an opportunity to re-engage.

Strategic programs that provide targeted communication to existing and prospective customers throughout their lifecycle are at the core of the program-focused services business model.

Direct marketing firms have established a similar lifecycle engagement approach. For this reason, some have said that print service providers should become marketing service providers. There is much more to this transformation, however, than simply the re-alignment of your services approach. To truly engage customers at a level that meets their lifecycle needs, all aspects of a program-focused engagement need to be in place and integrated. This includes a lifecycle engagement model, the cross-media production skills necessary, and a program-focused sales process.

A consultative engagement model is foundational to the selling, project management, and value extraction of program-focused services. Program-focused services are targeted at a customer's lifecycle in a specific vertical market. They move from the acquisition of that customer through a welcome period, the first transaction, and then some type of ongoing participation to keep the customer engaged. When the customer starts to fall away, there are other programs in place that re-engage that customer and keep them connected throughout their lifecycle.

Cross-Media Lifecycle Engagement Model

Creating a cross-media lifecycle engagement model to cultivate more effective customer dialog can be a powerful differentiator for your firm. It involves an immersive understanding of the communication needs of the target audience in a particular vertical market. This section explains how you can use the lifecycle discovery process as a useful tool to help unlock valuable requirements to build a breakthrough program-focused services offering.

The cross-media lifecycle model begins with a high-level view of the target audience and multiple audience "states." The concept comes from the realization that, as consumers and knowledge-workers, we are always in a state of motion, or "on a journey," in search of the best possible experience. In general, when we encounter a new offer or product, we try to determine its value to us. If it does not resonate with our need, we quickly discard it and move on. If we are curious, yet uncertain, we may engage, but with guarded intrigue. If the offer meets the original claim and sparks our interest, we use it and, accepting the offering, develop resulting allegiances and loyalties. As our loyalty builds, so does our trust, which in turn causes us to look for additional offers from the provider. Loyalty also leads us to tell our friends, family, and colleagues about our positive experience.

For the purposes of our discussion, we define the customer lifecycle stages as: Acquisition, Introduction, Retention, Growth, and Maturity. It is important to note that the number of stages, as well as the label and definition of each stage, is somewhat unique to each vertical market. For our example, we use these five stages since they tend to be a reasonable representation of most customer lifecycle needs at a high level. (To better reflect the subtleties of a different target market, however, it would make sense to change the lifecycle model.) The key point is to segment the customer database by lifecycle stages and to identify the unique cross-media communication for members at each stage.

1. **Acquisition:** Establish a smooth on-ramp.

2. **Introduction:** Ensure that the first experience is rewarding and renews further involvement.

3. **Retention:** Make certain that participation is a given, lifecycle stage to stage.

4. **Growth:** Increase active habitual participation.

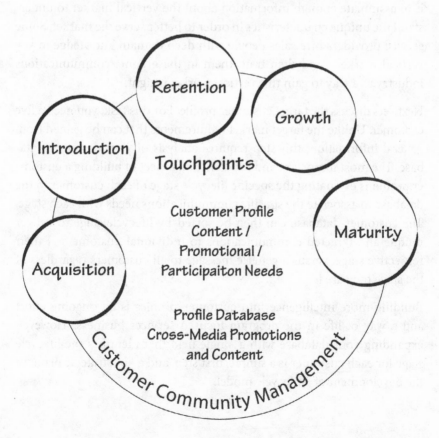

5. **Maturity:** Establish strategic participation (referrals and testimonies) to grow the overall customer base long-term.

A cross-media lifecycle engagement model is required for each vertical market. This model integrates three tightly coupled variables: (1) market requirements, (2) profile of the target customer at each stage of the lifecycle, and (3) the unique communication needs of the customer at each stage of the lifecycle.

Understanding the communication requirements for a vertical market can be done with secondary industry research on the Web, customer interviews, and perspectives from domain experts. You can combine all these valuable data points together in order to gain a better understanding of the target vertical market. Regulatory and security information, seasonality trends, best practices, accepted standards, demand cycles, and other industry specific information should be uncovered. Your goal is to assimilate enough information about the vertical market to understand the unique characteristics in order to better serve the market. Some service providers hire sales people with deep domain knowledge in key vertical markets, and then train them in the graphic communications industry as a way to gain this vertical market insight.

Next, let's discuss the target customer profile. For this task, you need a live customer. Unlike the target market requirements that can be gained from general information, this step requires analysis of your customer database. The most important and fundamental aspect of building a customer profile is evaluating the specific lifecycle stage of each customer in the database to associate the specific communications needs with each stage. The customer database can then be sorted by lifecycle stage to deliver unique and targeted communications to individual customers at their respective stage, versus a generic message to all customers regardless of the stage they are in.

Building more intelligence into customer profiles is an ongoing effort and a way of life in the program-focused services business. However, expanding your database with a single field that identifies the lifecycle stage for each customer is a simple, first step, and a key strategic plank in the development of a lifecycle model.

Beyond the basic data and the identification of the lifecycle stage for each member, more expanded member profile data (including other psychographic and demographic information) can be added to better understand current and evolving customer needs. Building an expanded database view of the customers is a requirement for program-focused services where "data is king." Building database expertise in-house, as well as defining and evolving your customer profile template, is key to more meaningful communications with your target customers.

The third and final part of building a lifecycle engagement model is to identify the specific communication needs of the target customer at each discrete lifecycle stage. To do this, imagine the journey customers take in that vertical market as they evolve, then document detailed communication needs for each stage. The lifecycle model requires very detailed insights that are targeted to the "who" at each stage of the lifecycle. If a potential member is, for example at the "acquisition" stage, you need to determine what, when, why, where, and how to communicate relevant and timely information that motivates them to join in. Customers tend to have three communication needs that need to be addressed at each stage in the lifecycle, (1) content, (2) participation, and (3) promotion.

Cross-Media Touch Point	Communications Objective
Content	Target customer relevant information (articles, instructions, pictures, messages, etc.)
Promotion	Offers or calls-to-action to be presented to the customer in exchange for participation
Participation	Invite for the target customers to interact with you and other customers via specific social media

When we define the cross-media lifecycle model, we need to develop a simple matrix that identifies each lifecycle stage with the content, participation, and promotional communication intended for each. This includes a list of the specific messages and materials you wish to communicate (content), what offers you will make to the customer (promotion), and how you wish your target customer to interact with you and other customers (participation).

For each offering in each area, you then document a number of critical points, including what the goal of each offering is, how the offering relates to the needs of a customer in that specific lifecycle stage, which channels will be used, what the desired outcomes are, and how success will be measured. Here is an example of an outline that you can use for planning purposes:

For each lifecycle stage, determine the Content, Promotion, and Participation characteristics:

- Description of content, promotion, and participation
- Communication Goal
- Customer lifecycle needs it will meet
- Cross-media Communications Channels
- Web, Print, Mobile, Social Media
- How success will be measured

Articulating your offerings at this level of detail for each of the cross-media lifecycle stages (Acquisition, Introduction, Retention, Growth, and Maturity) creates a roadmap that will allow you to design strategic and relevant communications to target customers. By articulating the specific objective and intended response mechanism for each communication, the lifecycle model also helps articulate how you will track the success of each product.

Remember to address the customers' content, promotional, and participation needs at each stage and to design the communication with a built-in response triggers, so that you design a participative dialog into the process that continues to enrich your knowledge about the specific needs of each customer.

Expanded Services = Expanded Skill Set

As the graphic communication industry expands service offerings upstream and downstream, so do the breadth and depth of the skills required to deliver cross-media communications expand. Evolving your workforce in stride with new services is an extremely important aspect of transformation in the graphic communications industry—so much so that we devoted a complete chapter to the "resources" needed to address transformation successfully.

In this section, we will complement our discussion of resources with some specific insight into the most important skill sets required to deliver the cross-media services that are in demand. To consider the most important incremental skills needed for a print service provider to transform to a cross-media communications firm, we need not look too much further than our previous discussion on technology.

Remember that we identified the three most important technology drivers for graphic communications: (1) Data and Digital Content, (2) Cyberinfrastructure (the Cloud), (3) Simultaneous Cross-Media Channel Deployment. From these three technology drivers, we can distill the vital new skill sets and future services that will be in demand. Thus the most important new services opportunities, and in turn, the most important new skill sets required by graphic communication service providers are (1) Strategy and Marketing, (2) Data Processing and Content Management, (3) Information Technology and Cyberinfrastructure, and (4) Cross-Media Channel Deployment.

Strategy and Marketing

It is not by chance that we have devoted an entire segment of *UnSquaring the Wheel* to the Customer Platform, including Business Development, Customer Experience, and Brand. Successfully transformed graphic communication firms present their services offering from a strategic perspective. They understand markets, marketing, customer behavior, and the strategic role of communication in all aspects of business. They are able to begin the graphic communication discussion with the development of a winning strategy.

The recent 2007-2009 recession imposed a new level of accountability for marketers/publishers and, in turn, graphic communication firms. The era of developing marketing and publishing programs on a hunch or lightly researched market trend are all but gone. To obtain the funds and right of passage to engage the market, publishers and marketers alike are required to develop rigorous business plans, contingency plans, test and rollout plans, and more.

These expanded strategy, planning, and testing needs present a services opportunity for graphic communication firms. If corporate marketers and publishing executives can be intercepted with strategic planning and a formal marketing regiment, they are more apt to trust and align with that service provider since this rigor represents the new playing field. Firms that have established methodology for uncovering and building on business strategy through effective and measurable graphic communications are well aligned with the market place.

The next generation graphic communication service providers will need to have a strategy/marketing competency. This competency may be an individual or a small team of people who understand how to have immersive discussions with executives about their business. These discussions will need to include the diagnosing the essential elements of the clients' business plan that can be partitioned into an actionable publishing or communications strategy with embedded metrics for measuring results.

Individuals with a marketing education or unique domain knowledge in specific vertical markets can become exceptional strategists. By introducing strategic planning and marketing strategy into the graphic communications services offering, firms are able to start upstream and engage with customers well in advance of the project inception. In fact, the graphic communication firms that are involved in strategic planning and marketing strategy are usually involved in the definition of the program in a manner that will ensure the plan is realistic and profitable.

Developing a strategic planning service, which includes a customer lifecycle roadmap, is an excellent way to engage marketers and publishers. Developing a lifecycle roadmap service is a non-confrontational and proactive approach that will turn the conversation in the direction of designing effective programs versus a cost-per-print discussion.

It is also useful to the services offerings of marketing/strategy firms and ad agencies to better understand the type of marketing and strategy services you might offer. A simple approach is to ask your customers if you can review their business plans for the next year. That way, you offer insight into areas to define or refine a communication plan that more effectively supports their business plan. Getting invited to this kind of discover meeting, or better yet, asking for a discovery meeting is key to selling program-focused services. We will discuss the services-selling approach later in this chapter.

Data Processing and Content Management

Many product-focused and almost all program-focused services begin and end with data. From basic variable data printing projects to integrated cross-media communication programs, there is an increasing opportunity for expanded data processing services. Developing a rich understanding of current and prospective customers, where they are, what they need, and how they want to be engaged is critical. To do this, you need a deep understanding of data processing.

Marketers and publishers are eager to better understand the demographic, behavioral, and transactional data of their customers. They are looking for a comprehensive, or a 360-degree, view of their customers' data so they can communicate more effectively. (Ackerman 2010) Marketers and publishers are looking for graphic communication firms with data processing services that can triangulate between transactional data (name, address, email address, IP address, and mobile number) and behavioral data (demographics, psychographics, buying habits, and preferences) in order to gain deeper customer insight. This customer insight can be directed to more effective cross-media programs. A deep understanding, core competency, and integrated data processing services are critical to the transformed graphic communication firm.

Direct mailers have historically offered data processing services as they relate to producing and delivering targeted direct mail. These traditional direct mail data processing services include address cleansing through a CASS™ process that standardize the address according to USPS guidelines and updates or appends ZIP®, ZIP+4™, Carrier Route Codes, Line of Travel (LOT) codes, and Delivery Point Barcode information in order to receive postal discounts. (Bondy 2010) Direct mail data processing services are foundational for cross-media communications; firms that have already integrated this level of data processing into their operation are well positioned to incorporate the next level of data processing services.

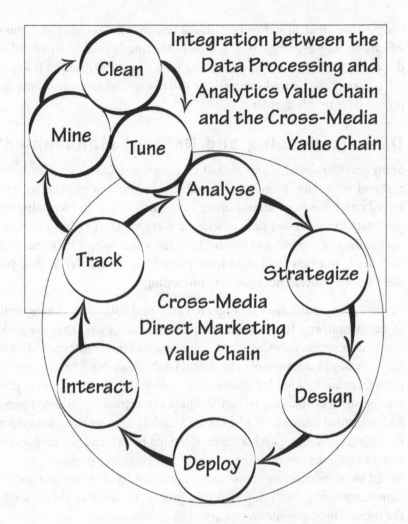

Integration between the Data Processing and Analytics Value Chain and the Cross-Media Value Chain

Clean
Mine
Tune
Analyse
Track
Strategize
Interact
Design
Deploy

Cross-Media Direct Marketing Value Chain

Marketers and publishers are looking for the next level of data processing services, including data mining, data analytics, and data hosting and reporting. Integrated cross-media communications requires a real-time dialog with your customers, and that dialog depends on constant access to your customer database for a what-if analysis. Service providers can expanded their data services in response to this emerging need for more accurate and timely data.

The core skill sets required for data services begins with handling and manipulating any fixed-fielded data though systems such as MS Excel, to understanding and programming a structured databases (e.g. Access,

FormBase), to programming relational databases (e.g. SQL, Oracle). These database skills are complemented by the use of specific applications that are designed to do core data processing functions, such as postal optimization and database d-duping (for example, using applications such as CorrectRight, BCC-MailManager, etc.). Investing in staff and applications in the data processing area is very important to tackling cross-media personalized programs.

As service providers expand to offer more data services, it's natural for them to integrate data management and reporting services into their offering, since they are working closely with the all aspects of the customer data. Leading service providers are hosting customer data, providing data governance (backup, security, controlled access, etc.), and advanced data analytics services. These services are very strategic, are high-margin, and allow the service provider to have access to a critical control point in the workflow that is the driver for all cross-media programs—the data.

The latest cloud-based data analytics solutions can be integrated with traditional data cleansing and optimization tools to provide a comprehensive range of data processing services. Companies (such as Tableau, Birst, IBM Cognos, Sisense, and many others) offer data analytics dashboards that can be branded by service providers to provide marketers and publishers with a graphical view into their customers' data. Data can also be acquired quite easily through online data services firms that sell custom data lists based on the targeted audience and the data fields of interest.

Offering data mining, data management, and data analytics services is an advanced services offering that can only be offered as a build onto an established core competency in data cleansing and optimization. For some service providers, offering data services presents a tremendous learning curve that might prove unrealistic. For these service providers, establishing a strategic relationship with a data processing firm where data services can be integrated as part of a cohesive and branded offering might be the best bet.

Managing collections also presents an emerging opportunity for service providers in much the same way that incorporating more data processing services is an essential offering. Managing collections is a new spin on an old concept, as we discussed previously in the Technology chapter.

For years, software vendors have claimed the value of digital asset management (DAM) technology, yet not all industries have been able to capitalize on the technology. Until recently, the price-performance of DAM technology was not attractive for smaller firms, and the need to have all content accessible and digitized was not a high priority.

Prior barriers to DAM adoption have been eliminated with low-cost cloud-based solutions, so there is now an easy on-ramp for smaller firms. Additionally, with the mass digitization of all media and trends in media consumption toward mobile, Web, and social media, there is a renewed interest in DAM.

Service providers can expanded their services in the area of managing digital collections to help firms better organize and coordinate all digital assets. Management of digital assets is becoming an important and integral component of delivering integrated cross-media services. It stands to reason that companies who control and organize their various digital assets are in the best position to deploy those assets in a swift and meaningful way for their customers.

Knowledge-workers are generating more digital content (and more types of unique digital content) than ever before. And the volume and variety of content comes from all facets of an enterprise— marketing communications, sales, finance, engineering, product development, human resources, and legal. Whether logos, sales kits, websites, videos, documents, photos, spreadsheets, and presentations, this digital content resides in a variety of different file formats (MSWord files, audio files, MP3, video files, PDF files for documents, etc.) on a range of computers, serv-

Many Content Creators

ers, thumb-drives, etc. It's easy to see that we have mounting challenge to organize digital collections.

The traditional physical storage of content organized in file folders is not practical with the variety of digital technology. Better efficiencies regarding the management of digital content will help minimize losses of employee turnover, help the loss of misplaced files, and increase the precision and efficiency of our cross-media communications.

Imagine the complexity of storing a variety of images for each media: high-res images for print versus Web and print versus mobile. When we include various textual content, illustrations, and video, the complexity increases. The variety, types, version, and iteration of content in its various formats are a complex challenge to marketers and publishers. Service providers who can incorporate DAM services into their offering as a complementary service to data processing service have will have a competitive advantage.

Files, files and more files

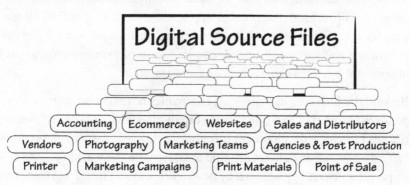

For service providers, there are a multitude of SaaS DAM options, including offerings from Amazon, Google, Microsoft, and many others. Graphic communications industry-specific DAM solutions (such as WebDAM, IntelligenceBank, Cumulus/Flight, Media Beacon, and many others) also provide a viable DAM option. Marketers and publishers will look for service providers who have the skill set and services to organize, store, and manage their digital collections. Service providers with customer-facing DAM capabilities that are integrated into their cross-media workflow will have a competitive advantage.

Information Technology and Cyberinfrastructure

Central to the discussion in this section on expanded services is a core competency in information technology, computing systems, and cyberinfrastructure. The graphic communications industry is becoming increasingly an information technology industry where a deep understanding of computing technology and software applications is essential. Computer automation from the make-ready process through to the machine interfaces that report productivity data has had a huge impact on even traditional printing.

It is important to consider the information technology and computing systems resources necessary to operationalize your services offering from these two vantage points: What skill set is necessary to run the operation? What skill set is necessary to support customer engagements?

From an internal or operations perspective, graphic communication firms need staff who are familiar with IT basics that will allow you to set up and maintain a network for a graphic communication workflow. This network will include client-server applications such as email, SFTP (secure file transfer protocol), Mac/Window operating systems, a variety of publishing software applications, configuration of printing systems and other input devices such as scanner, cameras, etc.

Beyond the IT basics, transformed companies have had great success expanding their base IT staff to include capabilities such as systems integration and software development (programming). Service providers with a systems integration skill set are able to streamline the workflow between disparate software applications by developing custom interfaces that provide automated connections between adjacent software systems. Linking a DAM system to a variable data composition system is an example of a workflow integration effort that can provide unique and streamlined services to customers through a systems integration effort.

Some transformed graphic communications firms have also expanded their technical staff to include application or software developers. This additional staff is typically both an operational and a customer-facing resource. Software developers may work on application development and user-experience software to streamline workflow operations. They may also be involved in developing customer-facing apps that provide access to job-related information. However, most of the customer-facing software development falls in the area of Web-based and program-focused experience.

Software development, coupled with cross-media communications, can prove to be an extremely strategic service offering for service providers who are proficient at program-focused engagements. Developing a unique customer portal experience that provides access to program activities and results data is a growing area for service providers. Software developers are also in demand for development and deployment of cross-media program that include personalized landing pages (PURL) and mobile apps.

Software development skills required for web development include experience with HTML, CSS, Javascript, jQuery, PHP, or Ruby. Software development skills associated with software integration require experience with C++ or Java, relational databases, IT infrastructure, in addition to the web-focused skills listed above.

Companies such as Direct Mail Express, Daytona Beach, FL (DME) have had great success with making a major investment in IT and software development teams. DME began with a commitment to Xerox XMPie variable data composition tool. They then took the standard offering and integrated these tools into their internal web platform to create a compelling customer experience for their clients. The company has also developed competency centers and tools in the areas of data analytics, video production (DME Studios), website production (DME Digital Media) to complement the expertise they have in personalized direct mail.

DME invested in building a strong internal technology integration team. This internal team is responsible for the development and integration of all the software systems at DME. By developing their expertise internally, DME can develop a unique workflow that is tailored to the way that they want the production process to flow. They can now also customize their customer experience in ways that provides DME competitive differentiation and a more program-focused customer solution. Combining IT and software development skills with graphic communication skills is a powerful and winning combination for the future graphic communication service provider.

Cross-Media Channel Deployment

As graphic communication firms extended their reach to include the simultaneous deployment of content to the Web, mobile, social media – along with print—there is an expanded services opportunity along with the need for unique skills. With the move further upstream, graphic communication firms have a better shot at leading high-margin programs. However, with this opportunity comes added responsibility for content creation and new media deployment.

First, let's evaluate the services opportunity and skill sets needed surrounding content creation. The creation of content involves the addition of "creatives" (designers, photographers, writers, etc.), either as staff resources or as a tightly coupled partnership. Core to offering any creative services is the addition of a Creative Director, a person with the responsibility to lead the creative process surrounding specific programs for a specific customer. These individuals usually demand a hefty salary, yet the goods ones are always well worth the expense.

The Creative Director is usually brought in at the start of the program to brainstorm with the stakeholders on the core creative elements. Items such as target audience, tone, look-and-feel, offers, call-to-action, program outcomes, media channels, etc., are discussed. The Creative Director then works with an internal or freelance creative staffer to develop the program context. This is a for-fee activity. Graphic communication firms that are unable to charge for content creation are giving away valuable profits and are reducing their services down to a commodity.

To engage upstream, service providers need to expand beyond a graphic designer to a Creative Director. A top-level Creative Director can keep a team of designers, illustrators, photographers, and writers busy. We recommend adding the Creative Director first, followed by the various creatives as the predictable demand of the firm can support the headcount. There are abundant freelance creatives available. The best way to test their competency is to have them work on a program under the leadership of your Creative Director to see how well the work together.

With new media deployment, service providers have opportunities to move beyond IT and software development and on to reoccurring content deployment. Leading service providers are looking beyond the functional deployment of a personalized landing page, or a single campaign to the ongoing delivery of through Websites, blogs, social media, etc. Using your creative staff to fulfill a consistent and timely flow of content (information, images, video, correspondence, etc.) to the target customer is similar to direct marketing firms offering telemarketing services to follow the mail through to closure.

One of the issues facing marketers and publishers today is the intense demand on their internal resources to keep current with their target customer base. For service providers who are defining the cross-media programs, it is a natural extension to propose an ongoing service to respond and populate all the media channels with content relevant to the target customers. This approach directly supports the lifecycle model, and it can help to ensure that your creative staff has a basis of contractual work that will cover their salaries. Services such as responding and posting to social media and blogs, posting technical information and white papers are all necessary, but are often overlooked by service providers.

Selling Program-Focused Services

The Services chapter would not be complete without a discussion on how to sell program-focused services. The key to a program-focused business model begins with the ability to shed the product-centric mindset where speeds, feeds, equipment specs, and price per thousand are the norm. The program-focused sales process includes these four steps: (1) Prospect Validation, (2) Business Opportunity Assessment, (3) Proposal, and (4) Project Implementation and Evaluation. We will review each of these steps in the program-focused services selling model.

Since program-focused services are more complex than are product-focused services, and the end-goal is to both deliver and to extract more value, it is very important that the sales process begins in the right context. The initial Prospect Validation step requires a preliminary discussion with the customer stakeholders. This is the person who has the scope, budget, and authority to direct the program. This is not a procurement person who does not have ultimate responsibility for the outcomes of the program.

The primary objective for the first step of the sales process is to validate the specific cross-media communication program needs. Are they within your capability? Does your firm have the budget and realistic schedule

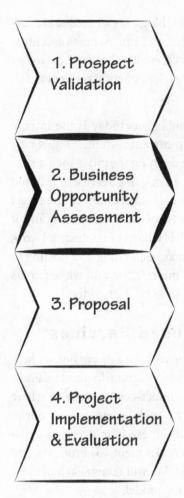

requirements concerning the program? There is often misalignment between the scope of a program, the schedule, and budget. Once you have confirmed the high-level validation, it is important to breakaway from the meeting, respond back with a summary note of the program and a request for a second "discovery" meeting to pin down the specific program details. This moves us to the second step.

The most critical step in the programed-focused sales process is doing a thorough job in second step, the Business Opportunity Assessment (BOA). Conducting a thorough BOA typically requires an onsite visit or web meeting that focuses on immersive discovery concerning the finite details concerning the measurable objectives, cross-media deployment strategy, content, cost, and schedule. The primary objective for this second step is to uncover enough detail so that you can produce a detailed proposal without further iteration with the customer.

The third step is the Proposal. It brings together the summary BOA, statement of work, project plan (with responsibility metric), performance metrics and program outcomes, schedule, and pricing. The proposal should be concise, easy to follow and well formatted. It is a good idea to develop templates for each of the sales process steps so that all BOAs, proposals, project plans, etc., are conducted in a similar way. By conducting the detailed BOA, the proposal can directly reference the specific program requirements in a manner that no details are overlooked.

Taking care to develop a clean, professional, and easy-to-follow proposal is essential to being able to sell program-focused services and is at the core of your being able to achieve high-margin sales. Each element in the proposal should be positioned to demonstrate value. One of the most important sections in the proposal is the coverage of performance metrics and program outcomes. When the program is finally delivered, your customers will refer back to this section to hold you accountable for the claims you have made. Putting time and research into measureable outcomes and realistic goals that align with the customer, yet are achievable by your firm, is extremely important.

The fourth and final step in the program-focused sales process is the Project Implementation and Evaluation step. In this step the project goes live—deposits have been made and the project team is assigned. In the Process chapter, we discussed agile development and project management process that are essential to delivering a predictable program. We cannot stress enough the need for a formal project management process, from the moment the project goes live through to completion. Your project management will drive and align your resources in the appropriate direction.

Schedule your project reviews and success metrics with your customer. Develop and test your prototype, which will lead to the initial test/trial. Finally, roll out and deploy your complete program, and gain your customer's acceptance. It is important to end each project with a face-to-face customer evaluation session to determine as a team whether the desired outcomes were met. You'll also uncover any insights and learnings that might be considered for future work. This is an extremely important step to building customer satisfaction. It is key to bring together the initial stakeholders with the project team and the sales person to reconcile all perspectives and pave the way for follow-on programs.

Summary

UnSquaring the Wheel services transformation involves evaluating your maturity as an organization to execute these critical dimensions: (1) uncover the unique needs of your customer through a consistent needs analysis discovery process, (2) integration of technology, processes, and services into a platform that can provide optimized services (services that can be supported and scaled), (3) scope and deliver a customer-driven services programs that can be project managed, and (4) deliver and extract value (satisfied customer with high-profit margin for you) from the services engagements (product and program focused).

UnSquaring the Wheel looks at specific services in terms of dimensions to help assess where you are at in your transformation and how you can put together a transformation plan to move your company into a fully transformed cross-media services business. The specific dimensions used in the services maturity assessment are as follows:

- Are you able to offer value-added services? Are you able to extract a profit margin from those services?

- Do you have unique solutions that you have developed inside your organizations that are tailored either at a product or at a vertical market that provides your company differentiation?

- Are you able to deliver integrated solutions?

- Are you able to meet with new customers in your target vertical market and bring them on board, assess their needs, and deliver integrated solutions?

- Do you have the ability to uncover the unmet needs and wants of consumers and knowledge workers through an organized needs assessment program?

These dimensions represent critical areas of transformation for a graphic communication service provider. Each of them can be evaluated on a continuum from the most basic to a mature and fully transformed organization. After completing the diagnostic survey using the *UnSquaring the Wheel – Business Transformation Assessment (BTA)* system, maturity levels can be assigned to the status of your operation for each of the four dimensions.

The maturity levels of each of the dimensions of your services will be:

- Ad-hoc

- Aware

- Informed

- Tactical

- Strategic

- Innovative

References

Akerman, K. *Using Data-Driven Decisions to Enchance Cross-Media Marketing. Experian Marketing Services,* http://www.dmnews.com/dataanalytics/using-data-driven-decisions-to-enhance-cross-media-marketing/article/170039/, accessed May 12, 2010.

Bondy, C. *Data and the Cross-Media Direct Marketing Opportunity - Strategic Assessment.* 2010. Weymouth, MA: InfoTrends, Inc.

Christensen, C. *The Innovator's Dilemma.* 1997. Boston: Harvard Business School Press.

Financial Analysis. 2015. US Department of Commerce, Bureau of Labor Statistics.

Johnson, Gerry, Kevan Scholes, and Richard Whittington. 2005. *Exploring Corporate Strategy.* Upper Saddle River, NJ: Prentice Hall.

THE THIRD DISCIPLINE

RESOURCES

by Joe Webb

All of the vectors in the *UnSquaring* "pie" connect at the center. All of the vectors rely on the best execution of each individual vector; in addition, each vector supports the other vectors. A few decades ago, it was common to think of businesses as systems, and there was a concept of "optimization." *Systems* were defined as independent entities working toward a common objective. The system needs to be optimized. Sometimes individual entities are optimized at the expense of the others. Just as there is optimization, there is *suboptimization*. An example is a printing business that has a world-class shop floor operation but can't issue an invoice in a timely manner. If all of the company's investments have gone to the pressroom, but the accountants are still using pencils and wearing green eyeshades, then the company will not operate in an optimized manner.

All of the vectors are connected to all the disciplines. This connectivity is clearly seen as all of the resources – finance, people, and alliances – are critical to all other aspects of the *UnSquaring* "pie."

What are resources?

Resources are everything that a business owns, or has an ability to influence or control in a way that meets their objectives. All of the vectors in the *UnSquaring* "pie" are resources in that sense.

Strategy determines the resources that will be transformed by the business into goods of higher economic value. Consider these simple examples: a recipe is a not a meal, and sheet music is not sound. All business resources need a direction, or a directed purpose. That direction includes the people in the organization and all of the relationships that those people create inside and outside the organization.

Money as a resource

Money is a standard we use to measure performance. It is the way we exchange resources when we interact with the outside world to secure the resources needed to create value. That's the purpose of finance.

A special aspect of a business that we often take for granted is people. It's not on a balance sheet like equipment or cash is, but we know organizations cannot exist without people. Alliances are especially related to that essential aspect of people within an organization.

A resource only has value if there are processes and knowledge that can transform it to higher value. Unused resources are actually a drag on a business. Money is a resource, therefore, if it has a purpose in the business. It is not the most important resource of a business. There are other resources of greater importance.

Resources might be better thought of as "capital." Some current-day economists use a very narrow definition to refer to investment alone, but the definition used here is more traditional. *Capital* is not just money or equipment, but also includes all of the knowledge and experience that is in the organization. Capital is what allows an organization to make that transformation of materials and knowledge into higher-value goods and services.

Money can have suboptimal uses, or it can be directed in ways that are not best. Money can become a matter of tax or estate planning in closely-held businesses that end up undermining the long-term health of a business. Owners may end up making decisions that protect their wealth at precisely the time when their businesses need new investments. After a while, the annual tweaks in accounting for tax purposes catch up with you.

Resources are easily misdirected without good strategy

The misdirection of resources occurs when management directs their efforts to making the current income statement look good, and end up doing that every year. That means the real business strategy is to make the next quarter look good, and then repeat that good appearance again. Any strategy documents developed in planning meetings that claim otherwise are meaningless. It's better to focus management attention on creating long-term positive directions for the data in the balance sheet.

Budgeting is not strategy and is not planning.

Wise use of resources is not just for internal management. The wise use of resources is a competitive weapon. The healthier the financial condition of a business and the more strategic its outlook, the more options that business has in its competitive strategy and its innovation.

Accounting statements are sometimes poor reflections of resources

The phrase "human asset" found itself into management books in the mid-20th century. Yet you can't find that phrase on an accounting statement as an asset. For all the high-minded thinking that people are human assets, our financial statements show them as expenses and costs.

Instead, we see the effects of people in the business by looking at the balance sheet over a longer period of time. The long-term decisions and actions of the people in a business today and its people of the past are all there in the trends of their accounting statements.

How can "alliances" be a resource?

Capital and resources are always scarce, no matter how profitable you are, especially for small- and medium-sized businesses. There are always more opportunities, and not enough resources and time, so we have to make judgments. How do we best deploy resources? And who is the best to deploy them to meet strategic objectives?

One way of dealing with this fact is to find resources elsewhere and to share those resources. The most important resources are the knowledge and skills that are used in creating products and processes. It is likely that the resources of printing businesses would be attractive to others.

Alliances are not the kinds of things that you can be half-hearted about. The clock is always ticking, and equipment is constantly getting older. But so is knowledge. Markets are always changing. Alliances are strategic. This is new to our industry.

The printing industry has a long history of outsourcing tasks -- to others who have equipment we could not justify to own in own plants or for services that were not cost-effective to staff in-house. So we created networks of specialists and trade shops that we used whenever we needed them. We think it has to be taken to a much higher, strategic level, and with a sense of urgency about it. You might have heard about this as a "make-or-buy" decision, but it's far greater than that. Our businesses have always had relationships with others, but they have not always been strategic. The concept of alliances needs the high-level executive attention that turns it from outsourcing tasks to an ongoing and important strategic initiative.

New markets, new perspectives about resources

The market is constantly changing, and this section about resources offers a new way to look at three aspects of our industry that are often taken for granted. Everyone knows the metrics for a financially healthy printing business, but that common wisdom locks us in the past. People were hired for specific tasks, but printing businesses often tell us that printing experience inhibits the ability to adapt to new markets. The communications planning and buying has changed so much that print businesses have lost their spot at the decision-maker's table to media and practitioners that practically did not exist ten years ago. Alliances let print businesses hitch a ride to the new marketplace and offer investment opportunities for capital that were not possible before. The world has changed, and catching up still leaves you behind. It's time to get ahead by taking a different look at the resources we've taken for granted.

9

MONEY

by Joe Webb

Finance refers to the systematic way businesses manage their resources of money, assets, and obligations. Not all financial resources are cash, but cash must be managed and invested and directed to acquire capital goods and support the production processes that create goods and services of value to a marketplace. Not all money is in the direct control of the business, such as current accounts receivable, and money that has been supplied by others (loans and obligations), and future requirements.

Financial management has a time dimension. Finance relates to the past, present, and future flows and uses of money in an organization. Businesses have many choices about what to do with money, and they have ways to evaluate the best purposes for their money based on current and future needs. From an *UnSquaring* perspective, the skill to direct financial resources according to a company-wide strategic plan over a long period of time is a critical skill.

This chapter approaches finance in an atypical way. There are only passing references to financial ratios, credit management, tax law, and other topics that are better discussed elsewhere. Instead, this chapter is about the strategic philosophy behind the financial decisions that an *UnSquared* organization makes.

Previous management decisions affect the nature of management decisions today and the ability and latitude executives have to make decisions in the future. Past decisions that were good create positive cash flows and profits today. Poor decisions limit the ability of current managers to take advantage of opportunities or deal with risks. Instead, they must first unshackle themselves from the constraints of past decisions, often at a financial loss. Taking that loss is often better than sticking with a bad decision that can only impair the future health of a business.

Very often, it's not that companies have problems adjusting their resources to the future. It's that their resources are locked up by past decisions. There may have been decisions made at that time, when markeplace conditions made them seem right, yet they may no longer be valid. This underscores the importance of strategic planning and the careful allocation of financial resources. It also means that the time horizon of decisions must match the financing of those decisions. Financing short-term opportunities with long-term debt obligations is unwise.

Why Financial Resources Must be Flexible

Managers move resources in response to and anticipation of marketplace conditions. Assumptions about the future, based on knowledge and experience of executives, produce a guiding vision of that marketplace for the months, quarters, and years ahead.

The first elements of plans are goals and objectives that become the foundation for revenue and market[1] forecasts. Spending and investment decisions emanate from that.

Every aspect of a business relates to finance because all business activities can be measured in terms of money.[2] Finance executives cannot know all aspects of a business; they rely on other managers to determine the best ways to use resources.[3]

---

1 "Market" refers to geography or business sector in which the business sales prospects and customers are. It does not refer to the economy or the stock market. Part of the planning process requires that a business define its market.

2 Later in this chapter there are comments about inflation adjustment and also the importance of finding business metrics that are not money-based.

3 In an upcoming chapter, the essay "I, Pencil" illustrates this circumstance.

A well-run managerial finance process is not limited to a person, department, or function. All top executives have strategic flexibility, a freedom of decision-making, and a wider range of strategic choices than competitors, based on the mutually agreed financial plan.

Financial acumen is a competitive advantage, if not a competitive weapon. Companies with financial muscle have financial insight and wisdom throughout their organizations.

Many companies have problems because they do not deal with their financial situations in a proper manner. Companies that have profit problems do not have problems with profits. They have problems with resources and the way they are used. Profits are the residue, or an effect, of management decisions. Because resources are scarce, companies need systematic ways of allocating those resources, usually through budget processes.

Transition: What is the Role of Finance?

The UnSquaring approach may seem to have a bias toward the idea that businesses need to make transitions to survive. Unfortunately, the history of the industry includes stories of supposed industry threats and imminent disasters for those who refused to adjust. A rising tide of general

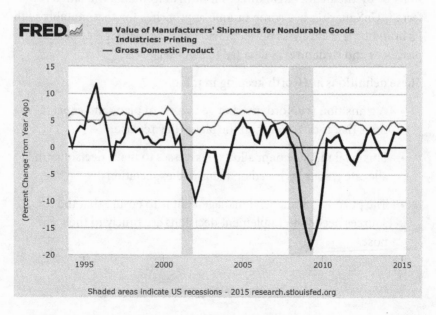

economic growth covered managerial sins and inefficiencies; that is not the marketplace today.

The chart below shows that the industry does not follow GDP growth, and printing shipments have been declining while GDP has been increasing. Yet we know that many individual printing businesses are profitable and growing. This means that good management makes a difference.

Unsquaring is not an attempt to invent a crisis with a single proprietary solution for the enrichment of the crisis-mongers. It recognizes that every business is different in terms of their resources and circumstances. That means there is no single "right" prescription to "fix" a company. There are managerial tools, like financial management, that help companies find what is right for them.

All businesses make transitions, adjusting to their environments daily, weekly, monthly, and all other periods of time. Without planning, however, those adjustments can pile up over time and move the business into directions that were not previously foreseen. This makes the business harder to manage and perhaps out of touch with its customers and prospects.

The question is whether the transitions are forced by short-term situations or by the deliberative direction of management. The latter is preferred. UnSquaring has some unique approaches for that, notably with its branding and business development, and the planning of production processes and structure, as detailed in prior chapters.

These definitions are worth keeping in mind:

- A transition is an orderly change to a set of plans and expectations that is different than the plans they replace.

- Financial management allows businesses to make decisions and allocate resources based on plans and expectations.

- The purpose of financial management is to ensure that the resources needed to implement decisions are timely to their purpose.

Budgeting Alone is Not Planning

The way resources are identified, managed, and deployed through financial management is much different than before. There are economic, social, and technological changes that have not been seen by the industry before. There are also many financial tools and services that are newly available to small and medium businesses that can make financial data easier to acquire, easier to analyze, and easier to use in decision-making.

Budgeting is not planning. In much of the printing industry, the budget process is the planning process. A budget process is an implementation process that is tactical and not strategic. Strategic processes are longer term, and they set the boundaries of budgets for many years forward. Those boundaries are based on a reasoned and logical evaluation of how to profitably match resources to the opportunities and risks of a marketplace.

When it was reasonable to assume that print was a stable, resilient, and growing medium, the lack of strategic planning did not hurt companies. Many printers had little formal planning processes beyond budgeting and the whims of ownership. They managed to survive. When demand is declining and non-print alternatives elbow their way into the minds and budgets of clients, budgeting alone can no longer suffice.

A Different Financial Philosophy is Needed

When the print business was growing, the penalties for bad decisions were often overcome by the higher rewards of the good decisions. In markets that are shrinking, bad decisions are harder to overcome because they sap the resources needed to implement better decisions. Good decisions seem to have smaller opportunities associated with them, and those opportunities may not be as enduring.

That means past decisions need to be undone or unwound in a manner that does not impair the ability of the business to adjust its operations to its new strategies. This is easier said than done. It is tempting to hold onto the assets and processes that supported the prior way of doing things while being tentative about the commitment to the new strategy.

The industry has not been highly regarded by the banking industry in terms of credit-worthiness. But it's not just printing. It's nearly all small and medium businesses that are viewed skeptically. This means that ownership must supply capital from their own savings and banking relationships, but small businesses also have to be self-financing after their initial investment.

If industry volume is declining, that means it will be harder for businesses to adequately fund their new initiatives. Management will have to be more selective about those initiatives or find alternative sources for funding, such as joint ventures and alliances.4

Consolidation and Finance

Efforts to consolidate should also be carefully considered with a wary eye. Usually, most consolidations are between similar businesses. These consolidations are rarely forward-looking, positioning the acquiring firm to be more competitive in the future. That kind of acquisition creates a company with similar problems and adds a new dose of risks related to the transition and integration of the operations, and perhaps future financial risks depending on how the deal was financed.[5]

Unless there is compelling value in a similar company combination, such as a customer base that that enhances market position or will add to bottom-line profits quickly, these deals are usually not worthwhile. If it's a deal to take a competitor out of the marketplace, the marketplace and competition from other media might do that anyway, given enough time.

Mergers and acquisitions that support the long range strategic plan with new products, capabilities, or markets (or all three) should have preference if only because they are better uses of capital.

There are printing companies that "pretty themselves up" so they can become attractive consolidation candidates. This is a situation to beware of. Companies can make themselves look better by eliminating purchases of new equipment, cutting back on expenses in the short term that only have to be stepped up later (such as marketing or maintenance), or by

4 The chapter about Alliances will explore the many options of alliances in greater detail.

5 Vertis was a good example of this situation. Its product lines and offerings were well-aligned with where the market was headed, but their junk bond financing limited their ability to invest in new technologies and to fight competition.

changing their debt structure from short term to long-term obligations. Good financial managers can't be bullied, and they don't play games like these.

Transitions Require Financial Clarity, Diligence, and Patience

Most transitions do not shift large amounts of resources from one place to another at one time. The resources move in incremental amounts in daily actions and decisions. Transitions are not like on and off switches. If one product area is being emphasized, while another is being de-emphasized, it is usually done gradually with a period of overlap. Both demand resources at the same time for legitimate purposes. This can create conflicts over funding priorities.

It is essential to be clear about what is being transitioned to and the reasons for it. The periods of overlap can be confusing to everyone involved unless there is a well-considered and well-explained plan. The financial plan must have great clarity because the overlap period may be a time of higher total costs. These higher costs may happen because neither product area will receive optimum resources until they reach their desired ends.

If more than one generation of managers is involved in company management, their personal experiences of prior industry changes affects the way they view the current and future marketplace. That means financial philosophy can become a strategic struggle in multigeneration family and other small businesses. These differences need to be sorted out carefully in open discussion.

If there is no constructive struggle over the deployment of resources, that may actually be a sign of an unhealthy company. Resources are always scarce, and markets are always changing, so there should always be questions about the right long-term path and best use of resources. If there is always one way of dealing with a marketplace that is unquestioned, the strategic planning process for that company is probably not working.

This does not mean that a company comes up with a new long-term strategy every year. "Long- term" means just that. Some executives talk casually about their "strategy this year," which is incorrect. Sales cycles with some prospects and capital investment cycles with equipment take years. If equipment will last five years, that means that the company has at least a five-year, or longer, strategy for it. That strategy is a long-term commitment that will withstand market changes and competitive challenges.

Tactics that implement those decisions fit within guidelines established in the planning process. They are used to navigate the daily interactions with the marketplace with minimal changes. If big changes are necessary, either something significant has changed in the marketplace, or the planning process mistakenly yielded an irrelevant strategy.

Financial Effects of Transition

Transitions are communicated through the business with communications and through visible actions. There are many constituencies who have roles in transitions: employees, suppliers, and competitors.

Employes are always concerned about transitions because the nature of their daily work, their compensation, and their employment prospects.

Suppliers are aware of transitions clients are having because the volume and nature of goods and materials used in production change. Because suppliers extend credit, they keenly monitor financial fortunes of their customers. It is good practice to review changes in business strategy that will affect them.

Competitors become aware of transitions because they sell to the same marketplace and are part of the industry grapevine. They take advantage of the disruptions transitions can cause.

These negative competitive aspects of transitions are often underestimated. In the case of a merger and acquisition (M&A), rumors can spread. Time spent on integrating staff functions and logistics reduces the time that can be spent on regular operations management. After M&A activities, financial resources can be more scarce than usual. Competitors use ambiguous and confusing situations to attract workers who are concerned about their future. They can "smell blood" and attempt aggressive actions to attract best customers. These disruptions are rarely anticipated and should be part of the planning process, which can make actions, should they occur, more rational and less emotional, and identify the ranges and alternatives of action in a time of calm, rather than in an end-of-workday panic.

When consolidations go well, however, the result is a healthier company with a more secure future, and one that can sensibly leap ahead of competitors.

Transition Risks of Expansion

Transition risks are not limited to mergers, acquisitions, or tuck-ins. They are also part of initiatives that add product lines or start new businesses.

Resources, already scarce, need to be stretched to support the current business and fund a new business. Management attention becomes divided, attempting to do two things at once. They have one foot in the past, while trying to lunge into the future with the other. The same occurs with monetary resources.

When a single businesses is supporting two tracks, the older side of the business has to fund the newer one, unless efforts are made to find outside funding.

This makes streamlining the old business very important. All businesses can be run more efficiently and effectively. Investing in a new product area or new business requires patience, as it is likely to have negative cash flows during its startup. This creates a competition for resources. There is always a temptation to go back to the prior way of doing business. Good planning manages those expectations, keeping the transition moving forward.

Many executives are familiar with the Boston Consulting Group's growth matrix. It's a good way to illustrate the issues of product line financial management. The BCG matrix has been used in training executives and by consultants for decades.[6] It is somewhat simplistic, but can be used used as a catalyst for discussions about the company, its marketplace, and its future. The chart of the matrix is below. (QuickMBA)

---

6 A good and skeptical summary of the BCG matrix can be found at
http://en.wikipedia.org/wiki/Growth%E2%80%93share_matrix

- *Cash cows* are products that are highly profitable, but have low growth rates because they are older and are encountering greater competition.

- *Dogs* are low-profit products with low growth rates.

- *Question marks* are products in high-growth markets, but enjoy little success.

- *Stars* are products that are growing and are highly profitable.

To use the BCG Matrix, executives need financial reporting that can characterize products in this manner. Printing companies have tended not to think of product lines with strategies, but as having job capabilities that are offered when needed. Cost accounting is usually in support of the job estimating process, with little concern about marketplace opportunities or market position. If organizing financial information for something as simple as a BCG Matrix product analysis is difficult, then it is likely that there are other problems with financial reporting, as well.

Cash cow products fund the company because of their high margins and because they can be "milked" to support other initiatives. The general assumption is that these product lines are dying and that no additional funding of them should be done. Theoretically, funding from the cash cows should go to new products only. But that may not be the case. Cash cows may be such because the company is able to produce them with great efficiency with a strong market position. In a printing market where traditional competitors are exiting the market, cash cow products may deserve greater attention from management to keep the offerings current and make their even more efficient. Even though the market size might be shrinking for the products, having fewer competitors might be a great opportunity.

Transitioning companies need their cash cows because they might not be able to get financial resources elsewhere. Don't walk away from cash cows. Just change their diet, and keep them prosperous.

Dogs are poorly performing products. Be sure to ask why. Eliminating these products should be an obvious choice, but their sales might be intertwined with other profitable products. Whatever the case, these products need to be scrutinized if they are using scarce resources inefficiently.

Perhaps sourcing these products elsewhere will allow the company to keep them in the product offerings, but free up resources for better reasons. Dogs may be candidates for business alliances.

Question marks might be new products that have not achieved sales levels worth their costs. Companies transitioning to new product areas will probably have lots of question marks, and that's fine. The question mark should be about how long one should wait for the products to become mature offerings that have consistent and predictable sales with superior margins. If "question marks" are headed for "dog-hood," then finding a different tactic or eliminating them are the right choices. Part of the evaluation should be whether or not appropriate resources were applied to the offering. Dogs can be rescued, but the decision must be the result of objective evaluation.

Stars are easy. You keep them and ride them as far as they can profitably go. But one should always remember that markets are dynamic, and today's stars might not be tomorrow's. The end goal of a star product offering should be to become a cash cow for a long time. Star products have higher marketing and sales costs when they are being introduced. Over time, the intense marketing support of a product introduction should not be needed, and their sales and production costs should decline over time because of experience and process knowledge.

Costs of Transitions

Transitions take time and resources. They often appear inefficient as they play out. Management's objective needs to be to minimize those inefficiencies and deal with skepticism about progress with a healthy planning process and truthful financial information.

All financial information needs three time perspectives: past (history), present (current period), and future (comparison to budget).

Financial information needs three attributes. The information must be correct, appropriate, and timely.

"Correct" may seem obvious, but it can be a problem. In many cost accounting systems, fixed costs are merely allocated and not charged as to their actual role in those fixed costs. There are situations where the Un-Squaring consultants have seen favored departments get preferred cost allocations and unfavored ones bear the brunt of decisions. We have also seen cost accounting allocations done "because we've always done them this way." The accounting data might all balance, but managers need internal accounting and financial reports that allow them to understand the effects of their daily decisions.

Hence, the importance of being appropriate. Do managers have the information they need at the time that they need it? Are management reports designed to make tax reporting easy, but turn out to make management reporting difficult?

Timeliness is important, of course. An easy example is whether or not a company can generate a correct invoice with the appropriate detail within hours or the next day after shipment. Many of the printing industry's financial consultants have found that the biggest problems in printing financial management is slow payments, and they often find that the guilty party is the printing company itself. If it takes ten days to generate an invoice, then those ten days are added to the usual time the client takes to pay.

The invoice is a good example about the effects of transitions. Many print businesses have accounting systems designed for job shop management, but are now in marketing services as a product line. Marketing services are not job shop arrangements, but are more similar to the accounting used in graphic design, ad agency, and consulting services, with retainers and negotiated services.

Many times, these subtle issues are not understood until after the transitions are begun, as sign of poor due diligence prior to starting a business. There are many other examples, such as not realizing that a new product area might require new types of sales and marketing efforts. Pioneers in digital commercial printing learned this the hard way in the early 1990s as the order sizes and customer demands were vastly different than selling sheetfed offset printing.

Debt Creates Impatience

Transitions are likely create intense internal competition for money. Unfortunately, much of finance is related to managing debt, rather than using resources in the most productive manner. There are appropriate levels of debt, but most of those levels were set during times of stable economic fundamentals and a growing industry. Printing companies may not be able to generate all of the cash that they need to fund the transitions they are likely to need. Debt can hang over a business, especially if some of the debts belong to the business owner.

A quote from international investor Jeremy Grantham (Debt, Be Not Proud) from February 2012 might be helpful. Grantham said "leverage reduces the investor's critical asset: Patience...It encourages financial aggressiveness, recklessness, and greed. It increases your returns over and over until, suddenly, it ruins you." When print demand started to fall, the penalties for riding the growing market using debt were finally felt. If the business did not close, the debt greatly constrained the abilities of print businesses to make the decisions they needed to.

The first rule of transition from a financial perspective is probably to have 25% of your current assets as cash in the bank as a starting point. It's important when making a transition to be a healthy company first. It is very difficult for companies that are having financial problems to be able to make successful transitions. Some companies may be better off not making a transition at all, and seeking merger and acquisition partners instead.

The Separate Roles of Budgets, Goals, and Forecasting

Annual budgets are essential parts of financial management, and rolling budgets with four-quarter time horizons make them better.

It is important also to separate forecasting from budgeting. Forecasting is the process of investigating trends of financial data for a period of time. They answer the question "if things continue the same way as the past, where will they be later?"

Forecasting can unfortunately become an intensely political process with some intimidation by top executives to interpret trends in an overly optimistic way. This is especially a problem when the forecasts are negative. This politicization of forecasting is a sign that goals and objectives are not being kept separate from forecasting and the budgeting process.

The purpose of management is to create a real-life situation where outcomes are better than underlying trends. Unrealistic trend analysis creates a shaky foundation for planning.

Management is the answer to the second question, "Knowing where the trend is, what do we need to do to reach our goals?" Cash needs to be managed to the rolling quarterly budget, and people need to be managed to the goals. If you manage finance to false high goals, the slightest downturn will create a resource shortage.

Using statistical methods as part of forecasting processes means that a systematic, objective, and disciplined method is part of the planning process. Forecasting software is relatively easy to run. Interpreting it may require some help, but it is worthwhile.

All businesses should adjust their financials for inflation. A 2% annual inflation rate means that the difference between the first year in a 10-year history will be 22% off, with compounding, the most recent year. So if a business is 25% bigger than it was 10 years ago, executives should not be patting themselves on the back for a 25% increase, but wondering why after 10 years their business is only 3% (25%-22%) bigger than it was. Use inflation adjustment to see your real trends.

Revise your forecasts no more than twice a year; more often creates needless bureaucracy. There are always trends in data that might be hard to discern by looking at them too often. Patterns need time to develop.

It's hard to stay objective in planning, especially if compensation schemes are tied with the processes. Compensation schemes should be consistent over long periods of time. Contests and short-term commission bonuses divert attention from the hard work needed to achieve the goals set in long-term strategic planning.

A final part of long-range planning are the creation of planning scenarios. These are especially helpful in the creation of disaster plans for the continuity of business, such as what to do if production is halted by weather or natural disasters, loss of key employees, and other situations. But there are also situations that need to be considered, such as new competitors, loss of key customers, increases in sales from major new customers and other factors. Identifying these possible events is important when understanding the risks of the business. These risks may be insurable or not.

They often involve backup production relationships with other printers, and resources that might need to be held in reserve should unlikely events occur.

There are always unforeseen events, but good scenario planning processes will create enough similar situations that the management, and the employees will have some guidelines about what needs to be done.

What Financial Ratios Really Say

There is always an interest in how companies are doing compared to others. For this reason, the industry publishes financial ratios about the performance of reporting companies compared to others. In the printing

Profit Ratios Data from PIA Financial Ratios Studies	All Printers	Profits Leaders	The Other 3/4	Leaders-Others Gap
2000	3.1%	10.5%	0.6%	9.9%
2001	1.0%	8.0%	-1.3%	9.3%
2002	1.6%	8.4%	-0.7%	9.1%
2003	1.7%	8.7%	-0.6%	9.3%
2004	2.5%	9.4%	0.2%	9.2%
2005	2.7%	10.3%	0.2%	10.1%
2006	3.4%	10.1%	1.2%	8.9%
2007	3.1%	9.7%	0.9%	8.8%
2008	1.5%	9.4%	-1.1%	10.5%
2009	-1.4%	7.0%	-4.2%	11.2%
2010	1.4%	9.5%	-1.3%	10.8%
2011	1.8%	9.6%	-0.8%	10.4%
2012	2.7%	9.9%	0.3%	9.6%
2013	2.6%	10.3%	0.0%	10.3%
2000-2013	2.0%	9.3%	-0.5%	9.8%
2008+	1.4%	9.3%	-1.2%	10.5%
2010+	2.1%	9.8%	-0.4%	10.3%
Data sources:	from PIA press releases		calculation by Strategies for Management, Inc.	

industry, the longest published series of financial ratio reporting is by Printing Industries of America.

Financial ratios are important in judging how a business stands compared to others in the same business area. They are averages, however, that include firms that are managed well and those that are managed badly. The preoccupation with financial ratios actually makes mediocrity acceptable—that is, unless one separates out the best firms, as the PIA Financial Ratios do. But even then, those are averages of profitable businesses, some of which are doing well and those that have outstanding and superior performance that average profit leaders would love to have.

The table below shows the financial ratios of all printing companies from 2000 to 2013. It is then broken out into two parts --the profit levels of the leaders, and then the remaining companies. It turns out that the profit leaders make virtually all of the industry profits, and the rest of the industry essentially broke even.

It's not that the profit leader's rates are that impressive on the surface, but in difficult years (such as the recession years of 2002-2003 and 2009-2010), the gap in performance between profit leaders and the other printers widens. Profit leaders profit rates fell, as one might expect, but they were still very profitable.

The table reflects just one ratio in the studies, profits divided by revenues. The full report has many different ways of looking at performance.

In studying the PIA *Financial Ratios* over many years, some basic characteristics of profit leaders become apparent:

- They have fewer employees than companies of similar revenue size

- They own less equipment in a general sense than others; they have just what they need, and not more

- They spend more on training; it is likely they spend more time on one-on-one training as well

The bottom line: They make better overall use of their limited resources.

The Nature of Capital Investment

Printers have always defined themselves to one another in terms of the equipment they owned. "I'm a sheetfed printer," one might say, while another might proclaim "We're a web offset shop." That was fine when equipment would last for more than a decade and a market for its output was assured. Now, there are more digital based presses, which are more like computer equipment rather than mechanical equipment. These devices have shorter life spans because they are part of the constant innovation of the computer industry.

The marketing life of capital equipment is different than the production life of the equipment. Nowadays, getting five years out of equipment might be a lot. From an accounting perspective, there is a question about how long the equipment can be depreciated and what the useful life is. Today, the marketing life of equipment is probably half as long as the production life for many digital printing devices. This has many financial implications.

First, leasing becomes a way of insuring against obsolescence. Though the cost of the equipment might be lower if purchased, the lease means that when the obligation is over, the equipment does not hang around on the press floor getting little use. The older the equipment, the more likely an employee needs to be retained to run it, and the employee is prevented from upgrading their skills to newer technologies. Obsolescence risk does not appear on any financial statements, but higher costs from leasing do. Managers need to see through those issues.

Companies need to be constantly investing and changing their capital base for to ensure a relevance to the marketplace. But that can be expensive, as noted, unless other strategies are employed. More print businesses are sharing resources and actively seeking out the business of brokers. Also, print businesses are seeking more trade work with other print businesses.

There has been a stated preference, and even an admonition, by past industry experts and advisors to refrain from this kind of sales initiative. The belief was that product margins are always better when the equipment is owned. This perception does not recognize some important ways in which the industry has changed. First, demand has been declining. When the industry was growing, many capital investment mistakes could be overcome, given enough time. Because there is no more "mainstream" printing business (such as brochures and other items that are now part of online information), the industry is left with specialty applications or data-intensive formats. It is hard to overcome low sales in product categories when the overall trend of volume is down. This means that specialty offerings have greater importance, but this requires specialty equipment. The only way to garner enough volume to make the purchase of specialty equipment financially viable is to establish trade partnerships and alliances with other printing and communications organizations.

There is also another factor that does not appear on company financial statements. By engaging in trade sales (that is, selling printed goods on a wholesale basis to other printers or print brokers) or reselling these items, the print business is reducing its risks of obsolescence and of poor investment decisions, and is increasing the utilization rate of existing equipment.

Capacity utilization is a misunderstood concept. The concept has little validity on an industry-wide basis. Using the Federal Reserve's data, there has been a 25+year decline (with some brief rises along the way) in capacity utilization. The industry had significant periods of high profits during the utilization decline, such as in the late 1990s. The burst of utilization in the 2006-2007 period (as shown in the chart below) was a period of sub-par profitability, even though utilization was at the same levels that produced significantly higher profits (about 2x to 3x!) ten years earlier.

Also, individual businesses can make their capacity utilization higher by using old, inefficient, equipment. Companies that have modern, well-maintained equipment may have lower capacity utilization rates, but lower costs and higher profits.

The main thrust of the capacity utilization argument in the industry has been that fewer presses mean higher selling prices. The argument is invalid. The industry has lost 1,000 printing establishments a year for more than 20 years, yet that has not helped to raise selling prices. It also assumes that there are no competitors for print budgets. As we have seen since 1995, digital media have taken more and more of marketing and communications budgets. Those digital media are now the first step in communications programs, and they are getting less expensive and more powerful from an analytic perspective almost every day.

Rather than focusing on utilization, it is more important to understand break-even points for each unit of equipment installed, as well as the overall break-even levels for the company (and separate divisions). There must be constant efforts to drive break-even points down, along with parallel efforts to increase the distance between the break-even point and revenue levels.

This means that financial management is not just about watching and cutting costs. It is about changing costs, understanding their dynamic nature, especially within a competitive marketplace.

There is also a desire to understand controllable and non-controllable costs. These are similar to variable and fixed costs in economics, but it can be more than that. Management may stipulate that certain costs cannot be changed because of contracts or their preference for operating. Even if those costs are objectively variable, individual managers cannot change them. For example, the company may have a no-layoff policy or a summer factory shut-down period. Management dictum has turned these variable costs into fixed costs, for practical purposes. These decisions affect all aspects of a business, including capacity utilization and pricing decisions. Capacity can be expanded by extending the number of shifts or days, but there may be company guidelines that do not allow that. Capacity can be increased with additional equipment. It can also be increased by sending overflow work to other printing organizations.

Capacity utilization is best used as a measure inside a business, not outside. Profit leaders have less equipment, they use them often, and they can turn them over with newer and more efficient versions. Also, by "wearing equipment out", it frees up capital for new and different capital investments. Owning equipment might be worthwhile for some years, but sharing it might be smarter in other years.

Beware of Contribution-Based Pricing

An aspect of capacity utilization is an understanding of how to allocate the fixed costs of a business. Under a targeted utilization rate, each job must bear a larger portion of fixed costs. When companies are above their targeted utilization rate, their profits rise quickly. There are a few important economic concepts here.

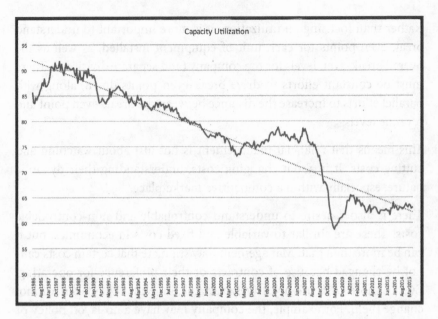

The first concept is the difference between fixed and variable costs. Fixed costs are hard to change in the short term; they are buildings, equipment, certain taxes and fees, etc. Variable costs are those that can change on the basis of usage, such as production supplies, electricity, and similar items.

The second concept related to this work is the benefit it has if it increases the volume of work beyond what they were expecting. Because of the concept of economies of scale, each additional dollar of revenue has a higher than usual percentage that "falls" to the bottom line. This extra margin can be flexible in terms of pricing.

There are times when it is may be in the interest of print businesses to accept or seek work that covers its variable costs and makes a contribution to fixed costs. This is attractive to print businesses that have open time in their schedule, filling in a period where there would have been no revenue. Most printers do not take on this work unless they are confident that it will not affect the pricing levels of their regular customers.

Contribution margin work is only profitable if the rest of the business is covering its fixed costs in other ways in the long run. The more volatile sales patterns are, the more unwise contribution pricing is likely to be. Many printers got caught in a bind with this pricing in the early 2000s when industry shipments were beginning to decline. That meant that most companies never met their sales plans, and seeking contribution-priced work did not work out as planned.

This does not mean a company should never take advantage of this kind of pricing. An order that is the equivalent of finding a $100 bill on the street should rarely be turned down. The question is whether the company gets "hooked on" this work and jeopardizes its operations. If this kind of work can be found regularly and makes sense, set it up as a separate business category where it can be watched, and possibly nurtured, but only if it does not undermine other aspects of the strategic plan.

Costs change in businesses, and all costs must reflect changes in the marketplace. There is reliable economic thought that market prices dictate costs, which is exactly the opposite of the cost-plus pricing method.

Market prices of print will continue to get lower, not higher, in the future. The competition from digital media pushes prices down as printers compete for the budget dollars and desires of communicators. It is essential not just to keep an eye on costs, but to be open to changing the processes that create the costs to better compete in the future communications marketplace.

Basic Metric: The Balance Sheet, Not Cash Flow, Not the Income Statement

Smaller companies and unhealthy companies focus on what's happening in their checkbooks and cash flow. But healthier companies have a focus on the nature of the balance sheet. In between the checkbook and the balance sheet is the income statement. The more that we move from the checkbook to creation of value as represented in the balance sheet, the time horizon of management and the planning process expands.

Owners and executives need to be directed to increasing the long-term value of the organization.

If ownership is deeply involved in the day-to-day operations of the business, there tends to be a more short-term focus and an inability to understand the future through a planning process. This is a very self-limiting proposition. Ownership needs to "let go" and move to professional management styles for themselves and for the long term health of the business. What if the owner is incapacitated? If they are greatly involved in day-to-day operations, then the company will fail.

The more owners are tied up in day-to-day operations, more likely they will be unable to detect marketplace changes that will affect their future.

Personal Taxation and Estate Planning

It may seem odd that this topic would appear in a chapter about finance in the printing industry, but it is an important one. Most print businesses are family-owned or closely held.

Because of the differences in personal and corporate taxes, there are distortions to the resources in a business and the decisions owners make. Some of these deal with double-taxation of profits, the timing of the recognition of revenues or expenses, and ownership of property. It is common, for example, for the building that a printing business is in to be owned personally by the business owner. Should the printing business fail, the owner still has a valuable asset. The owner leases the building to the printing business. For small storefront printers, it is not uncommon for them to own the small strip mall in which they are located.

The nature of taxation requires having wise accountants to maximize the net amount of money that is returned to the owner. Taxation is a fact of life, and choosing a course of business action on the basis of favorable tax treatment is wrong, but is also a fact of life and is done every day.

It is worthwhile to work with accountants who understand these issues. They should be asked to prepare a standard set of statements as if the business was truly standalone without tax strategy distortions, and keep that up to date. There are two reasons for this.

The first is to shed light about how those tax decisions affect business operations decisions. The second is that should the business be put up for sale for any reason, it will be easier for an outside buyer or business appraiser to understand the true economic value of the business.

Sometimes personal taxation strategies attempt to get "too cute by half" and cause problems. During the housing and mortgage boom, some cash-strapped printers took second or third mortgages on their personal property at low rates, and then loaned the money to their businesses at higher rates. When housing prices collapsed, the mortgages went under-water (loans were higher than the value of the property) and the printing businesses had cash flow problems and could not pay the loans back to the owners.

All due care is necessary in the financing of small business. Keeping things uncomplicated might be the best advice of all.

References

"Debt, Be Not Proud." *Wall Street Journal.* March 5, 2012. http://blogs.wsj.com/totalreturn/2012/03/05/debt-be-not-proud/.

QuickMBA Strategic Management. *BCG Growth-Share Matrix.* http://www.quickmba.com/strategy/matrix/bcg/.

10

PEOPLE

by Joe Webb

The most important resource of organizations is not finance, equipment, marketing position, or processes. It is people. No people, no company.

Missions, strategies, and tactics are designed and implemented by people, and day-to-day actions are performed by people. The actions and interactions of people define the nature and success of an organization.

There's No Accounting for People

Financial accounting for people is not easy. We've all heard the phrase "human assets," but no such thing exists from an accounting perspective.

In the bookkeeping process, people are recorded as an expense in the income statement, appearing as salaries and benefits. There is not a "people" asset on a balance sheet. On the manufacturing side, they appear as "factory labor," a component of costs of goods sold.

In the Money chapter, we saw that commercial printing industry volume is not connected to general economic performance. Yet we know there were very profitable businesses in the industry. It's not possible to create profits just by riding an economic wave upward. Few print businesses have high and sustained profitability. The barriers to competition in the industry are low, which means that many companies are trying to get their share of the pie. That means that good management, along with the choices those managers make in the long run, make a difference in creating high-profit businesses.

We can get a sense of "people strength" by making a series of comparisons to previous periods of performance and systematic comparisons to competitors. We estimate the value of people, their performance and decisions, by assessing how economic performance has changed over time.

"Your most important assets go down the elevator every night" is a quote usually attributed to legendary advertising executive David Oglivy. "The cemeteries are filled with indispensable men", offering the opposing view, is typically ascribed to Charles de-Gaulle. (The Graveyards) What's the right balance? Are people critical to a business, or are people replaceable resources of marginal consequence to corporate performance?

This means that positive balance sheet changes, judged on a year-to-year basis, are more important for managerial assessment than are quarter-to-quarter income statement analysis. You need both, but the printing industry tends to focus on the bottom line and not how the bottom lines build the long-term value of the enterprise.

Measuring Management

Measuring the performance of equipment, such as a press or binding function is easy, but it is harder to do for people. This is especially true for those in higher ranks of organizations, who are often involved in strategic decisions that do not have immediate effects, but may be seen three or five years later.

Performance, expectations, skills, and other aspects of managing people are hard to judge. The lower the job in the organization, the more likely there can be objective measures of performance because those positions have countable tasks in terms of output or time consumed.

Every manager has heard stories of employees with personnel folders stuffed with glowing evaluations, only to have those employees change bosses. Then those glowing evaluations are joined with new dour and depressing reports of incompetence and bad attitudes.

The higher the person is in the organization, the more subjective the decisions can become. We've all heard and perhaps known of seemingly incompetent managers who seem to produce good results. And we know of extremely smart and knowledgeable managers. Peter Drucker described them as "articulate incompetents," who can barely muster flat performance even in good times.

Why Do We Hire People?

Businesses hire people for what they can do and what they know, and for their expected contributions to meeting stated objectives. Even someone in a maintenance position, though low paid and sometimes disparaged, plays a role by making working conditions of others organized and more conducive to productivity and goal achievement. The skills to complete tasks may be widely available, but that does not mean the task is unimportant.

Like there is a time value of money, there is a time value for skills and knowledge. In the same way that reinvested earnings compound, skills and knowledge can increase in value with training and experience. Good investments need research and discipline: good companies make training systematic and consistent. If invested poorly, money loses value. If workers are untrained or do not have experiences that increase their knowledge or skills, the market value (and the internal value) of their knowledge and skills will decay.

> Dead wood? The phrase "dead wood" is an insulting term used to describe workers whose skills are no longer appropriate, but they remain in their positions within a company. The phrase refers to a gardening process, where healthy branches of trees and plants are kept, and weak or dead ones are removed, so that nutrients go to the healthiest parts of the plant.

"Dead wood" is actually a comment about management and ownership. How did the business allow its people to go untrained? Were they not aware that the market was changing and that new skills and knowledge were needed?

Many companies are revered because they "take care of their people," which usually refers to salaries and benefits. Great companies take care of their people by training them and cultivating their skills. The high salaries and benefits are the result of superior productivity from good management. This is why many companies with high profits also have higher than average salaries and wages. They also have high standards for employee selection. Productivity matters, and because it does, it gets rewarded.

Training Changes People: That's the Whole Idea

In a changing marketplace, what people do is best suited for goal achievement for only a short period of time. Well-run companies devote long-term resources to training, learning, and directing. They seek to overcome marketplace changes (if not otherwise leading those changes) by being adaptable to new opportunities.

People may not be assets, but the value of their actions and their time can be increased in the right environment. Changes occur inside and outside the business, and sometimes the pace of change can differ greatly. In recent years, the pace of change has been greatest in terms of new competitors. These competitors have forced companies to change the way they market, promote, and sell their products. Training, therefore, should not be limited to topics about internal operations.

Training is often viewed as "classroom time," but the most valuable training is what occurs on a one-on-one basis with supervisors and with other employees. Managers need to ensure that time is made available for those actions. Some kinds of training that are not always delivered in formal classrooms that have great value include:

- Cross-Training: Workers are trained to do multiple jobs, which allows shifting to tasks as needed, especially for coverage during absences and vacations, and changes to the volume and nature of work.

- Job Variety/Rotation: Workers share jobs and switch tasks on a systematic basis. This broadens their experience and knowledge, and also reduces problems with boredom.

- Job Sharing: Multiple workers share the same job, which can allow for flexible work schedules, especially when workers are not available on a full-time basis. This allows the business to keep certain employees inside the business, rather than have them work for competitors or otherwise leave the business.

- Team Building: These are events that are often generic in nature, but allow employees in the same or related departments to explore how they can improve the way they work together.

- Employee Events: No, these are not parties. Rather, they are times when employees can meet on a less-structured basis, often without the command presence of supervisors. Informal meetings can make formal meetings more productive.

- Customer Events: In many companies, only sales people and ownership meet customers. Knowing customers by sight and name changes the perspective about the jobs that they send to the print business, and the meaning and urgency provided to the work.

- Management Discussions: A way of breaking down walls between management and workers is have frank discussions about business conditions and operations. It is important to keep channels of communications between management and staff open with regular meetings (at least twice a year) and not just to report on business conditions during crisis situations.

- Performance Reviews: These are often neglected as training opportunities. Many reviews are done on a superficial basis, which means that they are of little value. Performance reviews can have significant training value when done properly. Goals and objectives need to be identified with clarity. In addition, the path to reaching the goals need to be identified, with training paths to those goals provided.

Of course, classroom time is important. Learning new software, equipment operation, management techniques, regulatory aspects of the workplace, and other topics keeps knowledge and skills up to date. When these are held outside the workplace, they add to the experience of the employee by seeing how the information applies to other businesses, and getting some new ideas to bring back to the office.

It is common, however, for workers who have gone for outside training to come back to the office full of ideas, only to lose the momentum as they return to day-to-day tasks. Managers should be sure they recap the information learned in an outside program, record the recommendations learned from participating in the program, and include those recommendations in meetings and in performance assessments. If that is not done, future outside training will be treated as unimportant and just a chance to be out of the office.

Key Concepts: Autonomy and Subsidiarity

The goal of management in the manner they work with employees centers around two important concepts – autonomy and subsidiarity. These are especially important for small and medium-sized businesses.

Owners can get tied up in shop floor details very easily, especially if that was the area of the business where they entered the industry. It's comforting to stick with something you know, and it puts the owner in the role of the expert, which is often good for the ego, but not necessarily good for the business.

The first concept is *autonomy*. Workers should know what needs to be done, have the skills and knowledge to do it well, and be able to work with minimal supervision. Autonomy is the ability to responsibly make decisions about their work and to cooperate with others as they jointly work to achieve business objectives and goals. A high degree of trust is necessary for autonomy to exist. The experiences that workers have with management interactions (especially management's willingness to allow people to learn from mistakes, diagnose problems, and self-correct) can contribute to this high degree of trust.

Subsidiarity is the concept that decisions are best made at the lowest levels possible, where the problems and the resources are, without having to rely on levels higher in the organization for decisions. In a small print business, where there is an owner and a few employees, this may be difficult to implement, but is essential to do so.

One of the most basic theories of management–that of Theory X and Theory Y –was expressed more than fifty years ago. Theory X managers assume that workers need significant amounts of direction and coercion. Theory Y managers belief that workers can be directed to goals, but make decisions about the best ways to achieve them within the resources and time constraints they are given.

Because businesses and the marketplace are always changing, it is impossible for managers and owners to know everything they need to know with complete certainty and in minute detail. They also need to rely on others to get their work done. Managers need to employ people who can be relied on to honestly and correctly interpret actions, events, results, and situations, and to report on them clearly. Whether it's a maintenance issue or a customer situation, resources and time are always scarce, and managers need to hire people who can be flexible and honest. Managers need to cultivate their staff and company cultures to encourage these behaviors.

Conflict and Consensus

When power over jobs and situations is dispersed in a business, it can lead to conflicts. In the long run, this is a good thing, because conflict in the right circumstances can lead to creative solutions. When two lower level parties agree to valid solutions prior to approval by management, it increases their understanding of the business and its functions. If the solution is based on trial-and-error experimentation prior to presentation to management, it trains workers on the process of decision-making. This prepares workers for unpredictable situations or periods of crisis. It also means they will have a better sense of what managers do. In Theory X organizations, management decisions can sometimes appear to be arbitrary and even tyrannical to workers. In Theory Y organizations, they are usually more accepted because employees have a richer sense of the business and what needs to be done to survive.

Consensus is often sought in businesses because, when people agree to objectives, goals, and procedures, things are more likely to run well. Oddly, striving for consensus before making all decisions can sometimes be the worst thing that can happen to a business. A change in the marketplace (such as a new competitor, or a loss of a customer) might require an urgent decision, and looking for consensus in those situations may indicate that management is reluctant to make necessary decisions. Waiting for everyone to agree can take forever (or longer) and give competitors time to create more mischief.

Organizational responsibility must be clear. Workers are most happy when their concerns and recommendations are thoughtfully considered and not routinely dismissed. Sometimes the answer might not be "No," but "Not now" in a participative management style such as Theory Y. The answer in the case of Theory X managers is often "No, never," which tends to discourage employees and limit their willingness to cooperate when needed most.

It must be noted that Theory X and Y are used as generalizations here. Not every employee, not every position, can have these ideas applied in the same manner. There are always situations that require the application of different management styles for a period of time. They are presented here as a means to stimulate thinking about goals and the nature of the workplace. The nature of management philosophies is a large topic, and worthy of separate and concentrated study.

Hiring Right

There are important legal and regulatory issues in hiring and other aspects of managing a workplace. (Discussion of these issues will be found in a later chapter.) This chapter explains strategies to gather the right resources in your business by attracting good candidates, selecting the right ones, and creating a positive, interactive, flexible, self-renewing and productive work environment.

The founders and owners of organizations have several crucial tasks: the identification, recruitment, selection, training, cultivating, directing, and otherwise managing the people they hire, along with the decisions and actions they take. Some companies perform these tasks better than others do.

Poor hires are usually done on an ad hoc basis when an opening occurs. Those sudden openings often occur at the worst possible time when managers are busy covering the work of the former employee, or helping someone else do that position, along with doing their regular job. Unfortunately, this means that just "getting somebody" becomes the hiring standard, rather than spending time and thought about recruiting the right person.

These kinds of situations mean that only experienced employees need apply. Inexperienced applicants can come back when they know something. When you hire only experienced employees, the opportunity to cultivate "the company way" is delayed or lost. Experienced employees who can participate in and improve the culture are hard to find. Make sure that the experience is right for long-term company goals. Doing things a "company way" is part of differentiating your business from others.

Hiring needs to be part of a long-term plan where workers become familiar with other jobs, cross-trained where appropriate, and the linkages between functions, departments, and positions, are always being reviewed. People are encouraged to reach for other positions, to learn more about their jobs on their own, and to be rewarded for self-motivation.

To cynics, delegation may seem like a sneaky way to get others to do your work. It is a critical aspect to training. It is a compliment to workers, an affirmation that they are competent and trusted to complete assigned tasks and programs.

The UnSquaring approach is different in that it recognizes how important it is that the company be understood and treated as a whole. Although there are three disciplines and nine vectors, they may look like they are all separate, but they are all connected at the center. They meet, overlap, and emanate from the center. All vectors work together because they share resources, processes, knowledge, techniques, goals, and objectives.

As with all resources, people resources require planning, direction, and control. There is a formal process of written plans and procedures that are understood through training and reinforced through daily activities. Their value is emphasized through informal interactions that become part of the larger culture.

How a the Culture of a Business Affects Hiring

Most print businesses were started by entrepreneurs who made their founding decision based on the experience and skills they had not long after their industry entry. They became convinced they could run their own print business better than others could. This is a common story, across industries, as the primary reason for starting a business is dissatisfaction with one's current job.

Those businesses are therefore built on knowledge applicable to a specific time and place, with assumptions that those experiences and skills will be applicable for many years into the future.

Owners, in the process of building their business from the bottom up, create a culture. That is, their experience, skills, knowledge, and business expectations ripple through through the business in the decisions they make. They become guidelines for future behavior in the company and with the overall business environment.

All companies have a culture, as do all types of groups, whether formal or informal. That culture augments a formal organizational structure and is the principal way that businesses get things done. This is why it is always important to watch a business in action, rather than to just look at organizational charts, especially in small and mid-size businesses.

The most important decisions managers make relate to the people they hire. Just as for the decision to begin a business, hires are based on the understanding of needs at a particular time and how those needs will change in the future. Also crucial is an understanding of the ability of those hired to perform tasks or direct resources is a manner that creates economic value that is greater than the costs of their services.

Hiring and Business Culture

Initial hires often come via family and industry acquaintances, from prior employers, or through their industry network. Those are usually worthwhile hires for that time, place, and market condition.

As time passes, the internal harmony of those interests and resources changes. Marketplaces change over time, and the congruence of the original business inspiration and the resources the business has tend to increase or decrease in relevance. Sometimes these changes can be anticipated as part of strategic planning. Organizations can adapt to marketplace changes by their communications, interactions with the market, and their ability to retain the match of market needs and company capabilities through formal and informal training.

Over time, one begins to realize that new hires are based on people who have the same business outlooks as part of their skills. There is always value in working together in a low-conflict environment, but eventually market conditions change to the point where they are no longer helpful. Managers always feel more comfortable when "hiring themselves," or people like themselves, but it may not be what the business really needs. Just as there is a time value of money, there is a time aspect of skills, experience, and knowledge. Culture plays a role in determining job requirements, hiring guidelines, and selection criteria. If you want to change a organization's strategy, you need to guide the culture to create that change; it cannot be done by edict, but by the culmination of management decisions and actions toward goals and objectives.

How does one judge the value of people in an organization or being considered for hire? The basic criteria for evaluating are their:

- skills

- knowledge and competence

- experience

- match of their skills and knowledge to marketplace needs

- ability to cooperate and collaborate

- ability to communicate with others inside and outside the organization

- interest in learning and applying training

- ability to create economic value beyond their costs, or to enhance the value created by others

- other factors appropriate to the position and the company

Where is the Talent?

There was a time when the industry could rely on graphic arts educational programs. Many of those programs focused on production techniques ("the how"), but not the reasons for media selection ("the why"). The opportunities in digital media means that many students have found themselves better off by taking classes in Computer Science and Information

Systems, rather than in traditional production. The era of production education is ending and is being replaced by a new era of digital imaging and digital deployment. Graphic design, content creation, and publishing continue to be very important, but now they are combined with skills related to media analytics and the management of media deployment.

This means that printing companies must be creative in their search for talent. In an upcoming section of this chapter, the nature of the new skills are detailed. Many of them will not be found in traditional sources for employees. Indeed, many print businesses may not be able to afford the skills needed because of the salaries available to them elsewhere, or because the volume of work requiring their skills will not warrant a full-time person. Alliances might be the solution; that topic is mentioned again in this chapter and is discussed more fully in the next.

How a Print Business Culture Grows

When companies are small, they are usually built on specific skills and specializations, and the trust and confidence in the owner. As companies grow, the employees' jobs expand to fill new requirements and, when necessary, new workers are hired when the general mold of who is already there are added.

Over time, a culture starts to form. Phrases like people "fitting in" or "working well together" are examples of cultures at work. That kind of chemistry is not solely a product of procedures or rules. It comes about from working together over long periods of time. Culture helps people figure out the "right thing to do" in those situations that are new and do not have established procedures, or when there is a crisis situation.

As the size of a business increases, job specialization and division of labor begins. At one time, the office manager was the bookkeeper who also answered the company phone, but now concentrates on bookkeeping. The sales manager no longer carries accounts and supervises multiple sales reps. The owner is busier, and walking onto the shop floor happens less and less often. A messenger picks up work and makes small deliveries, rather than assigning it to whomever was free at the time or was going in that direction anyway.

Companies just seem to grow organically, and hiring guidelines are often not created or written down. Managers tended to hire people who would fit in or people that they liked. In other words, new people tended to be just like them.

While culture is the tone of the workplace, and it ensures the smooth running of a business, it can make the welcoming of newcomers and new ideas difficult – that is, unless seeking newness is part of the culture. For that reason, we need to be very aware of the culture of our businesses. We need to be demanding about skills and competence, but we also need to be aware of adaptability, flexibility, and ability to learn.

How Culture Can Cause Trouble

Industry culture was one of the reasons that there was little proactive response to the changes that digital media brought to communications markets. The Internet and new forms of media depressed prices and lowered the demand for print. Digital media flamed desires for measurability and accountability of media. Few print businesses were ready for this kind of environment; in fact, many did not even know about it. Twitter was just for kids to send short messages with. Today it has 288 million monthly users, has 3600 employees (nearly half are engineers) (Twitter Usage/Company Facts) and is a publicly traded company (NASDAQ:TWTR) worth more than $30 billion. Facebook (DJ:FB) is worth more than $200 billion.

There is good reason to believe the issue is generational. A print business owner born in the 1940s worked in a craft industry of the 1960s, with major technological advances in computerization in the 1970s. Those digital technologies in prepress and manufacturing process management lowered the costs of production and increased print demand. Throughout most of their careers, printing was a steadily growing industry that was minimally affected by economic downturns and buoyed by upturns. Any pause in sales could be "toughed out" because print had great value. Desktop publishing was not a big deal because it didn't offer the quality of good typesetting. Offset printing was getting better every year and represented the best quality, which was what customers needed.

Business owners born in the 1970s, however, have a much different perspective. They grew up with computers, trained on desktop publishing, took pictures with digital cameras, barely remember a time without the Internet, has always used direct-to-plate, and considers digital printing as a mainstream process with unique benefits compared to other kinds of printing. These owners know that, because the market is so competitive, you need to offer something unique and better than others, because anyone can offer acceptable print quality. You need a range of product offerings, such as print, signage, data management and other capabilities.

The 1970s generation is slowly taking charge of the industry. This group of managers, who often complained that owners did not want to see how media were changing, are now in charge. If you became a manager in 1998, you have never experienced the commercial printing industry as a growth business. However, you have seen the industry adopt digital printing, e-commerce, data management, integrated media, and many other processes.

It's not just management. It's workers that need to have age and experience diversity. Having age diversity in a business is also experience diversity in terms of media use. Age diversity, especially in upper management, is a business strategy that minimizes the myopic effects of experience. If all management has the same business experience profile, it may make internal operations better, but adaptation to external changes may be difficult.

Market Needs Determine People Resources

There are systematic steps to gather and nurture the right resources in your business, by good recruitment and selection, and by the creation of a positive, interactive, flexible, self-renewing and productive work environment. These attributes need to be cultivated in a highly competitive marketplace that has changing tools and processes. That marketplace is increasingly defined by digital technologies with constantly lower costs with steadily rising performance. Matching naturally productive people with highly productive technologies is the goal.

Historically, employees in print businesses were craft workers, hired for their abilities to execute specific tasks that required physical training and, sometimes, physical strength. Decades and decades ago, union halls in big cities played a major role in training workers and serving as a clearing house for workers. Printers would often call to the union hall to seek workers for specific shifts or cover sick days or vacations. Yes, tasks were that well-defined.

Advances in computing changed the nature of work, with greater emphasis on workflow between functions, rather than on discrete and defined tasks. Each task had a unique tool or outcome. Modern workflows focus on collaboration, where many workers touch the same computer files, making cooperation critical. Previously, all of the crafts were self-contained within a company or a class of trade. The files used in today's work originate from content creators outside the business.

Originally, clients described work, provided sketches, models, and raw materials that had to be transformed into print. Today, clients take their own ideas, then edit, refine, and test their own ideas, and hand printers print-ready files (or near-ready, and if not, workable ones). The new craft is in the software and is accessed with keyboards and pointing devices, managing imaging and other data in ways.

Those client-originated data are deployed in many different ways to many different media. The tools they use, such as Adobe Creative Suite and Adobe Publish, make such deployment easy and nearly automatic. Print businesses are using the same tools that content creators and web developers use.

This means that, just as print businesses compete with other media providers for pieces of their communications spending budgets, they are competing with those providers and their own clients for many of the same workers. While they are not competing with press operators, they are competing with many other kinds of personnel. It was one thing to compete for bookkeepers or maintenance personnel that might be able to work in many businesses; but now print production personnel require skills that have great attractiveness in many media markets.

The chart below shows the average payroll per employee for selected industries. The general commercial printing industry average is $44,600, while public relations is twice that level. Graphic design is more than 20% higher, with others higher still. Printers pursuing the "marketing services" strategy are likely to have difficulty in pursuing experienced employees in those markets. This means that alliances, as discussed in the next chapter, are an important aspect of preparing for the changes ahead in the communications markets.

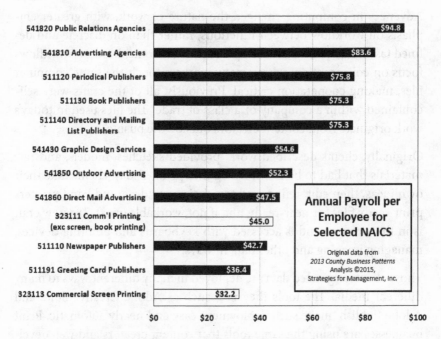

NAICS	Annual Payroll per Employee
541820 Public Relations Agencies	$94.8
541810 Advertising Agencies	$83.6
511120 Periodical Publishers	$75.8
511130 Book Publishers	$75.3
511140 Directory and Mailing List Publishers	$75.3
541430 Graphic Design Services	$54.6
541850 Outdoor Advertising	$52.3
541860 Direct Mail Advertising	$47.5
323111 Comm'l Printing (exc screen, book printing)	$45.0
511110 Newspaper Publishers	$42.7
511191 Greeting Card Publishers	$36.4
323113 Commercial Screen Printing	$32.2

Annual Payroll per Employee for Selected NAICS

Original data from
2013 County Business Patterns
Analysis ©2015,
Strategies for Management, Inc.

Mean Payroll per Employee
2012 County Business Patterns,
Adjusted to 2014$ Using CPI

These data also identify that recruiting of new workers will be difficult, as well. For years, those workers have been attracted by new media opportunities and the higher wages in those markets. This is one of the prime reasons for industry consolidation: the inability to attract new workers encourages consolidation similar to the scarcity of other capital resources. If the best companies have the best employees, rolling up the volume of others through tuck-ins or competitive actions allows surviving businesses to have higher productivity and to pay higher wages as part of the effort to retain skilled employees.

The marketplace is changing every day. Some of the skills needed to produce a modern cross-media program for a client are:

• Digital photography

- Digital printing
- Fulfillment and inventory management
- E-mail marketing
- Marketing automation
- Data hygiene/optimization
- Personalization
- Postal logistics and regulations
- Project management
- Website management
- Responsive design
- Mobile marketing
- Data management
- Data mining/analytics
- Media purchasing
- Social media
- Search engine optimization
- Content marketing
- Public relations
- Ad agency management
- Media buying and negotiation

Few organizations–and perhaps none–have every one of these skills in-house. Large agencies may have many of them. All who work in media, however, must have contacts to practitioners and organizations that can provide them. This also means that these skills must be part of the repertoire of sales people. They need not be fluent in them, but they need to be familiar with them and how those resources are identified and procured.

Tools for Better Hires

Print is a simple and familiar medium, but its use and specification is becoming more complex. As with the generational aspects of management, every generation of print user, media buyer, and employee, has a different frame of reference for its understanding of print media, print production, and print effectiveness. The same is true for employees. The generation gap in media makes hiring more difficult. Identifying skills and personal attributes necessary for current and future success in a position may come from generational experience and may not reflect current market conditions.

Unless managers are formally trained in personnel selection and evaluation, they should seek tools that can help them identify candidates for the best fit, even when looking at those who are internal candidates seeking a promotion or a lateral move. Interviewing techniques improve with use, but most managers do not get the opportunities to keep their skills sharp. There is something they can do to improve their skills, and that is to use employment testing.

Employment testing has evolved significantly over the years, and the Un-Squaring authors have become familiar with the approach used by the Harrison Assessments. It can be extremely helpful in narrowing down the number of candidates, but also in identifying key topics and questions for interviews.

Standardizing interviewing techniques can make judging candidates more objective and also minimize risks of employment litigation. This is especially important if the job requirements are for positions or skills that are unfamiliar to the executives who are responsible for employee selection. Because the Harrison Assessment compares the candidate to thousands of others who have similar jobs and are performing those jobs well, they can increase the probabilities of selecting the right candidate.

The three basic aspects to selecting the right employees are:

- Eligibility: Candidates have the right general skills to be successful in a new position.
- Suitability: Their skills and their temperament are appropriate for the tasks, and they will be able to work with the company in achieving those particular tasks and objectives.

- Interview: Verifies the eligibility and suitability, adds a personal dimension to the assessment, and creates an opportunity to judge motivations, knowledge, and reaction to the physical business environment in which they will work.

There is a problem with interviewing: They are rarely done well, and merely liking the interviewee can obscure whether or not the interviewee are really eligible or suitable. Testing can make the process more objective and prevent likability from creating the situation where executives hire someone exactly like themselves, instead of the right person needed most.

Businesses making strategic changes require different skills and behaviors than they had in the past. This means that the suitability and eligibility of employees need to be determined based on future needs, not on current ones. Those future needs are likely to be immersed in a future business culture that has not yet been established.

Using Tests for Coaching and Managerial Improvement

The Harrison Assessment is not just an employment selection tool. It can be used for current management and employees, especially when they are changing jobs in the company or making a strategic change. For the interviewing process, the Assessment can assist with questions that will enhance the interview process.

It is also a coaching tool that can bridge issues of age and business culture. Remember, companies have cultures, but so do professions. Designers have a different professional culture than computer programmers have, than truck drivers have, than accountants have, than maintenance workers have, and so on. Those professions need to all work together toward company objectives. Technically, a manager may have to assess specific skills separately (such as a background check that an accountant's claim to be a CPA is valid), but the structure of an employment assessment can make it easier for hiring managers who are not familiar with the nature of certain professions.

The coaching aspect of the Assessment identifies areas of improvement and also suggests methods for doing so. Most managers want to mentor or coach employees, but are not exactly certain how. This can help, especially when there are significant age and experience differences between manager and worker.

Putting People in the Right Positions for Success

The printing industry of the past trained workers for skills in specific departments, and even for the operation of specific equipment. This was a wise allocation of capital, but now it can create a misallocation of labor.

When companies and marketplaces change, some skills already in your organization need to be applied to more constructive and valuable uses. The Assessment can also provide insights that ensure that people are in the jobs appropriate for their skills.

This can be a real eye-opener, even to the employee. Because they do their jobs every day, they may not realize that there are different applications for their work. There are good examples in public relations, for example. How would PR professionals in 2005 know whether they would find a good use for their skills in social media or event planning? These were new jobs, and unless they happened to have an unplanned opportunity to work in that situation, they might never realize they would be suited for it. An assessment process can reveal new assignments or future assignments that can keep valuable workers in the company in positions they find interesting and satisfying.

Would the Owner or CEO Be Hired for Their Job Today?

If you are the owner or top executive of a printing business, are you still qualified for your job? This is meant facetiously, because if you started the business or survived the last few years with positive results, the answer is probably yes.

The Harrison Assessment is an excellent tool for self improvement, and can guide your own path for training and improvement. As marketplaces and competitive environments change, the underlying assumptions to the business may no longer be relevant.

Transitioning to the Current Era of Communications

Transitioning from one form of business to another, from the old ways of selling print because "everyone needed it" to the new form of print as "one medium among many" means that the organization will change the nature of what it does. Transitions that happen in a hurry do not usually go well. It is better to have an organization that adapts over time in a proactive manner.

When the pace of change increases, or there are major changes ahead, both the formal and informal aspects of businesses are stressed. Those stresses can intensify when there are financial problems, such as slack sales or sluggish profits.

It is during these kind of times when businesses decide to look at their strategy and re-evaluate their mission. These can be very trying times. Many businesses do not have the luxury of re-examining strategy when times are good. Most strategic re-evaluations are done when times are bad or when the business is threatened. That's not good, but it is necessary. It should actually be a constant process.

In recent years, many graphic communications businesses have established business development sales processes and are slowly eliminating traditional sales methods. The change is an adaptation to new marketplace realities. It would be better to be able to turn a switch and move directly from traditional sales to business development, but that is impractical. Current customer relationships may be disrupted by the change. The alternative is an organization that organically changes and grows with the marketplace without having to create a unique event that signifies a structural change.

Business development is covered in an earlier chapter, but it must be noted that it does not affect only the sales department. It affects all departments, and especially affects the people they train and the ones they hire in the future.

Traditional graphic communication sales management has always been based on selling something clients have always needed. That is no longer the case. Now, we are switching to a different approach where business development is based on understanding a client's problems and suggesting ranges of solutions. This usually means that more than one person, including production personnel, may find themselves in sales meetings.

It also means that the interviewing and assessment process for sales people is quite different. When everyone needed print, the sales process was a bargaining process. In the era when print is one approach among many, negotiating skills are important.

Negotiating has more to do with understanding goals and missions of the client, where there are no clear answers, and print is just one possible solution. Negotiating is about matching resources to needs in a unique manner for a particular situation or client. This requires a sales representative with analytical skills, is comfortable with researching alternatives, and can manage a mutual learning process. The employer must be willing allow time for these processes to occur because the sales cycle is longer. The representative must be good at teaching and instructing clients with new information about their approaches in a way that builds confidence. A team of people, as mentioned earlier, makes the negotiation a collaborative effort, ensuring that the client's objectives are met in a unique plan. Negotiations require the willingness to experiment, test alternative solutions, and have the persistence to see the right solution through to the end.

Printing was always a serial production process, and now the selling of it ties into other parts of media plans. This underscores the fact that the nature of employment requirements have changed in subtle ways that can be explored best by using employment tools beyond traditional interviewing and checking of references.

Factors that Improve the Likelihood of Transition Success

The four key factors that increase the adaptability and resilience of businesses in times of transition of difficulty are:

- Change in the manager-worker relationship

- Training is a constant, if not daily, practice

- Hire for future needs not current tasks

- Prioritize what is best handled internally and what is best handled through alliances

The first relates to the nature of management and the relationship of employees and the company. Organizations need resilient cultures that have strength, adaptability, and flexibility. In some cases, such as strength not being flexible and flexible not always meaning adaptable to new situations, these seem contradictory. They all work together, expressed in a mix of skills and abilities that are reinforced and prioritized at the right time depending on the need.

Second, in times of market change, tasks of workers and the purposes of management actions change. While the skills needed do not change when incremental changes are small, over time, those incremental changes compound and change context. Just as with financial resources being needed at the right time in the future, the particular skills and abilities also must be ready at the right times. These are times where the knowledge of the trainers is out of date, making the required training effort to be company-wide.

There is a more subtle and longer-term change the more sophisticated the organization becomes. Training shifts from being focused on well-defined tasks to self-improving and self-replicating training conducted by the employees themselves. This is fostered by the guidance of a strong culture under the coaching of the management staff.

Training is no longer event-related. Training is often linked with a new equipment purchase or a new hire. Instead, it becomes a constant activity among all employees on a consistent basis.

Third, business adaptability means that there needs to be new ways of allocating of skills to functional needs. As the needs change over time, those skills have to be adapted to those new areas that are opening up. The personnel hired today may not have the right skills or temperament for future initiatives. Striking the right balance of hiring for today while preparing for tomorrow can be difficult. These decisions are built on a strong planning process that is more than just budgeting.

There are never enough resources to staff a business properly, and especially a transition. Some resources will be needed just during a transition period and not after. Some will be needed only after a transition. Others will be needed throughout.

Because most graphic communications businesses are small and medium-sized, the alliances they create will be critical to successful business transformation. The next chapter, Alliances, examines these business relationships, how to craft them, and how to make them strategic instead of happenstance.

References

The Graveyards Are Full of Indispensible Men. Quote Investigator. http://quoteinvestigator.com/2011/11/21/graveyards-full

Twitter Usage/Company Facts. twitter.com. https://about.twitter.com/company.

11

ALLIANCES

by Joe Webb

Eight of the nine vectors, or "pie slices", of the UnSquaring Wheel represent typical aspects of printing businesses, as well as businesses in general. Alliances may not be so typical.

This ninth and atypical vector exists because the media marketplace has been in an accelerated rate of change, with more change on its way. This rate of change will stress the resources of all media practitioners, not just print-focused ones. The way to adapt to this changing environment is to share capital. Capital is not just money; it also includes knowledge, skill, experience, and management acumen. Communication markets will not be places where austerity and cost management can advance organizations. Constant investment and shared skill sets will be required as media change in their nature and their production.

For these reasons, alliances make more sense than do mergers, acquisitions, or single company investment.

What are Alliances?

Printers have always used the services of related businesses of their industry. Those businesses and their owners cooperated in associations and local craft clubs, working toward common objectives and sharing industry knowledge—even though they might bump heads in their sales efforts every day. Their work together in these groups codified trade practices, kept them abreast of industry events and technologies, not to mention scuttlebutt about customers, government agencies, landlords, and all aspects of running a business in their cities and towns. These meetings and associations often led to beneficial business relationships and long-lasting friendships, as well as the cultivation of mutual business opportunities.

Alliances are not the same as networking. *Networking* is a commonly used term today, usually referring to the sharing of business contacts or finding others who can assist in the completion of a task or a project. These contacts and sharing of assistance are tactical forms of alliances.

An alliance can be something more than that. The UnSquaring approach shows us that alliances need to be a key part of strategy. That longer-term perspective signifies a deeper relationship that

- advances organizational goals,
- minimizes risks,
- preserves resources, and
- creates opportunities.

What is an Alliance?

An *alliance* is a relationship where two parties have agreed to join together to accomplish an objective or achieve a goal of grand size. In geopolitics, alliances often occur in the context of treaties. In the history of some monarchical societies, marriages were often arranged as a means for achieving an alliance between tribes or countries.

The two key words are "agree" and "join." This does not mean that the two parties will necessarily join to become one organization, although it sometimes does when necessary. Treaties and royal marriages rarely combined countries, but they did share resources and plans for the future, and they created a circumstance for cooperation.

The shared desire for cooperation can take many forms, ranging from a substantial integration of businesses, to an unsophisticated purchase, to supplying of some products or services as needed.

Trust is an essential element of the decision to agree and join. Parties cannot create alliances quickly. Durable alliances emerge after a courting process with shared experiences that create an environment of trust. In business, that means that the two parties may have faced some confusing situation, such as determining which party should have the responsibility for a shared customer. Resolving those issues in a manner satisfying to both parties over a period of time can lead to fruitful alliances.

Marketplace Trends Require a New Look

The media marketplace has changed radically. Surviving print businesses will no longer be able to rely on inheriting business from deceased competitors, acquisitions, tuck-ins, or other shuffling of the deck chairs to wheedle their way through the year. Even printers who have been greatly successful in re-casting their businesses through investments in digital printing or by adopting marketing services strategies have only delayed their confrontation with significant challenges ahead.

Here are some of these challenges:

- Communications budgets are flat–or even declining–as businesses replace their traditional advertising and communications methods with digital media (especially in favor of social media, e-commerce, and content marketing strategies, and the automation and analytics they provide).

- The number of media choices are rising. In 2015, Super Bowl XLIX was streamed for free to smartphones, a confirmation of the trend away from traditional broadcast and cable distribution. It's becoming apparent that social media companies are valued far more highly than traditional media companies.

- Technology continues to provide faster computing and communications at lower prices. This allows for richer media (especially video) and more emphasis on on-demand offerings. Broadband technology continues to advance. By 2020, it is expected that an entire movie can be downloaded to a smartphone in 6 seconds

(rather than 6 minutes) when 5G networks replace the 4G networks that are the standard as of this writing.

- These trends came into prominence beginning about 1995, when
  print volume started to decrease. Per capita consumption of commercial printing is now below levels of forty years ago, back when
  letterpress was still a major production process in commercial
  printing.

What does this mean? Declining demand for print means that it will
be harder to create the financial resources for re-investment in printing
businesses. It will be harder to attract outside resources from the investment and banking community. Talent will be attracted to other media
markets.

Technological advances are bringing about these changes in media. How
can printing businesses keep up? How can printing businesses that have
not adapted to these changes make up for lost time?

Alliances are essential. They will give printing businesses greater access
to resources and will re-immerse print businesses in the media marketplace.

Alliances and the Printing Industry

Tactical alliances are part of the printing industry's DNA. Printers were
usually family-owned businesses which could not always afford to have
skills on staff beyond the ones they needed most often. Sometimes a production step meant having a particular kind of equipment. Sometimes
they could not afford to buy that equipment because they did not have
the volume of business for that specialized step to make it worthwhile.
But they did get access to them because specialty businesses that had
the skills and equipment were nearby. In New York City, many of these
practitioners would be in the same building, many along Varick Street in
downtown Manhattan. In Chicago, you could find them in a neighbor-
hood referred to as "Printer's Row." Printers shared equipment or skills
of workers by sending work to each other. They agreed not to seek out
each other's customers while working on a job for another printer. There
was a sense of gratitude for the fellowship of sharing craft skills, and there
was synergy— providing a sense that working together had a long-term

payoff. However, it was rare that the relationship became strategic, and their shared work was often on a task or project basis.

Why did these relationships exist? There were rooted in basic economic concepts of division of labor and differential (or comparative) advantage.

Economic purpose

Every business depends on the resources of its owners, the actions of other businesses, and its customers for its existence. Businesses share resources through purchasing, and selling goods and services to each other. Each turns to the resources of the other to have higher value. They guide the time and skills of employees in a manner that employees consider worthwhile in the process, and provide products and services that customers need and want.

This is a relatively simple concept that we know every day as consumers and businesspeople. The entire economy is made of interconnected buyers and sellers who depend on each other. However, they usually do not know each other, nor do they understand the processes used in great detail. No business has enough resources to own all of its factors of production. Economic concepts such as division of labor and differential advantage mean that there will always be specialists.

A favorite concept often used by economists to describe these relationships is called "I, Pencil." Its author, Leonard Reed (1999), describes all of the resources, skills, and knowledge needed to produce one pencil, making the point that no one person actually knows how to make a pencil on his or her own. One person would need to know:

- agriculture to plant rubber trees for the erasers, and to plant and nurture the trees that would become lumber for the shafts of the pencils,

- metallurgy to create the cylinder that holds the eraser and attaches it to the pencil,

- engineering to build the woodworking equipment requiring knowledge of electricity, materials handling and design, as well as all of the harvesting equipment, transportation, shipbuilding, and truck manufacturing,

- and now, computer hardware and software that would help manage the entire process.

No one person knows how to make a pencil, but there are thousands of people involved in making a single one. The point of this pencil exam-ple is that even the simplest goods are complex and are related to other goods. There are distinct areas of knowledge, skill, and experience that must be brought together.

Economists have always stressed the importance of differential advantage and division of labor, but many people find it counter-intuitive. Wouldn't it be cheaper and faster if they owned all of the factors of production and their transportation? Wouldn't there be great synergy in that?

There would not be, because the knowledge would be too great, and the resources are rarely in the place needed. Finally, skills and technologies are always changing. Combined with regulatory events, such as laws or government actions, the number of interacting factors cannot be antici-pated or understood unless someone is specialized in it. This is why we use accountants and lawyers, but also why businesses use UPS. The costs of personally delivering an item is very high, but when we can rely on a specialist, the costs are lower when we need to use that specialty. It is cheaper to buy a pencil than it is to build a factory to produce the single one you need.

For the same reason, print businesses will have difficulty setting up an ad agency on their own, create a social media management practice, or develop other kinds of businesses while they need to operate their core business.

Digital media are complex and constantly changing. They are still new, so their "rules" or "trade practice" have not formed yet, and might never form. The print business has a culture of investing in capital equipment that lasts a long time, sometimes decades. The time horizons of digital media and print production are so different that they cannot be com-bined. While offset printing may work because of the basic scientific ac-tion of oil and water not mixing, we rely on them not mixing to produce printed goods.

Like the pencil in the economics example, media budgets of all size companies will involve formats, ingredients, and competencies of many types. Not one company will have these specialists. Ad agencies, which have historically used outside resources to supplement their creative and art direction, may be a model for today's "marketing services" printing businesses. However, even they will focus on alliances and not tasks. This will be especially true for small agencies. "Marketing services" is too tactical an approach for the communications marketplace ahead.

Risk reduction through alliances

One of the basic assumptions of economics is that resources are always scarce, and needs and wants are always infinite. Fulfill one need, and another seems to appear. Once people were happy just to be fed. As agriculture grew, the plentiful foodstuffs led to new sets of wants. People wanted food to taste good, and when food became even more than enough, the needs and wants shifted to the way food was available. Food had to be convenient, and nowadays it has to meet more narrow demands, such as being organic, or range-raised, or in 100-calorie packs, etc.

Resources change over time, and knowledge and technology makes their use more efficient. The printing industry has gone through significant and traumatic changes since the public acceptance of the Internet, social media, and numerous advances in equipment and communications. These changes create new foundations for differential advantage and division of labor. Time and knowledge change all of these relationships, and they change the way resources are used.

As the size of the market for printed goods has declined, so have the resources available for investment. The applicability of the skills of the industry (the stored knowledge of industry production techniques) of its productive capacity (people and equipment) is less relevant.

This means that deploying resources to new investment is inherently more difficult. Resources are more scarce than before, which makes each decision to deploy them inherently more risky.

Alliances are part of entrepreneurship. Entrepreneurs are risk-takers, not gamblers. When it is said that entrepreneurs are risk-takers, that means that they study risks related to their resources and make judgments about the best way to use them. If they see that there will be negative or low future returns, they will not invest. Gamblers, on the other hand, will take some form of calculated risk. However, their actions are not investments because they do not require the accumulation and direction of resources. Gamblers bet on things that already exist. Entrepreneurs create new situations and new ways of organizing resources.

Because the marketplace for communications has changed so much (diminishing the need for traditional printed goods and creating what seems to be infinite demand for digital on hybrid goods), it is difficult for print business owners to support both their traditional businesses and position themselves for the future at the same time.

Therefore, the pool of resources is enhanced by forging alliances, especially related to digital technologies, for the opportunities in the new communications marketplace to be realized.

Remember the press that relied on oil and water not mixing? A printing press brings divergent materials together to reach a goal. Creativity is enhanced by having skilled practitioners look at client problems from different vantage points. By having carefully designed strategic alliances, that creativity and skill is brought together to provide new and different offerings that would not otherwise be possible.

How Alliances Differ from Mergers or Acquisitions

Mergers and acquisitions (M&As) involve the exchange of assets and liabilities from one party to another. Alliances allow each party to retain their ownership, but to align their strategies to support each other. Good alliances may result in a merger or acquisition after some time working together, but they avoid a critical problem in M&A activities: transition risk.

During a change of ownership, there is a period of adjustment as operations are integrated. If the operations are not integrated, but one party's process is adopted while the other party's is abandoned, then resources are used to train and to adapt to the new way of doing things.

Transitions often take longer and cost more than originally expected. During that time, competitors are active in the marketplace. They can create sales mischief while attentions are directed to the transition.

Look Ahead, Not Back

Many mergers and acquisitions are backward-looking, joining two companies of similar capabilities and interests, rather than forward-looking in terms of product offerings and market strategy. While a merger may create a more efficient company, the company still has problems adapting to a future marketplace dominated by digital media. Alliances allow businesses to move into new, growing product areas, gaining experience and knowledge, with a partner who is already active in those areas.

Flexibility of Capital Through Alliances

It's not always rosy with alliances. Some may not work out. In that case, the experience may still be rewarding, and the individual businesses still have their ownership and can ally again another day. Bad mergers can be avoided with careful alliance planning. Resources, especially financial capital, are naturally scarce. Tying them up unnecessarily creates new risks and reduces the flexibility of the businesses.

Alliances that work lend themselves to the creation of new businesses, not merged ones.

The long-term goal of alliances may not be mergers or acquisitions, but may be a jointly-invested new company. The alliance period provides time to understand each other's business, to evaluate problems and solutions, and to develop an appropriate market approach. Where transitions often involve "un-doing" one company's organization and methods, an alliance that leads to a new business from the ground up is likely to have a better chance of success.

Three types of alliances

The purpose of an alliance is to for businesses to provide relevant products and services to the marketplace to satisfy their customers.

The three types of alliances are

- task,

- project, and

- strategic.

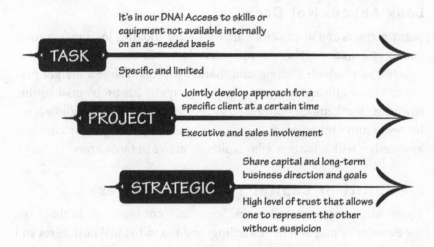

All three of the types are valuable to the wise operation of a printing organization. The strategic alliance has been rare and is the type that the UnSquaring model considers to be crucial to the future health of printing businesses.

Task alliance

The printing industry has always had alliances of convenience, working with trade services (such as color separators or binding and finishing services) that had specialized equipment or skilled staff. Some of them, like business card and stationery printers, had equipment and materials selection that other printers would rather not maintain, since sales volumes might be not be large enough to be a regular part of their sales efforts. Rather than turn customers away, taking orders for these products and having specialists produce them was became common practice. These are *task alliances*.

Task alliances are the most common in the printing industry and have been for more than a century. The invention of the Linotype was one of the reasons for the entire trade service business to begin, as the equipment was expensive and required a trained operator, which not every printer could afford.

Over the years, advances in photography created specialists in halftones, color separation, image assembly and stripping, platemaking, and a related business of photo retouching. Not all printers could have these skills on staff, but they had access to them because these businesses located near each other (as in the Varick Street area in New York City and "Printer's Row" in Chicago).

All of these task alliances, or inter-company purchases, were governed by trade practices, agreements that had stood the test of time and were jointly developed through industry organizations. When there was need to deviate from trade practice, the practices were a foundation for the agreement because everyone knew what they were deviating from and in what way.

Project alliance

A *project alliance* is a convenient assembly of businesses and practitioners to fulfill the tasks for a particular project. In a task alliance, the supplier has no knowledge of the total project and is hired when needed. In a project alliance, the suppliers are in on the discussions of the project prior to the bid. The suppliers may even join the lead company in information-gathering discussions needed to prepare a proposal. The relationship may include sharing of the project profits when the project is done. When the project is done, the relationship ends until a similar project opportunity arises again. Whereas task alliances are created for short-term convenience, project alliances are tactical. They exist for the duration of a particular project.

There may be situations where the client company has worked with project alliance members separately. In this case, there needs to be a project director. This simplifies the relationship with the client and allows the alliance partners to focus on what they do best. It also frees sales time to pursue projects from other clients. Alliance partners must be open to surrendering their lead to one of the alliance members.

An example of a project alliance might be the relationship of a home-builder and an architect where the project is defined by the length of time necessary to start and complete the project. They may use each other's services repeatedly, but there is no strategic, long-term intent. There is no intent to share resources over the course of multiple projects, nor for the builder to become part of the architectural firm or vice versa.

Strategic alliance

Strategic alliances involve the willingness to share resources and to make investments for future situations, and possibly to lead to the creation of a new business entity.

Businesses created for different reasons realize that they have shared resources and shared interests, but really have no intention of becoming one joined business at this time. The time horizon of the alliance also shapes its characteristics.

Some businesses desire to have revenue from multiple markets. Think of a landscaping business. Some landscapers work on individual homes, while others prefer to have commercial customers. A pool installer might want a relationship with the home landscaping business, but a relationship with the commercial business may not make sense. In this case, the strategic alliance may benefit the installer by having access to certain equipment, nursery stock, and skilled workers who can prepare a site and also add the finishing touches to a job. Landscapers would benefit by getting business they might not ordinarily get because of the installer's activities. This new business would be achieved without having to add sales personnel.

In a strategic alliance, you share goals, resources, and an organization structure. Ultimately, an alliance is a recognition that specialized knowledge and skills change in value and applicability over time.

For new technologies, it is a recognition that the acceptance of a technology has not reached a standalone critical mass that could support a standalone business. This means that two businesses share the resources and skills to complete whatever objectives and goals they have. They jointly invest in the process, resulting in lower cost to each company. This means that they have broader sales and production experience. They also may be able to buy a higher grade of equipment and employ higher skilled and more productive workers than they would not be able to afford otherwise.

Benefits

The benefits of an alliance are not always evident on the surface. The industry has experienced the benefits of task alliances for decades. Project alliances are just an extension of the task alliance experience.

Risk management

Financial risk reduction is obvious, but the alliance approach means that each party can gain practical experience by working together. Better investments can be achieved, and unique marketing approaches may be possible. This means that transition risk—frequently underestimated in mergers and acquisitions—can be avoided to a high degree.

New markets

Print businesses have been in a declining market, but there are printers who are currently doing well. Most of these successful printers have been leveraging digital printing and data base capabilities. Yet, many of the current generation of marketing managers have no personal experience with print applications, especially with how print can integrate with digital media. Finding specialists in marketing analytics, video, and app development can aid print businesses in finding new clients and developing new approaches in the process.

Alliances can also bring businesses into new geographies and new market segments.

New resources

Alliances should be directed to other organizations that can provide resources today that are not available in the current business. Gathering resources for new initiatives can take time, and there is trial and error involved. This effort also takes executive time away from supervision of the current business. Without experience in the new initiatives, it is also difficult for executives to understand subtle aspects of the new business. While an alliance is not the equivalent of flipping a switch, it does save time-to-market, and it can reinvigorate a current business with new talent and new knowledge.

Work with a different business culture

Working with different businesses experienced in different geographies, media, or markets, allows print businesses to go beyond the printing "culture." A business culture is a way of doing things such that employees and suppliers in that culture innately know the rules, boundaries, processes, and jargon. The printing culture, for example, was codified as part of its trade practices. Everyone knows that designers, agencies, photographers, programmers, videographers, and other content creators all have their unique cultures. The printing business was hampered in its understanding of the Internet's future effects on media because its culture and business practices limited the access to Internet creators and practitioners. Creating alliances with businesses that are already positioned where media advances will occur is critical to profitable future of a transitioned printing business. Working with a new business culture regularly is a better way to adapt than having occasional cooperation on specific tasks.

Make the shift to business development

A purpose of strategic alliances is to broaden and update the product offerings to include digital and other media. A printer may desire to offer more digital media, but enters into the alliances to participate in a larger media communications plan that would include some forms of print media. The sales process is different, and it requires participation in the planning activities of the client.

Changing from the old sales process ("Please consider us when you are sending out bids") to this kind of sales process ("What are your revenue objectives? What are your target markets and their media habits?") takes time, but the transition is legitimized by the new product offerings.

More than one alliance? Yes, definitely!

Most print businesses should have more than one alliance with minimal overlap. An example might be a printer who works with a web site developer, a social media manager, display designer, videographer, and a direct mail specialist. All of these skills may be involved in a media campaigns for their duration. If printers believe they are in marketing services, these kinds of skills need to be available and routinely included in client plans. Media planning is more complex than ever. Even small businesses need media plans, although they may never have considered the ad hoc ways they promoted themselves in the past as being part of an overall plan.

Finding Alliance Opportunities

Identifying the right alliance partners require organization and diligence.

Whom do I trust?

A successful alliance depends on the level of trust the partners have. This is why the development of alliances can take time. Candidates may go through the three levels of alliance with a printing business. They may be hired to complete tasks. If that is successful, they will be asked to participate in a project, including the proposal development. When several of those projects are complete, it should be clear whether or not a strategic alliance is worth pursuing.

You know you trust an alliance partner when he or she can visit one of your key clients and you do not have to worry that they will seek other business there without your knowledge. You know that they will keep you informed as to what their interactions are. You can trust them to offer constructive and creative advice about opportunities to satisfy the client.

What businesses are good candidates?

There are numerous businesses to have alliances with; many will be free-lance resources. The graphic design business has over 100,000 freelancers in the US alone, representing more than one-half of all graphic design employment. In the public relations business, there are about 54,000 employees in public relations firms, but an additional 32,000 freelance workers.

Everyone thinks of advertising agencies as requiring offices in order to accomplish their work. There are 375,000 workers in advertising agencies in the US in advertising firms, but they are also over 100,000 sole practitioners who report to the IRS that they work in the advertising agency business. Others include web developers, programmers, videographers, web analytics experts, postal regulation experts, logistics managers, copywriters, and meeting and trade show planners.

Are there new specialties?

The nature and pace of technological change has created new specialists. When technology changes so quickly and so often, it is hard to tell which ones are going to be sustained in the marketplace. Therefore, it reduces the risk of companies to work with new specialists in these areas first, rather than establishing the specialties in their business when demand for those specialties may not be well-known or well-understood. Smartphone app development as an occupation did not exist ten years ago. Smartwatch app development might be a new opportunity in these next years.

Creating Opportunities, or How to Attract New Alliance Prospects

Many print businesses have not been active in the content creation markets. While they accept business from designers, agencies, photographers, public relations specialists, and others, printers have never been considered part of that culture. (An exception may be the print business owner who has worked for some of those businesses in the past.)

To develop potential alliance partners, there is a new trend that might be useful for the process: co-working. This trend is where small and smaller companies (microbusinesses) share the same workspace and support resources. (Wikipedia nd) Many print businesses have downsized over the years and now have excess space. The establishment of a media co-working alliance incubator might be a good, long-term way of establishing relationships with creative personnel and other content creators with whom the print business might not otherwise work.

It is important to become involved in media and content creation associations. Some options include local chapters of advertising agency associations (such as AAAA), the American Marketing Association (AMA), the American Institute of Graphic Arts (AIGA), the Public Relations Society of America (PRSA) and others. In the experience of the UnSquaring team, so few printers are active in these associations that the opportunities are significant. Printers we have known who are active in these groups do not often speak about them because they like to keep opportunities to themselves.

It is important not to send sales people to these meetings. Sales personnel work with short-term time horizons, and always feel if they do not get an order from going to one or two meetings that they are not worthwhile.

These are long-term strategies and require patience and diligence to become a trusted member of the group.

Other sources of potential alliance partners are clients themselves. Find out which new media and other suppliers they have come to know and trust, then seek them out. If there are academic media and design programs in your area, meet with professors and teachers in the area and get recommendations from them. This can also be a great source of interns who might develop into partners or employees.

In Summary

In this chapter, we described how alliances ranged from just the focusing on tasks to a enjoying full-fledged strategic relationship.

The best and deepest alliances require planning client activities, workflows, and investments of money, time, and people. The ability of alliance partners to share business risks together to reduce their long-run risks is an essential part of the process.

Finally, the alliance partners are open to sharing their resources to reach mutually-set goals. The relationships allied businesses develop may not lead to their combination into one company, but may lead to the creation of a new company in response to future market changes and opportunities.

References

Read, Leonard E. "I, Pencil: My Family Tree as told to Leonard E. Read." 1999. Irvington-on-Hudson, NY: The Foundation for Economic Education, Inc.

Wikipedia contributors, "Coworking," *Wikipedia, The Free Encyclopedia,* http://en.wikipedia.org/w/index.php?title=Coworking&old id=648810672. accessed March 15, 2015.

12

ASSESSMENT

by Chris Bondy

Business Transformation Assessment (BTA) Framework

To be effective with any continuous improvement effort, you need to establish a baseline reference. We call this your "current reality". In addition to the current-state baseline reference of your firm, you'll need a set of realistic, reachable goals that you can attain from that baseline. *UnSquaring the Wheel* provides a web-based business transformation assessment system (*BTA*) that delivers a baseline view of your company from a variety of critical vantage points.

UnSquaring the Wheel – Business Transformation Assessment, or BTA, is the starting point for the "unsquaring" transformational approach. The *UnSquaring BTA* provides these three key benefits because it:

1. Allows you to discover where you are (your current reality),

2. Helps you to identify your gaps and misalignments, and

3. Enables you to determine what needs to be transformed.

It is important to look at your current reality and gain a perspective of the existing context of your firm as it relates to present and future market needs. The *UnSquaring the Wheel* assessment provides an easy way to evaluate your business in comparison to an ideal-state reference model. The assessment summary provides a graphical radar chart and a detailed status report of your current reality.

A Closer Look at the BTA

The graphic communications industry is very complex. Determining the priority and timing of continuous improvement efforts can be difficult and risky. *UnSquaring the Wheel* provides a consistent approach to evaluate the maturity of your firm along nine critical business areas (or "spokes in the wheel" that we call "vectors"). The *BTA* provides an easy-to-use web-based tool to collect and model the perspectives of a single or multiple leaders in a graphic communications firm. Using this tool enables a meaningful and focused evaluation of your operation as a foundation for future change.

Conducting a consistent assessment with your key company stakeholders provides you with a viable reference model and starting point to pinpoint your areas of strength and weakness. You'll also get the unique perspective of each person who conducts the *UnSquaring the Wheel BTA* assessment.

Within the *Business Transformation Assessment,* there are three key categories or "disciplines" (Customer, Platforms, and Resources), and within each discipline there are three transformational elements called "vectors". The assessment system provides an easy-to-follow framework to take you through a series of questions and statements that you select that best describe your current reality. To make the process more meaningful, we have organized the questions into four segments for each vector; we call these segments "dimensions". The table below illustrates an example of the assessment framework.

Discipline (1 of 3) e.g. Customer	Vector (1 of 9) e.g. Brand	Dimension (1 of 4) e.g. Clarity	Choose 1 of 6 Statements

After completing the BTA selections, you will get a graphic radar chart of a 9-spoke wheel that represents your current reality across all the disciplines and vectors. In addition to the graphic "wheel" representation, the *BTA* system also provides you with a report that provides details of the characteristics of your current reality. This *BTA* report is structured similarly to the assessment.

It also provides a maturity rating for each vector. For example, a firm with excellent "Brand" maturity might be rated with a Brand Dimension of "known for important things". This maturity rating is based on six different maturity outputs on a continuum from very basic ad-hoc operations to operations that are fully transformed. The *BTA* report will provide additional descriptions that describe the maturity stage in four areas: alignment, clarity, reach, and competitive separation.

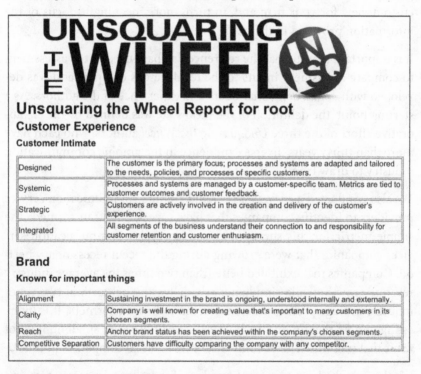

UNSQUARING THE WHEEL

Unsquaring the Wheel Report for root

Customer Experience

Customer Intimate

Designed	The customer is the primary focus; processes and systems are adapted and tailored to the needs, policies, and processes of specific customers.
Systemic	Processes and systems are managed by a customer-specific team. Metrics are tied to customer outcomes and customer feedback.
Strategic	Customers are actively involved in the creation and delivery of the customer's experience.
Integrated	All segments of the business understand their connection to and responsibility for customer retention and customer enthusiasm.

Brand

Known for important things

Alignment	Sustaining investment in the brand is ongoing, understood internally and externally.
Clarity	Company is well known for creating value that's important to many customers in its chosen segments.
Reach	Anchor brand status has been achieved within the company's chosen segments.
Competitive Separation	Customers have difficulty comparing the company with any competitor.

Conducting a structured assessment process, then getting a graphical representation and report of your current reality is a great way to get a macro-view of your firm. Remember that you are looking at your firm from these nine unique business transformational vectors all at the same time. Now you can determine the importance of the changes that you need to make in order to align with the current market conditions.

UnSquaring the Wheel BTA and the Book

The *BTA* system is designed to be an integral part of the *UnSquaring the Wheel* approach. The book provides a specific chapter focused on each one of the nine transformational vectors. The book is designed to be a "field guide" that provides detailed characteristics of the ideal state in each area of the nine spokes of the wheel, as well as an approach to achieve that ideal state.

By completing the *UnSquaring the Wheel* assessment first, target areas of the book come to life as real-world and practical solutions to areas that uniquely need attention for your specific company. Simply put, completing the immersive discovery exercise of the assessment provides a custom view for your firm and, in turn, more meaningful focus of the information provided in the book.

It is important to note that the reference database used in the assessment to compare assessment inputs to the ideal state is complex and was developed with actual benchmark data and experience of the authors. As a starting point, the definition of the ideal state was defined by the collaborative effort of the three *UnSquaring the Wheel* authors, who each have more than thirty years diverse experience in the graphic communication industry to draw from.

We also conducted a survey of over 300 graphic communication service providers to identify companies that have successfully transformed. The simple metric for this survey was to find graphic communication services companies that were growing during the recent recessionary period. Companies that exhibited better than two times the average industry revenue growth, while simultaneously delivering better than two times industry average profits, were considered to be transformers. It is interesting to note that, in our study, there were only a very small number of firms that met this criteria (only 6%, or less that 20 companies in total).

We then reached out to a good number of these leading companies and analyzed their characteristics from all nine critical vectors. In a very short period of time, we could see a pattern developing. This pattern was almost exactly aligned with what we had determined in our collaborated work together. We then took the results and framed the ideal-state definition across all nine transformational vectors. Form that point, we defined each of six different levels of transformation, from the most basic to the most advanced. With this model defined, we were then able to chart the exact position of a specific firm across all nine vectors, forming their unique "wheel". Invariably, that wheel was not round—hence the project became "How do you 'unsquare' the wheel and make it round or balanced?"

The *UnSquaring the Wheel* approach and *BTA* system has been tested with individual companies, as well as with a wider audience. In live pilot workshops we have held, two members of the same firm are often amazed that they each can have a unique perspective, varying greatly from each other. The assessment provides a springboard for discussion, and for planning and consensus building.

Business Transformation Assessment (BTA) - How does it work?

The *UnSquaring the Wheel – Business Transformation Assessment* (*BTA*) system web-based survey tool presents a series of questions, with six possible selections per question. The user of the *BTA* makes a selection for the statement that most accurately represents the definition of the current reality, as he or she has determined.

The assessment takes about 15 minutes to complete. There are nine sections (or vectors) that make up the spokes of the wheel. For each vector, there are four key areas, or dimensions, that each offer six possible selections. When the user makes a selection, the system presents the next question, and then the next, and so forth, until all the questions are answered. There is a status bar that provides users with a view of where they are in the assessment and indicates how much more they need to do to complete the session. (See graphic below.)

At the end of your assessment, the system accumulates all the information and provides a graphical radar chart that represents your "wheel", so you can easily determine how round your wheel is. It does this by referencing the profile database and retrieving the specific profile information that corresponds with the maturity you indicated during the survey. In that way, it shows you where to focus your efforts to "unsquare" that particular area of your wheel. The *BTA* report provides further details that characterize the current reality for each of your nine vectors and four

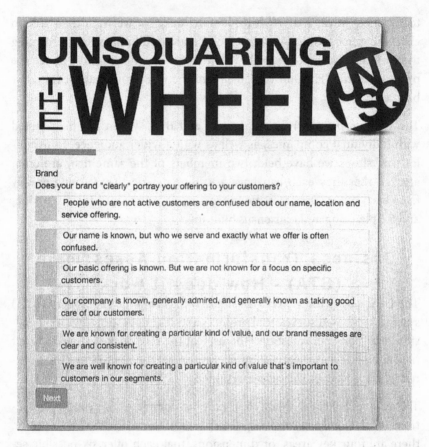

dimensions under each vector. The radar chart and report can be printed and/or saved to a file.

The *BTA* can be used by multiple users to compare the output, as well as at varying junctures in time to evaluate transformational progress. The assessment results can be useful in prioritizing continuous improvements across the organization, while balancing the effective use of scarce resources.

The *BTA* can be taken over again at key intervals of change. When taken by a variety of different individuals, it can bring out the perspectives of others and it be used as a communications tool to help promote alignment. Companies that spend time to investigate the critical issues and collaborate towards alignment on the specific transformational goals and priorities have the best chance for moving efficiently through the transformational efforts.

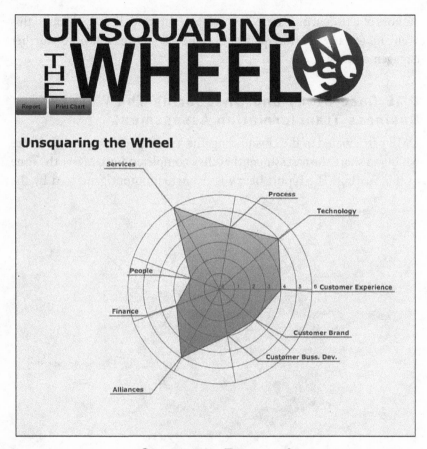

Support Beyond
the Unsquaring BTA and Book

The authors of *UnSquaring the Wheel* work with a variety of firms and associations to bring the material to life in a variety of venues. Depending on the specific needs that arise, they have delivered live presentations, seminars, and custom consulting efforts. Since the authors have extensive background in the industry and have a network of specialists whom they can count on for specific assistance, many firms have reached out to this team for assistance in the transformation journey.

For complete access to the "Unsquaring" - Business Transformation Assessment, and additional instructional information please register at www.UnsquaringTheWheel.com. Use promotional code: UNSQ50 to receive a $50 discount off the 60-day unrestricted system use for all purchasers of this book (60-day unrestricted BTA list price $199). The authors of Unsquaring The Wheel can be contacted directly through this Web-site for any specific questions or needs you may have for further engagement.

DME Case Study and Unsquaring The Wheel – Business Transformation Assessment

DME participated in the Unsquaring The Wheel pilot program and were willing to share the assessment that they completed for DME at the time of this writing. The report below is the actual output generated by the

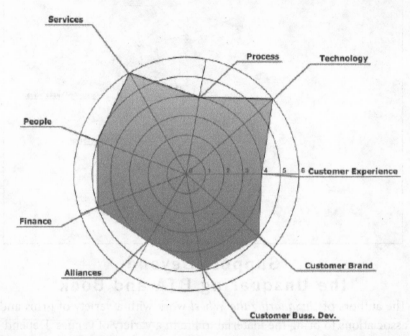

Unsquaring The Wheel Business Transformation Assessment system. This assessment report provides a visual radar chart indicating DME's specific maturity levels for each of the nine vectors of the "wheel" and the associated description for each vector.

Customer Discipline: Brand Vector

Maturity Rating: Know for good things

Dimension Characteristics:

• Initial brand strategy created and communicated internally.

- Admirable traits built into positioning, focus on "being of service.

- Widespread market awareness of value proposition and personality.

- Comparison with a "direct competitor" beginning to become difficult.

Customer Discipline: Customer Experience Vector

Maturity Rating: Customer centric

Dimension Characteristics:

- Routine customer interactions are planned, managed, and measured.

- Customer interaction processes begin to be customized for the largest and most important customers. Metrics are tied to customer enthusiasm.

- Customer preference and enthusiasm are understood to be strategic; policies and practices affecting both are under review across all departments and functions.

- Management of the largest and most important customer relationships actively crosses departmental and functional lines creating opportunities for the development of best practices.

Customer Discipline: Business Development Vector

Maturity Rating: Customer Expertise

- The company has assumed responsibility for identifying optimal prospective customers within chosen segments.

- A business development process is created.

- Customer segments have been chosen and targeted.

- Marketing, Selling, and Customer Support have been integrated around the business development process.

Platform Discipline: Technology Vector

Maturity Rating: Tactical

- Emerging ability to create one-off solutions to specific customer needs using existing technology.

- Able to acquire and integrate large disparate technology solutions with minor systems integration.

- Unable to define and deploy integrated software/services.

- Project management discipline is well developed, but limited largely to operations projects rather than cross-discipline projects.

Platform Discipline: Processes Vector

Maturity Rating: Strategic

- A workflow integration roadmap has been developed and adopted.

- Optimization culture established, widespread experience with process re-engineering across departments.

- Able to advise customers on strategic process improvement and implement customer facing programs.

- Needs assessment tools have been identified or created, and are in consistent use.

Platform Discipline: Services Vector

Maturity Rating: Strategic

- Ability to recognize market trends and construct services that meet market needs with measurable results.

- Integrated sales and software/services deployment platform to execute cross-media services.

- Solutions are integrated around specific customer objectives and metrics.

- Customer operational metrics are the primary assessment benchmark.

Resources Discipline: Finances Vector

Maturity Rating: Strategic and Innovative

- Balance sheet and value of enterprise has strategic priority; Bottom line >15%, EBITDA >20%

- Planning is strategic and specific, and guides budget preparation; reports compare to prior periods and budgets, and have predictive features for annual and multi-year performance.

- Interest in maintaining and growing a self-sustained business that can withstand disruption and is financially attractive to others at a future time; financial health is considered a competitive advantage; business attracts mergers.

Resources Discipline: People Vector

Maturity Rating: Insights into Talent Acquisition

- Workers are trained for specific tasks and transitions with the assignments of others; the need for supervisors interventions seen as problems with structures and workflow for which employee play a role in solving; job descriptions.

- Workers and management mutually seek ways to improve workflow and operations because of shared interests.

- Training is set to industry standard practices; regular performance review process directed to broadening experiences, adding new skills; new workers have training path for planned skill development.

- Mutually set goals with management, supervisors, and individual workers.

Resources Discipline: Alliances Vector

Maturity Rating: Strategic and Innovative

- Strong relationship with mutual investments in technology, companies, or departments.

- Rely on each other's profitable survival and growth for the realization for each business' long-term strategy.

- Desire to maximize areas of mutual opportunity in a way that conserves resources for each business and lowers financial and market risk.

- Strategic consideration of future needs for technology, acquisitions, and business structure to develop new capabilities and product offerings.

13

A ROUTE: MAPPING YOUR PATH FORWARD

by Wayne Peterson

The entire *UnSquaring the Wheel* process that we've described relies on two things: balance and traction. We've described why relying on a simple Job Shop business model is now high risk, and why designing a unique business model that balances the three disciplines and all nine vectors is essential. So how do you begin?

Do the Diagnostics First

Throughout this book, we've made the case as clearly as we can that there are no magic or silver bullets. There is no single answer to the question, "What first?" that fits every company. So despite the simplistic claims you'll hear repeatedly offered, there is no one thing that, if adopted by every company, would turn their fortunes right side up and guarantee their futures. That's true whether what's being offered is focused on selling, marketing, operations, purchasing, workflow, technology, MIS/ERP systems, or any other single aspect of your firm. Here's why:

What's missing from those claims, promotions, and offers is any effort to do the hard work of diagnosis first. The circumstances and needs of every company are different, and sometimes radically different. For example, even if the challenge is sales-related, there is a huge difference between a firm whose sales challenge is sales coverage and another firm whose sales challenge is sales effectiveness. Without doing the diagnostics first, there's no shared understanding on which to build a clear direction, and no context to choose between competing challenges and opportunities. So do the diagnostics first, and resist the claims and promotions from those who don't start with the essential diagnostics.

We created the Business Transformation Assessment (BTA) as the first step in the diagnostic process. And it's a self-assessment. It begins at the 30,000-foot level, looking at your entire enterprise to identify where it is well-developed and where it is under-developed. From there, you can dig deeper to understand where the development is needed, and where it will give you the most traction.

The Hub of Customers: Scale and Scope

A durable competitive advantage can be created by any enterprise if it begins where it should: with the customers. To repeat what Bob Bennitt (2015) of The Pace Group said earlier:

Pace's evolution from a printer into a provider of marketing strategy and execution began where all business should begin – with the identification of, and a commitment to solving, our clients' needs.

That's the best place to begin for you too. And the first, essential step is to identify a customer segment or group for which you can create incredible value and one which you can effectively monopolize. There are two dimensions that should enable you to decide how to describe that customer group or segment: scale and scope.

Scale

The starting line is identifying a customer group or segment that you can dominate completely by creating and delivering value that's more meaningful and useful than anyone else is offering those customers. Peter Thiel (2014) describes it this way:

> Brand, scale, network effects, and technology in some combination define a monopoly; but to get them to work, you need to choose your market carefully and expand deliberately. Always err on the side of starting too small. The reason is simple: it's easier to dominate a small market than a big one. If you think your initial market might be too big, it almost certainly is....
>
> The perfect target market ... is a small group of particular people concentrated together and served by few or no competitors. Any big market is a bad choice, and a big market already served by competing companies is even worse. (53 - 54)

For your firm, that customer group might be international, national, regional, or local. It could even be within a five-mile radius of your firm. The key here is to identify a segment you can genuinely expect to dominate to the exclusion of meaningful competitors. And geography is only one way to describe it, one kind of scale. But if you're a local or regional Graphic Communications company, geography may matter most. That's especially true if customer intimacy matters, and if you go to market through a direct sales force (even if that sales force is just you). In other words, the resources you can bring to bear to engage potential customers is the critical constraint here. To leverage those resources effectively, you need to answer this question: How wide a group of potential customers do I have the resources to engage with now?

Scope

How well do you understand the needs of that target customer group? And how many of their needs are you capable of fulfilling? This is where you need to gather real information, some of it ethnographic. How do your customers work? What's hard but essential for them to do? With what do they struggle that's material to their organization's mission and success?

As we described earlier, you're looking for needs that are worth meeting in the eyes of the customer. Failing to do this runs the risk of creating a solution for which exists no problem. Almost as bad is creating a solution that is only 1X or 2X better than what incumbents are offering, even if the incumbent is remote.

Proximity gets over-valued by Graphic Communications firms when they doubt that their local customers would choose to do business with someone remote. An under-served category of customers (very small and micro-businesses) is the foundation on which Vistaprint built a break-through business model. And few local commercial printers perceived those customers as especially valuable, or the initial loss of business card orders as especially threatening. Vistaprint offered those under-served customers a 10X jump in value by offering process color business cards for 1/10th what a commercial printer was prepared to charge. Roll the clock forward, and Vistarint has created a billion dollar business on a foundation of business cards, having captured a great deal of higher-value products from customers whose first need was a decent business card.

So the scope needs to be as broad and as important a business need as you're capable of fulfilling for your chosen customers. That's the essential answer to the question: "Why must your business exist?"

Balance: Rounding Your Wheel

Growth is the natural condition of a healthy enterprise. That doesn't nec-essarily mean explosive growth, and it certainly doesn't require growth through acquisitions. But a healthy business enterprise grows. Unfortu-nately, this focus on growth (sometimes a focus on growth at all costs) tempts us away from understanding that a business enterprise cannot long operate out of balance. A strength in one or two areas won't be suf-ficient to offset deep insufficiencies in other areas.

Beginning with the BTA, it's vital that a wheel be balanced before effort and investment is made to make it significantly larger. Here's why: Your business is a system. And the system will resist any counter efforts to push it out-of-balance. In fact, the failures of unbalanced change initia-tives are so common that they've been categorized and described as "ar-chetypes." Peter Senge (2006) describes it this way:

> In each case of limits to growth, there is a reinforcing (ampli-fying) process of growth or improvement that operates on its own for a period of time. Then it runs up against a balancing (or stabilizing) process, which operates to limit the growth. When that happens, the rate of improvement slows down, or even comes to a standstill.

Typically, most people react to limits to growth situations by trying to push hard .... It's an understandable response. In the early stages when you can see improvement, you want to do more of the same. But there's another way to deal with limits to growth. To change the behavior of the system, you must identify and change the limiting factor. (101)

The diagram below illustrates how this works in practice.

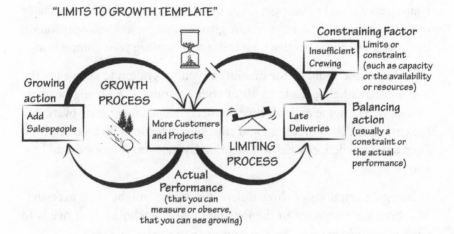

When essential elements of your organization aren't as strong as others, they act as governing, constraining or limiting factors. And those will slow both growth and improvement in performance. That's why they need early attention.

A good example is the ability to go to market effectively. Creating a remarkable service offering, but being unable to sell and deliver it effectively, is a recipe for failure. In most B2B relationships for Graphic Communications companies, some part of your organization will be responsible for making and keeping engaged customer relationships, whether that's a direct sales force or something else. But you will need people skilled and capable to create those relationships. Therefore, recruiting is a core competency for any company. If you're weak on the People vector of your business because you lack the capability to recruit effectively, that will become the factor limiting growth for you. And it will do you no good to push marketing or selling harder unless and until you remove that deficiency.

Another example could be insufficient ability to extend credit, to bill, and to manage your receivables effectively. If rapid growth (improvement in your sales effectiveness) leads to more projects and more revenue, but if you aren't able to extend the necessary credit to your customers wisely and effectively, if you aren't able to invoice quickly and accurately, and if you aren't able to collect payments in a timely and reliable fashion, you run the risk of running out of working capital as it is all tied up in accounts receivable. In that case, finance and accounting could be the factor most immediately limiting revenue growth, despite a sales organization that might be more effective than those representing your competitors.

A final example could be the inability of your operation to keep all of the commitments being made to all of your customers. A strong business development engine and effective financial management can't overcome the customer disappointment and customer defections that would result from failing to deliver what you promised, when you promised, and how you promised.

Offering descriptions of three different examples might seem excessive. But three are necessary to demonstrate that the whole wheel needs to work effectively in order for the enterprise to work effectively.

For your wheel to roll, it needs to be round. Advice to leverage only your strengths, rather than backfill to remove deficiencies, is misguided because it ignores the limiting effects that those deficiencies will chronically create. Therefore, round your wheel first.

Traction: Accelerating Your Performance

If you already have the wonderful luxury of a round or nearly round wheel, you're in rare company. And the next steps for you will involve designing the next steps to make your entire wheel larger. Since steady organic growth is the natural condition of a healthy business, it's logical to turn your attention there, once the deficiencies and limiting factors have been identified and corrected by reinforcing or strengthening those under-developed elements of your business.

Service design matters when designing for growth, and it goes well beyond the Lean mantra of a "minimum viable product." No, that's not arguing for useless additional features or needless complexity. Instead, deeper customer relationships and greater customer delight should be the dual objectives when you're ready to stretch beyond your current, well-rounded wheel. Rather than simply securing more customers and more revenue, the object should be to create better customers and better revenue. In essence, you're creating more and better traction with your customers and in the marketplace.

The BTA can be especially valuable here because it enables you to assess not merely where you are now in each discipline and for each vector, but it also describes what's next along each one of those radii.

Alignment and coordination is essential to avoid growing out of balance. And that's genuinely possible. The cautionary tale we recount early in the book describes Padgett Printing, which literally sold itself out of business as it tried to counter-balance a critical failure in financial management. Companies find themselves stalled when they embark on a one-dimensional initiative to grow or improve, while ignoring other elements of the business that will serve to limit that growth. And things are made rapidly worse rather than better when the focus is on leveraging strengths without removing or correcting deficiencies first.

Alignment between members of a leadership team is critical. Among ourselves, the authors have regularly remarked at how rarely we see a management team that understands and practices what we've described here, and how consistently high-functioning teams are present in high-performance organizations. That's no coincidence. The UnSquaring model provides a context within which to create that incredibly valuable alignment. Once members of a leadership team see and understand that it is impossible for the whole to thrive while one element is deficient, and that each element reinforces the effectiveness of the others, a basis exists to tear down silos and to expect team members to work in concert with each other.

References

Senge, Peter M. 2006. *The Fifth Fiscipline : The Art and Practice of the Learning Organization.* New York: Doubleday/Currency.

Thiel, Peter A., and Blake Masters. 2014. *Zero to One : Notes on Startups, or How to Build the Future.* New York: Crown Business.

14

THE ROAD AHEAD: PREPARING FOR THE UNEXPECTED

by Joe Webb

The purpose of planning is to ensure that a business has the tools, skills, and resources to navigate future marketplaces, to lower financial and other risks in their operations, and to be prepared to act decisively in unforeseen situations.

Not all unexpected situations are disasters, and many of those situations can be reasonably expected. Yet, there still are businesses that are unprepared for them, no matter how obvious and predictable they might seem.

That problem of being unprepared occurs when companies have flawed planning processes, or none at all. Planning challenges assumptions about a business and its marketplace. When those assumptions go unchallenged, events easily foreseen by others outside the business might be ignored or dismissed by those inside the business. Going back barely twenty years ago, we can see a good example of this.

Unprepared for the Expected

The printing industry was flying high in the mid- to late-1990s. The booming economy, enhanced by the Internet revolution, saw the value of printing companies soar. Owners who started their businesses after the Second World War began to retire and exit their businesses. The financial reward from this, as well as the ease with which this happened, was rare in industry history. A CEO of one of the consolidating buyers described the period by saying, "Our investors did not just want to know what companies we were looking to buy. They wanted to know how many printers I drove by on the way to work that morning."

They were heady times, for sure. It was commonly thought that the Internet would create a boom in print, and the proof of that was all around them. Computer magazines were among the thickest on the newsstand. "Dot-com" companies were spending lots of money on broadcast, print ads, and promotions. The stock markets—especially the NASDAQ, where all of the high technology companies were traded—had its index rise through the late 1980s and into the 1990s.

There were naysayers to the revolution, however. Louis Rukeyser, host of Wall Street Week on PBS, fired the show's technical analyst in 1989[1] and refused to allow one of his long-respected guest experts[2] to return because they were always saying that NASDAQ stocks were very overvalued. He believed they caused his viewers to miss one of the greatest stock market run-ups in history, and his credibility was hurt.

Then the bottom started to fall out.

The Internet Bubble burst, and stock markets crashed. By 2002, the NASDAQ fell to 1997 levels, and as of this writing, is still about 15% below its peak reached in that period. The index has to break 6500 to be near its inflation-adjusted historic high.

Print volume started to decline; for some products, it was precipitous. Magazines, one of the beneficiaries of dot-com ad spending and a strat-

---

1 Technical analyst Robert Nurock was let go in 1989. http://www.nytimes.com/1990/11/11/business/enduring-not-always-endearing-wall-street-week.html?pagewanted=1

2 Investment technician Gail Dudack was let go in 1999 after 156 weeks of missed forecasts, despite many years of generally accurate ones that ranked her among the show's best guests. http://www.nytimes.com/2006/05/03/business/media/03rukeyser.html?pagewanted=print&_r=0

egy of creating titles aimed at niche targets, had to retrench. Newspaper inserts declined as newspaper circulation fell, with more consumers finding their news online. Catalogs decreased their print run lengths, mailing frequency, and page counts, as retailers lured their customers to their websites where product selections were not limited by pages or postage expenses. E-commerce gained attention, especially as Amazon changed the very way books were sold.

The Internet was never a secret in the 1990s. Behind the Internet boom was an expanding infrastructure of telecommunications and computer networks used with increasing regularity. The declining cost of computing and increased speed of communications have also been in plain view since the 1960s. Businesses and consumers had already started to install high-speed communications that increased the use of and satisfaction with the Internet as a source of information and entertainment.

Graphic designers and ad agencies reported spending more of their time working on websites and e-commerce. They were being asked to design the look and feel of Internet sites and online campaigns for advertising and delivery of consumer information. They were spending much less time designing print materials. Client budgets for advertising and communications grew with the strong economy, but print budgets were shrinking, elbowed out by Internet fever.

And about those computer publications: It seemed that no one considered that computer users would look for information about computing online. Indeed, they preferred to do so.

All of these trends and technologies were hidden in plain sight. Printers evaluated them in terms of past experiences, even though every new day was offering up new experiences that ran counter to the past.

The changes to the pace of life during the Internet Bubble were tangible. Surprisingly, the Internet's advance in that time did not include most of the companies we associate with digital media today. Google was a startup, having only been incorporated in 1998. Apple had fired Steve Jobs, and it was unclear if the company would survive. Social media did not exist in way we came to understand it by 2007. There were no smartphones or tablets in the consumer market at that time, either. The closest thing we had to them were PalmPilots.

Why Were Printers Unprepared
for What Was So Plainly Seen?

How were the effects of the Internet missed? First, the printing business was good. For many printers, it was really good. The high prices being paid to buy printing companies affirmed their optimism. There is a tendency in planning to assume that the current situation is likely to persist within a narrow range of variation. This meant that it would go on forever. Or longer.

The most worrisome one reason for the lack of preparation was generational. Most owners never knew a time when the industry contracted significantly. They always assumed that print was in a lockstep relationship with the economy. Their real-life experiences showed them that they could wait out slow economic times and count on a definite rebound ahead. Experience was an impediment to recognizing and assessing a changing marketplace.

There is an old saw in business about investing in the technologies that can put you out of business. Many print business owners dismissed the new technologies as trendy gadgets used by kids. Like hula hoops and Pet Rocks, they would pass. The enthusiasm about the new technologies by young Silicon Valley executives might have been overdone and too hyped, but they were dismissed by printing's elite leaders. This caused print businesses who misread the upcoming media shift to invest in new traditional presses. Just a few years later, that malinvestment would cause many printing companies to default on their leases and surrender their presses in bankruptcy. There was little desire on an industry level to look at new technologies as new opportunities. Planning processes often focus on threats, but don't always flip over the threats to see what new products or markets they might lead to.

An important aspect of planning for the unexpected is knowing what is important to watch. Was there an Internet Bubble? Sure there was, but watching the stock market and its crash obscured what was really happening. The actual behavior of individual people in a marketplace is far more important than how the stock markets value them at one particular moment. Stock prices can be manipulated by many factors, and the market was seriously overpriced. But actual behavior in the market should be viewed as it is. No matter what the stock prices were, there was still a massive new communications infrastructure being built. New technologies were coming to market, and people were using them. News about the Internet was found in books and newspapers in the early 1990s, but they read about the bursting of the Internet Bubble online.

Printing prices were also misleading. Printing profits at that time were among the highest in decades, and prices were very good (despite the complaints about overcapacity that seem to have started in Gutenberg's time). But no one looked at the behavior of print buyers and consumers. Today, we know that printing volume was flattening at the time and shrinking on a per-person basis. Printing volume disconnected from the economy and started to grow more slowly in 1997. By 1999, printing employment was starting to decline. Prices are supposed to be an indication of market conditions, but they can be misleading unless you carefully investigate the price-setting forces at work.

Few printers had a plan for the digital media scenario. Most all printers had heard about disaster planning or succession planning, yet no one seemed to have a plan for the natural course of business and innovation that they saw every day.

The Planning Habit Needs to Permeate a Business Culture

Curiosity is at the heart of all planning. Planning is always about the future, but not one future. Planning is about multiple futures that may or may not occur, but always have a possibility of occurring.

The by-product of planning will be a knowledgeable staff that is flexible and resilient as it works toward a desired goal.

The worst planning creates a bureaucracy that protects and perpetuates itself. Planning bureaucracies become out of touch with the marketplace. Coordinating planning is an important management skill that should bring out the best of top management's knowledge, skills, and experience. It should not be confined to a department.

Basic planning always includes financial projections and evaluations of possible courses of actions. Many printers tie planning to budgeting, and so do not get the full value of the planning process.

If planning has value in the future direction of a business and its engagement with the marketplace, how does one create the situations that should be studied in a planning process?

Scenario planning is a process that started decades ago at Royal Dutch Shell.[3] It is commonly cited as an example of what good planning should include. Two examples that follow, one from the Internal Revenue Service and the other from NYC's response to the 9/11 attacks, show how the purpose of planning helps to put into perspective the scenario concept.

What if...?

Good planning requires the carefully considered business scenarios and the managerial actions that will be needed should they occur. These scenarios may not happen as foreseen. The process of analyzing the situations, circumstances, resources, and ranges of possible decision alternatives reveals important information about the structure, resources, and skills of a business, as well as several other key factors.

For example, the Internal Revenue Service has a plan to ensure that the government has the funds needed for defense and operations of agencies in the case of nuclear war.

The "National Emergency Operations" section of the *Internal Revenue Manual* (as reported by the *New York Times* on March 28, 1989) states that "operations will be concentrated on collecting the taxes which will produce the greater revenue yield."

As of the publishing date of *UnSquaring the Wheel*, the IRS has had no need to implement these directives. Therefore, the IRS should discard these guidelines, right? Of course not.

Operational directives need to be updated regularly, but the need to be prepared for unlikely but high-risk situations may never change. There is still a threat of nuclear war, and its likelihood will be argued by experts as it always has been. Whether the risk is considered high or low at a particular time, there is still a risk. That means the plan is still needed.

The operational directives from that plan might be usable in a different situation. Such was the experience of New York City in the 9/11 attacks.

---

3 http://www.shell.com/global/future-energy/scenarios/40-years.html

After the 9/11 attacks in New York City, the police, fire, and emergency services all had to find ways to deal with the situation. The City had no plan for terrorist attacks that used passenger planes. They had developed and refined some plans for terrorist attacks at the World Trade Center after its parking garage was attacked by a car bomb in 1993.

On that September day in 2001, the City had a variety of emergency plans created for other purposes over many years that they had studied and rehearsed. There were plans for natural disasters, blackouts, medical emergencies, rioting, transportation system breakdowns, labor strikes, bombings, building collapses, and many other calamities.

Those plans gave the various municipal services guidelines for their actions. They were created when managers and officials had the time and discipline to consider them in deliberate fashion. This allowed them to examine many options and alternatives as they created procedures and operations guidelines for the City's future managers and executives. While there are always disparaging comments about planning documents created by government bureaucracy, their purpose is simple and essential. They capture the knowledge and experience of management for use at a future time when those managers are no longer in the same positions or left those organizations.

While there was not a planning book titled *Terrorist Attack with Commercial Airliners* in the archives, the emergency management teams were able to select portions of other plans that seemed to be the most applicable. The attack's chaotic aftermath had the police, fire, and emergency services using procedures about evacuations of tall buildings, managing fires, handling crowd management, traffic control methods, and many other procedures for dangerous situations. In the end, all of the services had experiences that prepared them for dealing with 9/11 issues.

There was one critical area for which they were not as prepared as they should have been: interagency communications. Post-crisis reports that studied their performance indicated the need for improved communications among the different agencies. There were bureaucratic aspects to the communications problems, in that departments held many of their exercises and training within their departments with little interdepartmental practice. Despite large investments in communications technologies, the 9/11 disaster disrupted communications that were originally considered reliable. Landlines for voice and data were damaged. Cell phone systems were overloaded. Technology was not as reliable as was once thought.

The City used the new knowledge and updated their infrastructure and procedures accordingly. This is an example that planning is constant. Every situation provides new information about the efficacy of the prior procedures and focuses attention on improvement of the implementation of those plans.

Scenario Planning[4]

For many companies, scenario planning is very limited. It has three aspects, all related to forecasting. They have forecasts that are optimistic, pessimistic, and likely. The optimistic plan forecast might be 10% higher than a baseline likely forecast, and the pessimistic plan forecast might be 10% below the baseline forecast. Unfortunately, that's where the scenarios end. These are cash and budget forecasts. They are not scenario planning.

The previous examples show how scenarios can lead companies through complex situations. Scenarios place the company in a set of circumstances designed to stress its capabilities and challenge management to deviate from a previous plan with calculated actions of a new plan. Managers have to identify and reallocate their resources in a set of actions that they had not anticipated. When they review the effects of their decisions, they formalize them into plans and procedures that would be used if a scenario similar to the one they dealt with had actually occurred.

Very briefly, the Shell experience led to five guidelines for scenario planning:

- Make it plausible, not probable. The likelihood of a particular scenario event is not that important. The fact that such a scenario can happen is critical. Probable events should be part of the usual course of planning and operations. Scenarios are grander and riskier, requiring difficult choices about company resources in response to the scenario.

---

4 Some of this section draws from a summary of Shell's approach that can be found online at the website of the *Harvard Business Review*, "Living in the Futures." https://hbr.org/2013/05/living-in-the-futures

- Tell stories that are memorable, yet disposable. The lessons of the scenarios are more important than the story. The narrative story behind the scenario gives context to the scenario, but the procedures and operating decisions might be applicable to possible, but yet unimagined, scenarios. But most stories start in the present and extend the known trends of today into the future. Scenario stories need to have a different foundation of assumptions that start in a different place than do today's circumstances. What's learned in the scenario is more important than the story.

- Add numbers to narrative. Managers manage by numbers and reports, and scenarios need to provide similar kinds of data to illuminate the scenario and make it more realistic. Planning teams have diverse personalities and disciplines in them. The company controller may not be able to envision a scenario without hard numbers. Design personnel may be more comfortable with less verbal and more graphic descriptions of scenarios.

- Scenarios open doors. The purpose of scenarios is to get all aspects of the organization to consider ways that the scenario will affect them and their potential actions. The interactive process allows members of organizations who do not typically interact in a transparent way to do so. The scenario exercise can therefore have a positive effect on overall management cooperation in daily operations because they have a greater appreciation of their skills and expertise.

- Manage disagreement as an asset. Scenarios must be thought through as completely as possible. That makes it important to explore all areas of disagreement and different perspectives. It is far better to have examined those differences in the scenario process than to work out differences of opinion as real events unfold. In this way, the disagreeing perspectives learn why they disagree and learn the subtle aspects of their actions.

Lessons about Planning and the Unexpected

Most businesses will never deal with disasters of the magnitude of the 9/11 attack. They will be confronted with problems in staffing, production, investment, weather, communications, transportation, competition, regulation, health or availability of key personnel, and legal issues.

Some of the issues are simple, such as which employees are cross-trained to cover for vacations, which backup suppliers a business has, and similar issues. The more difficult events, such as what happens if the plant is lost to a fire, pose special challenges. Any event that has not happened yet, but can, requires a planning process that includes the participation of experts with specific knowledge. Sometimes, there needs to be combination of insurance companies, trade associations, and the advice of others who have experienced the event.

Changes in the nature of the marketplace require the same process. It is easy to see how, when business is good, a myopia to the grander scheme of things can affect management's desire to plan. Many businesses enter planning processes only when business is bad. Planning must be constant and systematic, conducted in good times and in bad.

Not all events can be foreseen, but enough of the possibilities can be planned for and provide the background, knowledge, and procedures needed. Unexpected events do happen, and they always seem to find the most inconvenient time to occur. When they do occur, but there has been no planning for them, even a small problem can cause great disruption.

When businesses make the mistaken assumption that budgeting and planning are the same, they leave themselves open to severe downside risks that jeopardize the survival of the business, and the safety of the personal and family wealth of the owners, and that of all employees.

Some of these events can be insured for financial loss, but they cannot be insured for strategic and logistical losses. A recent study of the economic conditions of countries hit by national disasters[5] showed that the negative effects are felt for fifteen years. This is despite the abilities of governments to create money through monetary policies, deficit spending, the seeking of aid from other countries. No business has these kinds of resources and relationships. Even with all those resources, countries suffer negative economic consequences for a decade and a half, and probably more. This means that businesses are at greater risk of permanent impairment to their business than most realize.

---

5 http://www.nber.org/papers/w20352

Not All Disasters are Sudden: It's the Slow Ones that Can Kill

Some disasters are subtle, such as losing a customer here and a customer there, losing a key person, making bad hires, tolerating illegal activities (such as large gifts to a customer if it serves a supposed larger purpose), lax auditing practices, and many other creeping problems. Most business disasters originate in behaviors like these.

Preparing for the Unexpected: Summary Guidelines

The concepts about planning of this chapter are summarized in these guidelines:

1. View planning as a larger process than budgeting. It is a constant and systematic process in which you learn more and more about your business and the marketplace.

2. Use planning as a means to establish a structure for a business that allows it to minimize direct supervision and supports your desired business culture.

3. Avoid plans that simply extend the present trends into the future.

4. Always be on the lookout for generational myopia. Generational perspectives can affect the way the business environment, threats, and opportunities are perceived.

5. View experience as a double-edged sword. It can allow for quick managerial action and high productivity, but it can also lead to the discounting of new processes that are unfamiliar and not consistent with that experience.

6. Question everything. Everyone has assumptions that they have found to be true in the past. What was accurate then, might not be accurate in the future. Be skeptical and inquisitive. Curiosity is the most important ingredient to put into planning.

7. Look at threats as opportunities. Threats might be opportunities, but they can require changing a course of action or negating prior decisions that were right for their time. Alliances might bridge the gap between the two.

8. Measure change in ways that are realistic. This chapter showed how easy it was to misinterpret some commonly accepted measures, while the real and permanent changes were masked by them.

9. Use scenarios to explore the nature of your business and the marketplace. This process is much more than optimistic, likely, and pessimistic views of trends that are already entrenched or actions that should be a natural course of business.

10. Beware of creeping and small changes that accumulate over time. Many of these are undetected by the planning process. They may be small decisions and observations that become part of the culture and are never challenged.

11. Don't let planning become a bureaucracy. All managers and staff have an aspect of planning to their jobs because they have the responsibility to manage resources in a way that meets company objectives. Creating a planning department might be the first sign that planning is becoming planning for its own sake, rather than a means of enhancing operations and creating a more flexible and resilient business.

12. Don't hide the plan. Not every employee needs to know all aspects of business plans. There should always be concern about competitors learning about the plans and acting against them. But there should always be important elements about the plan that are shared with employees, certain vendors, and alliance partners. Everyone needs a sense of direction, and your company's direction, especially.

15

CONCLUSION: RUBBER ON THE ROAD

by Wayne Peterson

Comprehensive and scalable. When we set out to describe how the graphic communications companies with whom we're working are changing and thriving, and why "business as usual" isn't viable any longer, we began with a live "proof of concept" presentation to a dozen industry leaders. They offered incredibly valuable and actionable feedback, in addition to their hearty encouragement that we were on the right track. Among the actionable feedback we received was the charge to insure that what we produced was both comprehensive and scalable. Taking that to heart turned a project that might have required months into one that's taken three years to complete.

We've made the case that no graphic communications enterprise will find a single, magic bullet enabling it to transform itself from struggling into successful, from shrinking into growing, or from marginal to vital in the eyes of its customers. Real transformation requires looking at the whole enterprise comprehensively. That comprehensive perspective is what you hold in your hands.

Transforming a company into something else, something different and better than what it was certainly isn't for the faint of heart. But we see so many owners and executives working so hard already, we know that if they faint it will be from weariness rather than timidity.

We've only rarely encountered a defeatist attitude among the owners and executives of graphic communications companies. But in too many cases, we've heard confusion and frustration as they work to stiff-arm a sense of dread about their possible futures. Fortunately, it's easy for us to offer substantial hope because we can point to companies well down the path of transforming, of reinventing themselves. And we've described how they have learned to transform themselves into something new, unexpected, different, and strong.

Those transformed companies have dodged the temptation to "stay the course" and avoid change, and its evil twin temptation to become a "marketing services provider" that's offering the execution of a wider array of services while still chained to a business model that's outlived its value. We've seen firsthand that neither of those courses holds much hope for sustainable growth and a viable business enterprise. Fortunately, we know there are alternative paths because we've watched a number of companies create new paths for themselves. And to a one, they've understood it as a comprehensive reinvention of who they once were.

Our friend, Sid Chadwick, consistently refers to graphic communications as "our great industry," and we agree wholeheartedly. That we need to change our business models and to create new futures doesn't diminish either the companies or the people with whom we have the privilege of working day in and day out. That understanding doesn't diminish or disregard the histories of great companies by assuming that they have seen their day and should quietly exit the stage. Instead, that perspective sees existing companies and their customer relationships as the axles for newly round wheels.

The necessity to transform graphic communications, to reinvent an industry by reinventing the companies in it, has been evident for more than a decade. Fortunately, that's entirely possible, and the reports from the trailblazers are in your hands. We're looking forward to seeing you on the road.

INDEX